Eleanor, the Firebrand Queen

Helen Rayson-Hill

Eleanor, the Firebrand Queen

Glass House Books
an imprint of IP (Interactive Publications Pty Ltd)
Treetop Studio • 9 Kuhler Court
Carindale, Queensland, Australia 4152
ipoz.biz/glass-house-books/
ipoz.biz/ipstore

First published by IP in 2021

© 2021 Helen Rayson-Hill, and IP

All rights reserved. Without limiting the rights under copyright reserved above, no part of this publication may be reproduced, stored in or introduced into a retrieval system, or transmitted, in any form or by any means (electronic, mechanical, photocopying, recording or otherwise), without the prior written permission of the copyright owner and the publisher of this book.

Printed in 12 pt Book Antiqua on 14 pt Avenir Book

ISBN 9781922332370 (PB); ISBN 9781922332387 (eBook)

A catalogue record for this book is available from the National Library of Australia

Glass House Books
Eleanor, the Firebrand Queen

Helen Rayson-Hill trained as an infant teacher, and taught in country Victoria, Melbourne and the UK. Later, she became a drama teacher following a long interest in the theatre.

After a family transfer to Brisbane, she was appointed Queensland Manager of the Australian Elizabethan Theatre Trust. For two years she co-ordinated National Arts Week in Brisbane working closely with the Queensland Government's Ministry of the Arts and Brisbane City Council.

On returning to Melbourne, Helen held a position at the Victorian Arts Centre in the Membership and Fundraising and Development Department. For two years she was an adjudicator for the Victorian Drama League.

Helen has also performed both on the stage in Melbourne and Brisbane and on television in *Neighbours* on Channel 10 and *Something's in the Air* on the Australian ABC network.

Writing has always been an interest of Helen's and she is a member of the Writers' Circle at Melbourne's Lyceum Club. She has written plays for her drama students as well as sketches for amateur theatre. Also an artist specialising in oils, Helen has held several successful exhibitions at several Victorian galleries.

Helen's short stories and memoir pieces have been published in anthologies, and she has written a children's book, *Kid Detectives*. The story was inspired by her grandson who wanted to know how children entertained themselves before electronic devices filled their lives.

Helen has long been interested in Medieval history, especially in the life of Eleanor of Aquitaine. After many years of research, inspired originally by the play *The Lion in Winter* by James Goldman, Helen was motivated to write about Eleanor's amazing life. Consequently, *Eleanor, the Firebrand Queen* became the first in a planned series of historical novels about this Medieval feminist.

Glass House Books
Brisbane

For my family,
Glyn Rayson-Hill
Tristan, Ingra, Jojo and Pippa
Freya and Jovan
Jonathan, Simone, Charlie and Madeleine

Acknowledgements

Author photo: Glyn Rayson-Hill
Cover image: courtesy, Armstreet.com
Book design: David P. Reiter

I am grateful to my friend Jocelyn Paterson for introducing me to Eleanor of Aquitaine through a production of the play *The Lion in Winter* by James Goldman. Wanting to get into the head of this powerful Medieval queen, I started reading historical biographies about her, including *Eleanor and the Four Kings* by Amy Kelly, *Eleanor by the Wrath of God, Queen of England* by Alison Wier, and biographies by Ralph V Turner and Marion Meade, whose books kept my interest firing.

For years Eleanor ran round my head till I was given a mighty prod by author Toni Jordan, whom I thank for getting me started. The Lyceum Club of Melbourne's Writers' Circle listened patiently to my readings of the early drafts, encouraged me, and gave me the conviction that Eleanor the Firebrand Queen could be published. Susan Pierotti, who knocked the early manuscript into shape, I thank for her keen eye and discerning judgement. Thanks to Jennifer Bryce who urged me to send the manuscript to Irina Dunn whose diligence found me David Reiter of IP, who has faith in my work and is sending my book on its way.

To my friends and family who have put up with my lectures on Medieval History and Eleanor, and especially Peggy Cochrane who read the manuscript to assess its suitability for book groups, thus boosting my confidence. Finally, thanks to Pearl Longden, who ran her eagle eye over the final draft not missing an ill-placed comma or apostrophe.

Lastly, my love and thanks to my husband Glyn Rayson-Hill, my computer guru, who calmed my fits of despair with his sense of humour, through corrupted USB sticks, my general lack of computer knowledge and horrors when the screen went black or when some other minor glitch occurred.

Contents

Chapter 1. Inheriting the Duchy of Aquitaine	3
Chapter 2. The Reluctant Bride	11
Chapter 3. Crowned Queen of France	25
Chapter 4. Marie the Unwanted Heir	37
Chapter 5. The Lure of the Crusade	44
Chapter 6. Unholy Holy Land	62
Chapter 7. Antioch Discovered	73
Chapter 8. Love and Prophesy	87
Chapter 9. Raging Queen	119
Chapter 10. Shipwrecked Marriage	134
Chapter 11. Reluctant Return	148
Chapter 12. Determining the Future	155
Chapter 13. Short-lived Freedom	171
Chapter 14. Tigress Marries Lion	191
Chapter 15. Burying Gamma and Epsilon	205
Chapter 16. The Dawning of a Prophesy	224
Chapter 17. A Destiny Fulfilled	248

Eleanor, the Firebrand Queen

Chapter 1. Inheriting the Duchy of Aquitaine

Petronilla was gazing out the door of the old school room in our palace at L'Ombriere as Papa recited a chapter from the multitude of laws of our Duchy of Aquitaine. A well-thumbed copy of Cicero lay on the table. The aroma of freshly threshed hay drifted in from nearby fields mixed with the scent of the blossoms from the garden.

Papa's voice broke into my reverie, 'Eleanor! Are you listening? Nilla, why do you not run off and play? You are daydreaming.'

'That is not fair! Nilla is always allowed to miss lessons.'

'Elea, it is you who is destined to be Duchess of Aquitaine, not your little sister.'

'But Papa, I already know them off by heart. I feel like a talking parrot, over and over, law after law, till my eyes cross.'

Papa chided me for being rude but at times my heart is heavy with the responsibility I know will be mine one day. I hung my head and stared at the gold, bejewelled girdle round my waist, fiddling with a loose pearl. I must ask Renée to restitch it before it falls off. Papa gave me the girdle for my twelfth birthday.

Although I have been encouraged to question everything from Latin verbs to discourses by Aristotle, it was no use arguing with Papa. No, I was stuck in the schoolroom while Nilla and my friends, Clotilde and Jerome, played in the gardens, breathing fresh air instead of ink and parchment, practising, practising, practising, a never-ending education. Papa's voice rang in my ears, 'Do your duty, Eleanor'.

The wealth of the Aquitaine surrounds me. The opulence of our palaces and estates I take for granted as I do my education, music, poetry and the love in which I am enveloped. But the weight of my future duty hangs over me. I hope Papa lives forever.

***

We played many games around the old Roman walls. Renée was always darning our hose and kissing better scraped knees. I remember trying to learn the names of all the herbs in the Herbarium one summer. Everything grows so well here in the gardens, flowers as well as fruits and vegetables. The vines produce the most delicious wine. There are olive trees, too, some so old and twisted our gardeners say they were planted by the Romans. L'Ombriere has always been a favourite palace, but now it is carved on my heart as the place where the Archbishop broke the news that Papa had died.

Archbishop Geoffrey told me I was special in the eyes of God. If I was so special to God, why has He taken away all whom I love? He took my *Maman* before I knew her or can remember what she looked like, and my little brother also. He was only a baby named William after Papa. Everyone was crying. Renée came to look after Nilla and me because *Maman* died with William.

And now God has taken my beloved Papa. The Archbishop said Papa was in the bosom of St James in his shrine at Compostela and therefore mightily favoured by God. If I were not so bereaved this would be funny. Papa only went on this pilgrimage because the Pope had excommunicated him again. Maybe His Grace was trying to be kind. That I am now Duchess of Aquitaine is too fearful to comprehend. I think I am too young.

In this old school room Papa told us many stories about our Roman ancestors. It was here he read *The Aeneid* to Petronilla and me. He said I was Juno and Nilla was Dido. I love Aeneas' adventures. Whatever fate awaits us, I must keep *The Aeneid*. I know Nilla will not want it. I will find some special trinkets for her.

Archbishop Geoffrey told me King Louis of France was to be my guardian. It was Papa's wish to keep me safe. I find this most odd. Papa had no liking for the French. He said they were pious and dirty and spent more time praying

Chapter 1. Inheriting the Duchy of Aquitaine

than bathing. There was little I could do. I must obey Papa's wishes. Renée said Papa would never have made this decision if it was not for a good purpose. I have heard King Louis is grossly fat.

Renée is calling me to get some fresh air. She grumbles if I stay at my journal too long, and worries I am becoming melancholy which is not my usual disposition.

But my head is whirling with the abrupt changes in my life when all around me life seems normal. Birds are tweeting, Petronilla's pet monkey Simian, has stolen the laundry maids' freshly washed linens and has dragged them though the dirt. The maids are furious. Nilla tried to catch the naughty monkey. He is now in a tree.

***

I was summoned back to the Archbishop's palace. I was nervous, fearful of his tidings. He had a most official looking missive in front of him, with grand looking crests and seals from King Louis VI of France. He read the Latin screed to me that requested my hand in marriage to his son Prince Louis. Surely, it was a jest. I do not want to live in Paris. It was not fair!

When I returned from Archbishop Geoffrey's palace, I ran to the ruins of the Aphrodite temple. I had a long hard cry. Why must I marry? I am barely thirteen years old. Renée found me, dried my eyes and encouraged me to talk to her. She listened with patience to my ranting as I cursed my fate. She tried to comfort me by telling me what she knew about Prince Louis. He is fifteen years old, supposed to be quiet with a pleasant disposition. When his brother Phillip was killed, he became heir to the throne. Before his ascension he lived in a monastery.

Nothing Renée said helped. I hitched up my gown and ran.

Our head groom found me in the stables with my horse. I had put on her bridle, but I could not manage the heavy saddle.

'Lady Eleanor, what are you doing?'

I could not think of an answer. I did not know. Next, Jerome arrived. He looked like I felt, miserable. Since he was six years old, he has lived with us because he is an orphan. Like me, his happy life has been upended. He must go to the Benedictines.

I dropped the saddle and bolted. Jerome ran after me and caught me. I said I was going to run away.

'Where Elly?'

'You can come, too!'

'Come on, Wild Child, you know we cannot. Your fate is determined, like mine. We have to obey your Papa's wishes.'

I stamped my feet and swore in dialect. Papa would have been disgusted, but I got some of my frustration off my chest. I just wish I could be as carefree as Nilla's monkey.

***

I saw the courier arrive. I have since been informed Prince Louis is two days away. The French are travelling by night to avoid the heat of the day. Are they afraid of the sun? It is not that hot: where is their fortitude?

My maids laid out many gowns for me to choose to wear for my introduction to Prince Louis. At least this was exciting. I like wearing pretty gowns. Every seamstress within the palace has been weaving, embroidering and stitching for my trousseau. The lace on the chemises was made by the nuns at the abbey. It is so fine, so beautifully finished. My lacemaking attempts always look clumsy because I get the bobbins tangled; also, I do not practise. Nilla likes this sort of occupation and is more adroit than I am.

I chose a yellow gown embroidered with many brightly coloured flowers. It was also stitched with precious gems and pearls that will sparkle like stars when I move. The chemise was made of the finest linen, with lace at the neck, sleeves and hem. The girdle for my waist was woven in gold thread. Renée said I will be a marvel for all to see.

I was bathed and scrubbed (no more inky fingers), and my hair washed and rinsed in lemon juice to highlight the

Chapter 1. Inheriting the Duchy of Aquitaine

colour. Finally, my tangled tresses were brushed and brushed till my scalp tingled. My body was scented in a specially prepared perfume made from an essence of lily of the valley. My cheeks were given a hint of rouge; my eyes rimmed in kohl. It took hours to get me dressed in the beautiful gown with all its intricate lacings and long train. I think the bells rang more than thrice before I was finally on my way to the audience chamber which was especially hung with new tapestries and laid with carpets from Byzantium for my first meeting with Prince Louis.

My maids, Renée and the pages escorted me to my throne. Everyone was fussing around arranging my train, making sure the crown of Aquitaine sat straight on my head. It was altered to fit me. It is heavier than any coronet I have worn before. I felt like an ornament on display. Everyone stepped back as the doors opened and there stood my betrothed. Prince Louis looked as ill at ease as I felt. There was a deathly silence, no fanfares. Prince Louis was surrounded by attendants who looked like priests and nuns at a wake; all were darkly robed. They reminded me of the black *cafard* that scurry in dark corners. The Prince wore a plain cream tunic. He looked like a monk.

Archbishop Geoffrey entered the chamber with a dour-faced French cleric, the Abbé Suger, who made me feel uneasy. They escorted Prince Louis to stand in front of me. He gave a little nod as we were introduced, then sat next to me. After the introductions were over, as quickly as they had flurried in, they flurried out, a blur of faces and strange voices speaking in Langue d'Oeil. Papa had not taught us the language of the French, saying it was barbaric. My entourage followed the French.

Prince Louis and I sat aloof from one another. A long silence ensued. I am sometimes considered garrulous, but I could think of nothing to say. I glanced at Prince Louis out of the corner of my eye, he was staring at the floor his hands clasped in what could have been prayer. I wondered if I was that frightening.

I got a little braver and managed to look at him more carefully. His hair was fair and curly. He seemed to be slight in build. He was pale, his nose a little prominent, but mine is a bit aquiline too. I could not see his eyes.

I was about to ask him if he would like some wine when a piercing twitter caught our attention. My heart sank. Simian was capering across the top of the tapestries on the opposite wall. Prince Louis let out a cry. Even in Langue d'Oeil I understood the word *Satan*. As Simian is small and black with a long tail, I suppose he does look like a little devil. Prince Louis stared in horror and made the sign of the cross. He looked so funny, I had difficulty keeping my face expressionless. In Latin (I presumed he spoke it), I explained it was not the devil, but a pet monkey. I had to disentangle my train from my throne to move across to the tapestries where I tried to coax Simian down from high above my head. But no, he was having a great game as he chattered and scampered from one side of the tapestries to the other. Simian would have to be bribed. I excused myself from my terrified betrothed, dragged my burdensome train to the door, and alerted the guards outside to fetch my recalcitrant sister to collect her wretched monkey.

Petronilla sidled into the chamber with half the palace guard grinning like gargoyles behind her. I had to kick her in the ankle to get her to concentrate on Simian and not the Prince who stood as far from the tapestries as possible. Simian will do anything for a few almonds and dried apricots. With excited squeaks, he leapt down the exquisite faces of knights and unicorns to land on Petronilla's shoulder who swung her eleven-year old hips towards poor Prince Louis to introduce him to Simian. I hissed at her to get her revolting little pet and herself out of the chamber or Simian would not see the light of day, followed by a few choice epithets for good measure. She did not bat an eyelid. Hampered by my train there was little I could do. I would have loved to have boxed her ears as she simpered past Prince Louis with doe eyes.

Chapter 1. Inheriting the Duchy of Aquitaine

At least the atmosphere had thawed. I took the opportunity to pour us both a goblet of wine. Prince Louis took a hasty gulp. I apologised for Simian and my saucy sister. He said he did not notice my sister. (I could not wait to tell her that!) He wanted to know about Simian and where he came from. I told him Papa brought the monkey from Morocco as a pet for Petronilla and me. We were supposed to share him, but he soon became my sister's most favoured playmate because I was not so enamoured after he destroyed one of my necklaces.

We fell into silence again. I broke it by asking him if he liked to read. He nodded. I asked him if he had a favourite book. He lisped, The Confessions of Saint Augustine. I said I had many favourite books; The Aeneid, The Iliad and The Odyssey, and that Greek was my favourite language. Prince Louis looked at me in a most peculiar manner. I wondered if something had gone awry with my gown.

'Can you read?'

'Of course, I can read.'

How foolish, I thought, are the French.

When he said he thought learning in one of my sex and status was unwomanly, my face flushed! I took a deep breath to control my ire. I informed Prince Louis that not only could I read I could also write, and I was fluent in three languages along with a smattering of Basque. Furthermore, if it was not for my fluency in Latin, we would not be able to converse because His Lordship did not speak my dialect and I had yet to learn his unless he thought it too unwomanly for me to do so. He did not answer, but I noticed his ears had turned pink.

I swallowed my wine in haste and stood as gracefully as my heavy gown would allow. If my eyes were basilisks, he would have been a pile of ash. I announced I would take my leave. I stormed to my quarters. The crown hit the bed as I entered and bounced on the floor at Renée's feet. As I tore at the lacings, I announced I never wished to see this gown again to be reminded of what was before me.

***

I ran to Papa's library. The diamond patterns were darkening on the floor as the last rays of sun filtered through the tall glass windows. I have recorded what took place. I yearn for my Papa. I need his help and advice. My life is a catastrophe. Furthermore, I have broken two quills and blotted my journal. Renée called, so I let her in. She was saddened when I related what happened. I was still fuming,

'How can I marry such a pious-looking fool? Does he expect me to unlearn all that I know? Prince Louis is an ignorant barbarian. He cannot string two words together or even recognise a monkey when he sees one!'

Renée reminded me of tonight's banquet. Ink and quills bounced as my fist hit the desk. I yelled at her,

'I do not want to go!'

***

I went. I decided to show those oafs of Frenchmen how we do things in the Aquitaine, to display our learning and sophistication. I wore a lighter gown so I could dance. Before the evening proceeded, I instructed the minstrels to play at their best to produce their finest songs of chivalry and courtly love as well as *Chansons de Geste*. I brought my lute so I could join in their music, to display to that bumpkin Prince more of my abilities. I cared not what my betrothed thought of me. He cannot change who I am. I am everything I have been trained to be since I was declared Papa's heir. I am proud my father spent his lifetime educating me, inspiring me to learn. Moreover, I will never stop learning.

His Lordship made no attempt to engage me in conversation though I was seated next to him. His mouth flapped open like a gasping fish as he took in the opulence of his surroundings. His courtiers wavered between shock and amazement at what there was to behold in food, wine and entertainment. Not a sou was spared on the lavish banquet. The treasury Prince Louis had brought to impress my people made him look like a beggar.

Chapter 2. The Reluctant Bride

I fled to a far corner of the school room to write. It may be many months before we arrive in Paris and I can take up quill and ink. I must pinch myself now all the formalities are over – I am a wife. The wedding ceremony attracted people from far and wide who came on carts, on foot, on donkeys and all manner of carriages to see Louis and I paraded through Bordeaux as husband and wife. I wore a gown of scarlet silk encrusted with jewels. The guests were numbered over a thousand I was told. The wedding feast was of such munificence, words could barely describe it. I ate not a morsel.

We will be leaving here soon to ride through the Aquitaine to introduce Louis as my husband. He must be presented to my vassals as the Duke of Aquitaine and Gascony and Count of Poitou. He will rule in my name. But by my troth, for as long as I draw breath, I will never let him forget he rules because of my name.

***

My stomach is like a butter churn. I am anxious. What will happen when I must go to my bed chamber? All my life I have been surrounded by intriguing trysts, grandparents who loved but who were not wed to each other, strange moans in bushes and shadows, songs of courtly love and innuendo. But since Petronilla and I reached marriageable age, slobbering mastiffs have slept outside our bed chambers. For all the lascivious talk about the immoral House of Aquitaine, I know little of the ways of men.

I tried to express my concerns to Renée, but all I did was turn bright pink with embarrassment. She was doing her best to prepare me for married life. I am late in years coming to my monthly cycle, being a somewhat tall slender girl. At least that is what I have been told. I am still not well formed in a womanly way. The thought of Louis coming to my bed is so abhorrent I want to run away and hide.

Renée succeeded in keeping Louis out of my bed chamber till we get to know each other, but I do not know how much longer our marriage can remain unconsummated. The French have made it clear they want an heir. Not that Louis was beating down my door to demand his connubial rights. But I do not believe we are ready for babies. I think I am too young, though I am certainly more mature than Louis who behaves like a monk. He is so naïve.

***

We arrived in Paris and I have found a corner in my new quarters in which to write. It is not as satisfactory as I would like because I must keep the activity secret from members of my new court who, like Louis, do not approve.

It was a long slow ride from Bordeaux and Poitiers to Île de France. Our progress through the Aquitaine was well received. Papa's vassals welcomed me as their Duchess and were willing to pay homage to me. The French could not but notice Louis was given only passing recognition.

Since arriving, I was introduced to Louis' mother, who I sense does not like me. I have tried to be polite. I overheard Queen Adelaide complaining to Louis I was gaudily dressed, far too beautiful, and therefore could not be trusted. I am puzzled to know what one's face has to do with trust. Her Latin is rather odd. Maybe I think too much. I have yet to meet the king who, I am told, does not keep good health. No wonder. The palace is built on this island in the river and is damp, dark and draughty. I am suffering mightily from the cold as are all the members of my household. It is also smelly. Everything bad is tossed in the Seine. Papa was right about the French; they do not burden themselves with cleanliness.

***

Today Louis and I were summoned to the king's bed

Chapter 2. The Reluctant Bride

chamber. Before we entered, Louis surprised me by giving me a beautifully worked scented handkerchief. I was touched by his gesture until I realised why. The door of the king's bed chamber opened, and we were ushered into his presence. At once I was overwhelmed by a stench far greater than anything I had ever smelt. I retched as the odour enveloped my senses. I thought I was going to faint. Louis had to almost carry me over the threshold. In a bed, propped up on many pillows, was a white slug, a mountainous maggot of a man issuing the foulest fumes I have ever experienced. This was King Louis, the man my father made my guardian.

It took every ounce of inner fortitude to approach the bedside. Louis was nudging me, little by little, from behind. Scented handkerchief or no, I was trying not to breath. King Louis wheezed at me to come closer, so he could see me more clearly. His eyes were slits in rows of folded, pallid flesh. I stood leaning as far back on my husband as I could while trying not to look repulsed. The old king, after eyeing me as if I were a tasty morsel, remarked how fortunate Louis was to have such a beauty for his wife. He addressed me in Latin, saying he had heard I could read and write. I nodded. I was trying to think of a way to escape. When he asked what I liked to read, I blurted out '*Cicero,*' the first author who came into my head. This was followed by a crescendo of guffawing, coughing and spluttering, as the whale of a man laughed. I thought King Louis was going to die, as, I am sure, did his attendants. He gasped for breath and repeated 'Cicero' to his son. Not only was Louis married to the most beautiful creature he had ever seen but she was a Roman Advocate as well. After I regained a little composure, I muttered I also liked *The Aeneid*. King Louis surprised me by saying he liked Virgil too and would I come back and read it to him. I nodded.

I had to keep my word. I also had to get up enough courage to return to his bed chamber without vomiting at the smell. Louis and his cohorts were probably thinking I was getting my comeuppance for being precocious. Renée as usual came to my rescue by dousing my gowns and veils in heavy perfume. Also, King Louis would readily fall asleep, so I did not have to stay long in his presence. I discovered this giant lump of blubber held a man of great intellect and sensitivity. He was astute; his reign was good, and he was liked and respected by his people.

I grew fond of him and I think he liked me as well. King Louis would make little jests to get me to laugh, but this used to make him cough. One day I was brave enough to say I would laugh and cough so he could save his breath, but this only made things worse because he thought what I said was hilarious, such a dear man. He does not disapprove of my learning either; he said he hoped I will be able to help Louis in the future which I do not want to think about.

Louis is mightily influenced by the clergy, especially Abbé Suger. I think I can understand why Papa wanted King Louis to be my protector. What Papa would think of his son and heir, I know not.

***

It was not easy settling in. My life could not be more different to how I was brought up, let alone the expectations of my role as Louis' wife. I miss Papa with all my heart, and Nilla too, as we continue to mourn his death. Poor little Nilla, though she was trying to be brave, she was like a lost soul. I am doing my best to make sure she is not left alone when I must attend the French Court. Where possible I take her with me, and insist she be given status as my sister. I need her as much as she needs me.

We have both been accustomed to learning with our father. It is a mighty void in our daily lives. Yet Paris is full of scholars, students and learned men discussing, arguing and reading philosophical extracts. Lectures are held on the Left Bank. Peter Abelard is here. Everyone is flocking to listen to his theories on metaphysics and ontology. I have heard he has been giving daily dissertations in Notre Dame. Papa was greatly interested in Abelard's teachings. He discussed

Chapter 2. The Reluctant Bride

his philosophies and tried to pass them on to Nilla and me, but I think we were a little too young to fully understand. I am curious to hear Abelard speak. Louis I am certain would have a pink-eared fit if he knew I wanted to attend a lecture by this great thinker. He would consider it unwomanly. Damn his eyes!

I tried to work out a way I could get out of the palace to attend one of Abelard's lectures. I knew it would be easy to get into Notre Dame with the scholars and students from all over Paris. I put my idea to Nilla. It would be easier to go with her if we could come up with a suitable disguise. She told me she thought it would be boring. I had to coax her,

'Come on Nilla, where is your sense of adventure. It will be fun to escape. Look, I'll give you my ruby and emerald bracelet – come on, little Sis.'

That managed to convince her. She put her sneaky mind into the project and found two monks' robes from goodness knows where. I did not ask. We explored the palace for a way out. The rickety old water-gate on the other side of the cloisters off my quarters looked the most promising. There is a bargee's towpath along the Seine leading past Notre Dame and reached by the water-gate. All we had to do was to get out without being seen at the time of one of Abelard's lectures.

We escaped with ease. So much for the French guards! Our plaited hair was tucked down the back of our robes with the cowls pulled low over our faces. We looked like any one of the young acolytes milling about.

Soon we were safely in the Cathedral with hundreds of eager people all waiting to hear Abelard. We were jostled and pushed, not something we had ever experienced, but it added to the excitement and fun. We pushed back. Nilla swore at some scrawny character in our native dialect when he stepped on her foot, hardly in character as a monk. I told her to keep her voice down when I noticed she was wearing the bracelet I had given her. I hissed at her to take it off. She shoved it further up her arm under her sleeve.

The hubbub reached fever pitch as Peter Abelard arrived and mounted the pulpit. A hush spread through the throng as he began to speak. We were transfixed by his oratory, his voice echoed through the great cathedral. To Nilla and me, every word of his discourse was like a precious jewel. We were mesmerised by his ideas like the crowds around us. After his voice died away silence hovered over everyone before a crescendo of cheering and clapping soared through the vaulted arches of Notre Dame.

Nilla and I wrapped our arms around each other in excitement. It was incredible we were part of that moment. We jumped up and down with not a thought given to our disguises or dislodged cowls until over Nilla's shoulder I espied Abbé Suger. I pulled Nilla's cowl over her face and buried my head in her shoulder. I prayed he had not seen us. Since the day we met at Louis' and my betrothal, we have never liked each other. He does not approve of me.

Over the hullabaloo, I yelled at Nilla that we had to get out of there. But she could not hear me. I hoped by my expression she knew something was amiss. I managed to adjust my cowl. It was difficult to move. We were pummelled and shoved. The crowd was so thick it was like wading through porridge. The cowls impeded our view. I was terrified we were going to lose our footing as hordes of adoring participants swarmed towards Abelard. It was hopeless. Nilla and I were forced to move with them. All I could do was hang onto the cord belted around Nilla's waist so as not to be separated.

We were swept close to one of the side chapels. With all my might, I pushed Nilla off into its stepped entrance. We both fell together at the foot of a small altar. Our robes were all awry, but heaven be praised, Abbé Suger was nowhere in sight. We straightened ourselves. It looked like the whole of Paris was streaming past; we had to wait to make an exit. By now, I knew we would be missed from the palace. Our adventure was looking dire.

Time dragged on but the crowd started to thin. When it

Chapter 2. The Reluctant Bride

became safe to move, I gripped Nilla's hand and we edged past the soaring pillars and managed to reach a side door. With a sigh of relief, we were out in the open, except we had no idea where we were. It was late afternoon. I began to panic.

I scoured the architecture of the mighty structure for a familiar gargoyle or statue. Nilla started crying, which did nothing to calm my fears. I yelled at her that howling was not helping and told her to keep quiet. She told me, as I had forced her to come, I had no right to tell her to shut her mouth. I demanded my bracelet back. It was no longer on Nilla's arm. I boxed her ears for wearing it. She hit me back. So, there we were, the future Queen of France and my noble sister from the House of Aquitaine lost and fighting like fish wives beside Notre Dame.

Red faced and breathing like bellows, we heard footsteps. With haste we adjusted our cowls. I hoped we looked like two young monks having a conversation. A tall man strode past. He looked familiar to me. One of Louis' knights from our court perhaps? I decided to follow him in hope he would lead us to a landmark I could recognise. I pushed Nilla along in front of me and hissed at her to stop snivelling.

He led us to the front of Notre Dame; a relief because I could see the bank of the Seine where we had come along the towpath. The shadows were getting longer so we had to run. The towpath was muddy in places; sure enough, much to Nilla's amusement, I slipped over. We slunk inside the cloister door to my chamber to be greeted by a relieved but furious Renée. There was uproar because we had been missed; the palace searched from tower to dungeon. Renée demanded an explanation as to why we were dressed as we were, why I was covered in mud and how come Nilla's face was scratched. By the time the tongue lashing ended, I felt we were six years old again.

We bathed and dressed, giggling with relief. But I had to face Louis and Suger who, I hoped and prayed had not recognised the two young monks at Abelard's oratory. With my fingers crossed, I said Lady Petronilla and I went to the towpath to watch the water traffic on the Seine and had lost track of the time. Suger looked at me with suspicion written all over his face. I stared back with every bit of hauteur I could muster.

When I re-read what I wrote about Nilla's and my escapade, I can see it was an essay in foolishness, a risk for more than one reason. The clerics of Louis' court, particularly Abbé Bernard de Clairveaux, consider Abelard a heretic. Is that why Suger was there, to build a case against him? Nilla and I were lucky to get away with it, but it was worth every minute. My mind is still reeling from the powerful thoughts and philosophies of that inspiring man.

***

Our unconsummated marriage is causing more and more consternation throughout the court. Abbé Suger is insistent that the event must take place even though Louis is showing no interest in me as a woman. The rumours are flying around that this is because I am not a virgin. Renée did her best to quell the tales and stressed to me there was only one way to stop the gossip. I protested there was little I could do if Louis showed no interest in me.

Renée, bless her, approached Suger. She told him Prince Louis was showing more interest in prayer than an heir, that it was up to Suger to step in to encourage him, because the king was too ill to advise his son on such matters. She emphasised I was a virgin and a beautiful one at that so what was wrong with the prince? Was he incompetent or impotent? I had to ask her to explain what she meant. I am still blushing.

Suger got the message. Their conversation would have been something to behold as the dour, celibate cleric advised the reluctant Prince on how to lay with his wife. I am hesitant too, but I do not want my reputation sullied any further because Louis is naïve.

So far, no romantic meetings have eventuated. Sometimes

before bed, I play chess or backgammon or play music and sing with Nilla and our maids. But after they leave for their beds, I am left alone.

***

What I relate now is embarrassing. Last night, after everyone had gone to their chambers, I was disturbed by a rustling beside my bed. It was cold so I had the curtains closed. To begin with I thought it was Nilla, who at times had bad dreams and climbed into my bed for comfort. Within the cocoon of drapery someone had arrived, someone heavier than my sister. Whoever it was had been drinking wine. The odour filled the enclosed nook. I was so frightened, my heart thumped. I pulled myself from the bedclothes on to my pillow and demanded whoever it was identify themselves. Instead this person grabbed at me. I kicked with all my might. A cry of pain echoed as I contacted a head or shoulder. It was Louis. I shrieked 'by Lucifer,' and demanded to know what he thought he was doing in my bed. A wrestling match followed. Louis was inebriated and it was dark, so I won. Louis landed with a thud on the floor. By now my yells had brought palace guards, my maids and Renée with candles aloft. Louis bolted. Renée calmed my humiliation.

The next day, prompted by Renée and my maids, I went to speak to my husband who I discovered had a blackened eye from my kick. I told Louis, if he wanted to come to my bed, to warn me of his intentions and to come sober. Suger, who was present, gave me a lecture on duty to my husband. I could not believe how bad his Latin was. I told Suger I did not believe it was a husband's duty to terrify his wife by attacking her in her bed. Then, unable to help myself, I corrected his Latin, which sent him into purple spasms. Of course, I was now in trouble for impertinence and answering back. Louis uttered not a word.

***

Louis' unsuccessful attempt to 'deflower' me reached King Louis' ears. Two days later, when I was reading Aristotle's philosophies to him, the old man cleared his throat and asked what I thought of his son. I had to stop and think. There was no way I could lie to this dear man, nor could I tell him I thought his son, weak. Couched with, I hope, tact, I told King Louis I was finding it difficult to get to know my husband. He spent most of his time with Abbé Suger and other priests. I said I thought I frightened Louis because he knew little about girls. A snort erupted from the bedclothes. I fixed my eyes on Aristotle as the tome shook in my hands. King Louis looked across his vast middle deep in thought. He asked if I would have Louis sent to him. As I scratch my thoughts across this parchment, a drumbeat of trouble pounds in my head, with Suger beating the rhythm.

For the next few days, I kept out of sight. I am learning Langue d'Oeil with Nilla. It has not been difficult, because both of us have learnt languages all our lives with Papa. I do have a slight Langue d'Oc accent, but I can now hold a simple conversation.

***

I was awaiting the arrival of carpets and tapestries from Poitiers. This cold draughty palace was getting into my bones. I have had the broken panes replaced in the windows and fireplaces installed in my quarters as well as Louis' and his parent's. Of course, the French think we Aquitainean soft, but as it has improved everyone's health to be warm, they have little to complain about. Suger had to shut his mouth when I reminded him whose treasury was paying. But the biggest upheaval occurred when I had the rushes removed from the floors, carted by barge across the Seine and burnt. You would have thought I had brought hell's wrath down on their heads. They could rant all they liked, but my actions removed most of the vermin infesting the palace along with years of filth. I also stopped sneezing from the dust the rushes created or screaming when a mouse ran out.

Chapter 2. The Reluctant Bride

***

The carpets and tapestries arrived and were installed. My new home at last was looking more attractive and no longer resembled a garrison, though I think the stark monastic quarters of my husband and his bevy of monks will remain dreary. I have a plan to develop the garden outside my quarters. It is surrounded by cloisters on two sides. Opposite is a high wall where the water-gate leads to a dilapidated quay with steps to the Seine. At the far end towards Notre Dame is a swampy morass which attracts swarms of mosquitoes. I thought it could be made into an attractive lake as well as controlling the mosquito problem. The garden is now a tangle of plants, vines and weeds. There is a gardener with a few ragged looking churls, but they have little idea of how a garden should be laid out. Renée will be invaluable. Her knowledge of herbs, shrubs and flowers is vast.

To prevent another furore, I needed to consult Louis about my plans, which meant Suger will be hovering like a dragonfly. I find it most irritating I cannot consult my husband a jot without that dome-headed, scrawny cleric in the background flapping his black robes. He reminds me of a carrion-eating crow.

In the meantime, I have heard not a word of what transpired between Louis and his father. The old king's health is deteriorating. I have not been called upon to read of late.

***

As chance would have it, I met Louis walking from his chapel to his chamber alone today. He almost jumped out of his skin when he realised he could not avoid me. I thought I would surprise him with my Langue d'Oeil, so I greeted him in his tongue, not that he commented. I asked him for a little time to discuss some plans I had for a garden. From there, I thought I could move to more intimate topics. He relaxed a little and agreed a garden would be an attractive addition to my quarters. Before he could leave I requested he spare me a few moments to walk with me to the cloister where I could elaborate on my ideas for paths, rose arbours, herb beds or even a fountain or two as well as my vision for a lake to help eliminate the mosquito problem. He said little but admitted a lake would be beneficial if it rid us of the biting insects. We looked in silence towards the muddy swamp.

It was pointless shilly-shallying any further, so I enquired about his father's health since I saw him last. I guessed his father wanted to talk about me, so I asked Louis how the meeting transpired. Louis reddened. We were now in the awkward situation where our conversation was becoming personal. But this time I was determined he talk to me, even if I had to squeeze the words from his throat.

I put my hand on his arm. If needs be, I would hold him fast. His Adam's apple worked up and down. Did he ever want to kiss me, I asked? Waves of horror wracked his face. It was too much; I burst into tears and begged to know why he hated me so much. I reverted to Latin. I promised him I was a virgin, pleading with him not to believe the rumours about me being promiscuous. I admitted I knew as much about men as he knew about women. With damp, flaming cheeks I stammered if we were to have a child, we would have to consummate our marriage regardless of how much he loathed me.

He entreated me not to cry. He said he did not hate me but blurted out that he did not know what to do. His father suggested he practise in a brothel. That was anathema to him. Suger had given him wine the night he came to my bed chamber to give him courage.

He said, to my surprise,

'And all I did was frighten you, Eleanor.'

This was the first time Louis had ever used my name. I looked at him, my feelings for him thawed a little. I wiped my nose on my sleeve. Louis gave me his handkerchief. We both shuffled and stared at our feet. Dear God, I thought, we are little more than children. I supposed I was sophisticated, but

Chapter 2. The Reluctant Bride

I am only fourteen years, and poor Louis is a sixteen-year-old naïf. What were we to do? Both of us are unenthusiastic lovers.

Our conversation had run its course, so I requested to take my leave and walked towards the door. Louis called after me.

'I could come tonight if it pleases you.'

My stomach lurched, but I nodded.

***

I have not been able to write for weeks. Each time I face a piece of parchment, my hand starts to shake. Is this a woman's lot? My innocence has been sullied, my girlhood, once a carefree magical place has gone.

I was being smirked at by the French court. How I hate this place! I begged Renée to find a way for me to go home. But she is as ensnared as I am, trapped within *my* fate. I am forcing myself to write, to purge myself of the revulsion I feel.

They strew my bed with rose petals and dressed me in the finest of linen edged with the nun's delicate lace. My hair cascaded to below my waist. Candle flames winked and danced. My night of nights was a disaster. I am still a virgin though the rumours persist I was never one in the first place.

I can barely describe what eventuated. Louis arrived and flung himself on top of me. I lay rigid with embarrassment and distaste. I knew I had to open my legs, but our gowns got in the way. I could feel something hard, poking and thrusting. Louis let out a sort of strangled groan. I felt something warm and sticky on my inner thigh. Louis scrambled from my bed and ran away. I felt filthy. There was no blood on the sheets. I was hysterical.

Some days later, I overheard a group of Louis' men snorting and laughing that the prince preferred men to women, that he was a catamite. I have no idea what a catamite is – a religious order maybe? Their laughter had a nasty edge which I did not like. I was going to ask Renée about it, but something prevented me. I think I do not want to know.

Suger sent Louis back to my bed after Renée told him she would go to the king if the court persisted with the rumours about my virginity. She was emphatic, stating that, until the prince could perform his duty to his wife, I would remain a virgin and there would be no heirs for France. Her parting words to the Abbé were; if Louis were a stallion he would be castrated or worse. I cannot believe she was so bold.

It took four visits to my bed before Louis eventually succeeded in penetrating my body. It hurt. I felt more defiled than ever, but I am no longer a virgin. There was at last blood on the sheets, proving the gossips wrong. Now all I must do is produce a son.

Chapter 3. Crowned Queen of France

Some two weeks have passed since my last cycle. Mornings have been miserable. I cannot eat a morsel without vomiting. Renée is sure I am going to have a child. I swing between fear to exultation. I have begged her not to say a word to anyone. If anyone asks why I am sick, I have implored her to say I have eaten something that has upset my stomach.

It was a tumultuous time in the palace. King Louis was failing. His physicians think he is not long for this world. I have only visited him for a few minutes. He was not conscious most of the time and rambling when he was. Louis and Queen Adelaide have barely left his bedside. He was surrounded by priests. Abbé Suger was praying with such fervour, it would be enough to send him to heaven in desperation, I thought.

I will miss this dear old man. He has been so kind to me; the only person in this palace who has welcomed me. It is terrifying to think Louis will become King of France. Never will there be a more reluctant nor unsuitable monarch to grace a throne. The king has often said I will be able to help Louis, but I do not think Suger will allow my husband to seek my advice on matters of state. I can advise a little regarding the Aquitaine. I know its laws backwards, but I know nothing of the affairs of the French Kingdom.

I was hoping King Louis would go to his Maker in the knowledge I was with child. I had a miscarriage. I am heart broken. Only a few people knew or suspected my condition. I had only told Louis a few days before I became most unwell with cramping pains. Renée did her best for me with my other maids, but nothing could stop the bleeding. I feel so weak.

Bad news always seems to howl down like a winter storm. I was called from my convalescence to hasten to King Louis' bedside. He died shortly after I sat beside him. Perhaps he waited for me. Louis amazed me by throwing himself into my arms. I did my best to comfort him. Poor Louis, his Papa and his baby within days. Maybe the dear old king and my little one are together with Papa, in the arms of God.

***

I find little time to write these days though I now have a proper place to do so. King Louis bequeathed me his library and all his books, a haven in this bleak palace. How kind of the dear man to realise I needed a place to breath, to be myself. He understood I would struggle to adjust to my new status as a decorative adjunct to Louis. Suger and Abbé Bernard de Clairvaux take every opportunity to remind me my duty is to produce the next in line. With much finger wagging, it was made clear the loss of our first child was a black mark against my suitability as Queen of France. They have no sympathy for my distress or sorrow. Nor was anything said about Louis finding my bed abhorrent. There is something amiss in our marriage. I am sure there must be more than the tussling, groping copulation that takes place between Louis and me. If I touch him or try to kiss him, he either freezes or whatever it is that occurs with men happens too soon. He says he loves me, but I think not my body. He has never seen me naked nor I him. On his rare visits, he slinks in the dark to my bed. Afterwards he runs away in shame. I am left angry, full of revulsion.

***

Our coronation was a grand occasion. Throngs of citizens lined the streets to gasp as we paraded from the cathedral. Louis and I were greeted by all manner of nobles, clergy and simple folk paying homage. Louis found the ceremony deeply spiritual. It was inspirational with its prayers, rituals, plain song and triumphant fanfares. The crown is heavy.

Louis was trying to take control of his kingdom. With unusual stubbornness he is ignoring all advice, even Suger's,

Chapter 3. Crowned Queen of France

which is most odd. I have tried on the rare moments we are together to show interest in his duties, to give him my support regarding the heavy burden of his new responsibilities. But he is more taciturn than ever, and often, for one of usually mild temperament, angry. Oft times I find his mood strange. The only way I glean any information about France is when I overhear Louis' advisors or knights whispering in corners. I do not know why, but I suspect trouble is brewing.

***

To my surprise, Louis announced we were going on a royal progress to Poitiers. It will be exciting riding through the Aquitaine to the homage of my people. I have not been home since we were wed. It will also take my mind off the tension in the palace. Louis' mother has decided to leave us, to return to her lands at Compiegne. Although Queen Adelaide has never liked me, we did have one thing in common, our distaste for Suger. I think he drove her out.

On arrival in Poitiers, and to my amazement, Louis informed me he was going to invade Toulouse to re-regain control of the county on my behalf. It would be more than honourable if he could restore Grandmother Phillipa's usurped inheritance. I hope Louis and his knights give that upstart thief Alphonso Jordon, who dares to call himself Count of Toulouse, a good hiding. But I worry about Louis' abilities. He is no soldier; he can barely stride a horse, and Alphonso is a seasoned knight. I fear Louis may be over-ambitious.

As I dreaded, it all ended badly. Louis did not prepare well enough. He and his men were routed and suffered many casualties. Louis arrived back from Toulouse humiliated. He sulked all the way back to Paris. I also have a suspicion Petronilla is hiding something; she has been behaving very skittishly of late.

As soon as I could, I went to visit the newly laid out garden. It was wonderful to see how it has grown and developed since we have been away. It looked splendid. The lake has attracted water birds. I intend to stock it with fish. I was talking to the head gardener who is now an enthusiast for my favourite roses when Nilla appeared. The expression on her face alerted me all was not well. I dismissed the gardener and was engulfed in a tearful tale.

God's teeth she has fallen in love with Raoul de Vermandois, Louis' Seneschal, and he with her. Raoul has been in his governing position for some years, appointed by the old king. Nilla tells me the attraction blossomed in Poitiers while he was travelling with us. But Raoul is married to Theodore of Champagne's sister Eleanor, for heaven's sake. Also, he must be many years older than Nilla. She wants me to persuade Louis to have Raoul's marriage annulled. Theodore will explode for sure regarding his sister's honour even if her marriage was one of convenience.

I want Nilla to be happy, but I fear this will be a problem of great enormity. Suspicion prods me to wonder how much her dower and her being my sister has prompted Raoul's passion for her. She told me they have already lain together. Heaven forfend, what advice do I give her? She has shown no sign of heeding me in the past.

***

I was returning from the library when I heard an uproar coming from Louis' quarters. A gaggle of knights had congregated outside his chamber. They did not see me, so they made no attempt to lower their voices. I waited in a shadowy recess to eavesdrop.

It appears Louis' tilt at independence has thrown him into a dispute with the Pope. It has to do with the vacancy of the Archbishopric of Bourges. The knights were mocking a decision made by Louis to appoint Chancellor Carduc to the position. I was shocked. This was not a sensible choice. I have met the man several times. He is weak, a fool! The Pope has chosen someone else. I was straining my ears, but I could not overhear anything more as they walked away from their huddle. No wonder Louis was bellowing in his chamber.

I will be the last to be told who the Pope has selected. This will not be a good time to petition Louis on Petronilla's behalf. I will have to wait a few days. Nilla will pester me I know, but she is going to have to curb her impatience, not a family virtue I am afraid.

I was being attacked on all sides. My sister was wailing and beating her breast. She says she will die if she cannot marry Raoul as soon as possible. I leapt to the conclusion she was having a child. She swears she is not. I have warned her to keep out of his bed. I asked Renée to try to talk some sense into her. Renée rolled her eyes. Louis was ignoring me. To be honest, if it were not for my little sister, I would be happy with the status quo.

I had to give in. Petronilla's nagging was worse than iron being hammered by an armourer. I sent a page to Louis to ask to speak to him. I have not received a reply. In frustration I decided to go to his chamber and damn the consequences. Either that or I will strangle Nilla.

I entered the hallowed chamber. An atmosphere akin to a winter's frost aroused my suspicions. Suger and Bernard de Clairvaux were in a corner with their heads together. Louis was muttering to himself, agitated. With malicious glee, Suger pounced before I could utter a word. Petronilla and Raoul's affair had reached their ears via Theodore of Champagne.

Venom dripped from every syllable as Suger smirked the House of Aquitaine was showing its true colours again. I spat back it was a pity he did not find its wealth equally contaminated. He flushed puce to his tonsure. Bernard 'harrumphed' but said nothing. I requested to speak to my husband in private. Louis dismissed them. Snails could have departed at a greater pace.

I told Louis I knew about Carduc's appointment. An inane grin fixed his face. He was mightily pleased with himself. He boasted how he had defied the Pope and the Canons of Bourges who prefer a man named Pierre de la

Chatre. I thought it best to remain silent. I let him rant about how his status was being undermined by subordinates. In this mood, if I do not agree with him, he will not cooperate to help Petronilla.

I was anxious after I left Louis' chamber, but whether to please me or to spite Theodore, Louis agreed to help Raoul have his marriage annulled. There were three Bishops with whom he was on good terms. He told me they will comply. I did not expect Louis to help without more debate. I think he was still smarting about Toulouse. I will not get Nilla's hopes up too soon, however. Louis' enthusiasm could be ill conceived.

***

To keep up with events in the court has turned me into a spy. I am eager for information. The Archbishopric of Bourges continues to cause major problems. I was told Pope Innocent thinks Louis is immature and needs to grow up. Louis threw a tantrum. He has sworn on some ratty old Holy Relics that he will never allow Pierre de la Chatre into Bourges, and has had the gates locked. The Pope, in retaliation, is threatening to excommunicate Louis. If it were not so serious it would be hilarious. Louis proclaimed he cannot go back on his word because he has sworn on the Relics. It is like a game of chess; who is going to checkmate whom?

Further snippets came to me about the Pope's chosen man for the Archbishopric of Bourges. Pierre de la Chatre, I hear, has gone to Rome, as a guest of the Pope. Louis is in trouble. The Pope is not pleased that Louis locked la Chatre out of Bourges and followed up on his threat. A Papal interdict has been placed on Île de France. Everyone has been denied the sacraments, with all the implications that ensues. The pious French court is self-flagellating, tearing their hair and moaning hell has descended upon them. Louis is nervous but stubborn. My household has not batted an eyelid. The House of Aquitaine has incurred so many excommunications and Papal interdicts over the years they are almost considered a

Chapter 3. Crowned Queen of France

sport like jousting. If knocked off one's horse, pick yourself up and get back on again.

***

At last, Raoul has had his marriage annulled on the grounds of consanguinity. He and Theodore's sister were distantly related it seems. Raoul and Petronilla are now husband and wife, having been married by one of the same Bishops who approved the annulment. I am delighted she is happy. I wish I could say the same about my marriage. It is, however, one less problem for me. But it has caused bad humour with the Pope, let alone Theodore. There has been friction on and off for years between Île de France and the Count of Champagne, so I am not surprised. Oh, Nilla what have you got yourself into?

Papa never trusted Theodore. He said he was mad, belligerent and as cunning as a fox. At least he was looking after his sister Eleanor and her children since the annulment, by taking them under his roof. He was also giving shelter to Pierre de la Chatre, no doubt to incite Louis. He succeeded. I hear a precious challis bounced off the wall of Louis' chamber. (And I thought I was the only one who threw things!)

To add to Louis' fury and giving me concern, the Pope has acted against the bishops who annulled Raoul's marriage. Bernard de Clairvaux, who should remember where his loyalties lie, was meddling. The Pope has excommunicated everyone involved as well as putting interdicts on their land, including Raoul's. He ordered him back to Theodore's sister. I foresee no good coming out of this.

***

Louis went mad. In ill-fitting mail, he charged out of Paris leading a rabble of mercenaries and roustiers into Champagne. Louis will have no control over these men; they are a law unto themselves.

I have had little to no contact with Louis, but the

information that made its way back to me was shocking, to write it down, sickening. Men, women and children of Vitry-sur-Marne were being slaughtered by these brutes; their crops and animals destroyed, and churches burned. I could not believe what I was hearing.

Louis ordered an attack on the castle at Vitry-sur-Marne which was a wooden structure. I remember Papa related once how a construction of this sort can catch alight with ease from flaming arrows. My maids, Renée and I prayed that something of this magnitude would not occur.

But our prayers were unanswered. Terrified townsfolk, the old, women and children fled into the cathedral where we heard the doors were barred. The town was engulfed in flames. The cathedral where everyone had sought sanctuary became an inferno. There were no survivors.

***

Louis witnessed the conflagration. Now back in Paris he no longer speaks. His grief, guilt and shame have driven him to despair. He does not eat; he has hacked off his hair. He has flailed himself till blood soaked through his gown. I have tried to contact him, but he shuns all who want to give him comfort. He has locked himself in the stone cold of his chapel.

My tears have blotted the pages of my journal. Louis, Louis what have you done? All I can imagine are the screams of our trapped people. Whatever in God's name entered your head? Where was your judgement? I cannot salve my conscience either. I knew your decision to appoint Carduc was ill conceived, but I said nothing, not because I was afraid you would not heed me, but because I did not want to prejudice Raoul and Petronilla's chances to be together. We are all implicated. Louis, you are a naïve fool, but you are not cruel, nor are you a tyrant. Why did not Suger stop you? Maybe he tried. I do not know. But Suger and Bernard look at me as if I stood there and lit the arrows. I am guilty by neglect. I feel useless. There is not a jot I can do to ease your

Chapter 3. Crowned Queen of France

pain or be a balm for your conscience. I am no wife to you. I cannot give you comfort or consolation. We started ill the day we met. Whatever flare of affection there was between us has guttered like a candle in a pool of wax.

I pray Raoul and Nilla will find happiness together. One day the excommunications and interdicts will end. Theodore, may his conscience keep him from sleep, was not without blame either. Papa knew he was vindictive.

We are living with heavy hearts. I am searching my brain for a solution out of this mess. If I could have the interdicts against Nilla and Raoul removed it would help. I am trying to find the courage to approach Bernard or Suger. They are the only clerics I know who have some influence with the Pope, although they disapprove of me. I am so distraught; I am willing to try anything for relief.

***

I decided to ask for an audience with Abbé Bernard. He is the more approachable of the two. He fears women though, and once I heard threw himself into a freezing lake when he was attracted to a pretty girl. If I dress in a plain gown maybe he will not notice I am no longer the skinny stick of a girl who married Louis. I have grown more womanly with rounded breasts, a waist and hips, and of course, there is the 'face' that cannot be trusted. Will he despise me with all my other conceived faults because of my features? Dear Lord, I know not, but I must do something for my sister and for my conscience.

It did not go well. Bernard chastised me for interfering in affairs of state. He berated me for not having produced an heir. I felt humiliated.

'Milady, your appeal is irrelevant, it degrades a woman of your status. A man would never challenge the interdicts of a Pope so what right do you have in such matters? You seem to misunderstand your purpose, your responsibilities, your duty to continue the succession of France. Instead, you waste your time with literary pursuits, which should be left to your betters thus preventing your feminine abilities to have a child.'

I was shocked, hurt, and incensed by the ignorance of Bernard de Clairvaux. Has he no sensitivity? I felt my fertility was compared to that of an animal. I cannot produce a child without it being made by a father. Who does he think I am, the Blessed Virgin? He accused me of being barren. I reminded him I had conceived a child that miscarried. I told him I prayed to have another, but my husband was reluctant to come to my bed. What more can I do? Louis is too depressed to desire his wife if he ever did in the first place. I begged Bernard to speak to Louis.

***

I summoned the courage to approach Louis. He was a shadow, gaunt, dishevelled and red eyed. He did not acknowledge my appearance, slumped in his chair. I knelt before him and took his bony hands in mine. I begged him to come with me. I thought if he walked or left his chamber it would be of some benefit. He did not move. I was about to rise and leave when he suddenly stood. I led him to my bed chamber. He was like a mannequin. Once I had him there, I had no idea what to do with him, so I lay him down and lay beside him. In exhaustion, we both fell asleep. When I awoke, he was gone.

Louis came to my bed a few nights later. I was surprised and tried to control my normal revulsion when he attempted his connubial rights. I lay there waiting for the inevitable thrusting and grunting. When it was over, he did not run away but fell asleep, though he was gone by morning. I do not know what Bernard said to him, but he came again on two other occasions, but did not stay afterwards.

***

On the first day of September, a courier arrived from Rome. Pope Innocent has died and the newly elected Pope, Celestine, has revoked the interdicts and excommunications on Raoul and Petronilla and freed the French court as well. Louis can again find succour from the sacraments. It was such a relief, because I discovered I was having another child, a miracle seeing Louis and I have now been married for five years.

My joy was marred, however, by the addition of an austere woman to my household. Angelique is her name. She was appointed by Abbé Suger. She is his sister. More nun than maid, this woman gave us all concern because she did not come alone but with a cohort of handmaidens in dark robes. It was as if all the black beetles from every dank corner of the palace had assembled in my quarters. When I complained to Louis, I did not need ladies-in-waiting foisted on me by Suger, he said they were to help with our expected child.

Deep suspicions ran through my mind. What was afoot? We soon found out. Every loom attended, every stitch put into a piece of embroidery, what we sang, whether we played chess or attended the archery range, how many times we prayed, or did not, was reported in exaggerated, elaborate detail, back to Abbé Suger. I bolted to the library and locked the door. God bless dear old King Louis!

I flopped at my desk to catch my breath. A light cough startled me. The inkwell was in my hand as I swung around. In front of me was a slender young monk. He looked askance at my raised heavy pewter weapon.

'Do not throw it, Milady! I am Brother Joachim, the late King Louis' archivist and librarian. I am sorry if I frightened you.'

He continued that he had just returned from a long pilgrimage to Compostela. Oh! For several minutes, I could not speak as the memories of where Papa died flooded back, a grief I cannot erase. Brother Joachim's face flushed. I was embarrassed, flustered as I tried to explain how I missed my Papa.

I could tell this man was a gentle, kind soul. He dashed out and came back with a mug of lemon barley water. He sat down on a stool in front of me and waited for me to regain my composure. I asked him to explain his duties. With a sparkle in his eye, he told me how he cared for the books, looked after their bindings and kept a catalogue of the library contents. I had found a kindred spirit. I asked if he read them as well as maintained them.

'Oh, yes Milady!'

For the next hour or so we talked non-stop about our favourite books and authors from the Greek philosophers to Cicero and even Saint Augustine. Brother Joachim's cherubic face flushed with excitement while we discussed *The Aeneid*. I told him about the books I had brought from Poitiers still packed in crates and chests. He said he would be delighted to find space for them and build more shelves if necessary.

After we had exhausted our topic, I asked his opinion on educated women. It was a joy to listen to his voice full of pride. His eyes glowed as he told me about the girls in his family.

'All my sisters were taught to read and write. Two have taken the veil, and two are with God. I am the only boy in a family of scholars.'

The shadows through the windows and the bells of Notre Dame reminded me I must return to my quarters. Before I left, Brother Joachim offered to prepare my ink and quills if I desired. He suggested, too, it would be wise to keep this and my other journals under lock and key. He said he had his own key to the library and apart from the one I possessed, he did not think there were others, but he would make discreet inquiries. Not only a kindred spirit but one sensitive to my predicament.

Chapter 4. Marie the Unwanted Heir

With relief, Renée and I think I have passed the danger period for myself and my baby. I calculated I have about five more months of waiting. My shape is changing too. I now have a rounding to my stomach and my gowns are having to have the laces loosened to accommodate my belly.

Yesterday, while wandering in my flourishing garden, I was surprised to find Louis down by the lake. We see little of each other, except for royal progresses to visit our estates, or occasions when I am the decorative Queen of France there to charm and be witty for visiting vassals. I have almost given up trying to meet Louis alone without Suger. At least Bernard has left the palace for other holy pursuits. I think, seeing the fruit of our coupling becoming obvious was almost enough to make Louis faint. There was no escape, so he was forced to say something. He asked if I was well while casting his eye around as usual for a way out. I said I wished him to sit with me awhile on the marble bench I had positioned to take in the pretty view of the lake. It was most amusing. Much to his chagrin, he found my middle fascinating while trying not to look at it.

I was feeling mischievous. I asked Louis if he would like to place his hand on my small bulge.

'I have not felt the baby move yet, but Renée tells me soon I will sense a little flutter which says the baby is kicking from within.'

Louis blushed to his ear tips, so I grabbed his hand and placed it plumb in the middle of my abdomen. His reticence was beginning to annoy me, so I teased him with fluttering eye lids to get a reaction.

'It is a shame we cannot go to bed, because women in my condition often feel quite sensual.'

His face registered horror. Like Bernard, I think he wished he could jump into the lake. He tried to pull away, but I tightened my grip. My humour dissolved. I flung his hand away in scorn. I stood; my eyes flashed.

'What sort of father are you?'

Silence.

'You are nothing more than a pitiful fool. After this child is born, keep out of my bed. Entertain your catamite friends instead.'

Louis sprang up. The stinging slap stunned me. I hit him back. Disbelief reddened his face. I turned and ran.

Poor baby got a bouncy ride.

***

I arrived out of breath in my chamber. Thank God, Angelique and her black beetles were nowhere in sight. I sought out Renée for a bowl of water to bathe my flushed face. She was not pleased when she found I had been running. Renée pointed out a slight red mark on my cheek bone. She wanted to know how it got there. It must have been from one of Louis' rings. I did not want to tell her what had happened between us, so instead I asked her what order of monks were the catamites? She laughed till she cried. I had no idea what was so funny. She was surprised I did not know. I was getting cross. Louis had tried my patience and now Renée was jesting with me. I wanted answers, so I related how I overheard some knights referring to Louis as one and therefore assumed it had something to do with his early monastic life.

An expression crossed Renée's face changing it from one of mirth to seriousness. My heart sank. I pushed the bowl of water away; my fingers gripped the stool. Renée paced, not a good omen.

'Elea.'

My pet name, another bad sign.

'Elea.'

In a rush she blurted out, 'A catamite is a man who prefers the company of men over women.'

Chapter 4. Marie the Unwanted Heir

Is that all. I could see with my own eyes Louis is always surrounded by men and it is obvious he does not enjoy my company. Renée cleared her throat before she added in a rush,

'Catamites prefer also to lay with men'.

My jaw hit the floor! My hand went to my face, while my mind tried to work it out. How? Men and women are not built the same way.

I bolted to the library. I have had to find the courage to write down what transpired between Louis and me as well as Renée's thunderbolt. To be honest I feel sick. Papa, what have you ordained for me? Did old King Louis know this about his son? Does Suger know or is he one too? Renée says maybe it is not true. It could be malicious gossip. But why did Louis strike me? Was it because I accused him of something, he would find abhorrent or had I scratched a festering sore? Renée said it was a sin. I am sure Louis would not partake in something so wrong in the eyes of God. He is so pious, always prostrate in prayer. God's teeth, I was so grateful to Brother Joachim for the secret shelf he built in the library for my journals and parchment. Although I feel a greater distaste for Louis, I do not want others to discover his secret if it is true.

***

The time is getting closer for the birth of my baby. I have not written much of late. Instead I have been stitching tiny gowns and bonnets as well as weaving little swaddling blankets and such like. I have made some lace which looks presentable rather than my usual lumpy, bumpy threads. The only worry in my joyous state is the unknown experience of the birth itself. Renée told me I should not be concerned because I am strong and healthy, and she will be there to look after me. I know I never seem to suffer ills except for the odd headache or sniff, but I know of too many women who have lost their lives giving birth and it is so painful by the pitiful screams one hears. My miscarriage was bad enough.

The whole court was praying for a boy-child, an heir to the throne. I want a boy, too, for France. As for Louis, I only see him at a distance. We are avoiding each other. I receive little information about France's affairs of state these days. The occasional knight's or cleric's gossip filtered my way, but it was scanty. Louis' desire to carry the Oriflamme of France from St Denis to Jerusalem was exciting news, however. Before he was killed, Louis' older brother Phillip had promised to go on crusade to lay the sacred Oriflamme on the altar of the Church of the Holy Sepulchre. Louis intended to grant his wish as well as his own desires; to purge his soul, I am told, for Vitry-sur-Marne.

***

Christmas and New Year have come and gone. I am tiring these days. When I write I often find myself leagues away in a dream. My body has changed shape. I think I resemble the old king. I have developed an ungainly waddle when I walk. I must look like a duck. Yesterday I was daydreaming in the sun in the garden, a favourite destination, when I was alerted to an uproar in my chamber. I returned as fast as my bulk would carry me to find out what was amiss. Renée and my Aquitaine maids were screaming in hysterics surrounded by the black beetles and a scornful Angelique. Several black-robed clerics were in attendance with guards. I pushed my way through the throng. I demanded an explanation, demanded why my nurse and maids were being harassed. Silence fell except for Renée's and my other maids' sobs. I enveloped her in my arms and insisted they tell me what was occurring. Renée cried they had been dismissed from my service and must leave on the morrow for Poitiers at Louis' and Suger's orders. I know not what happened next; I fainted.

***

In the library, Brother Joachim tried as much as he could to calm my nerves. Louis has locked himself away nor will

Chapter 4. Marie the Unwanted Heir

Suger give me the time of day. Renée had to be removed by force. She fought like a tigress. She had been at my side since I was little more than a baby after my mother died. I ran to the Seine in my despair. I wanted to throw myself into its murky depths; only its filth prevented me doing so. I wanted to die but not to sink in that sludge.

Except when I am here at my desk, I wander from place to place, listless. I live in terror of the birth of this child with no-one now to give me strength. Every twinge in my belly sends me into paroxysms of fear.

I have banned the black beetles and Angelique from entering my chamber except to help with dressing and other necessities for my wellbeing. Although I have difficulty walking, I went to the kennels to ask the dog handler for six of his largest mastiffs. I do not like dogs much, but I trust no-one in my entourage, especially Angelique who reports everything I do to Suger. Now she cannot get in my door.

The mastiffs have proved a boon. Angelique and the beetles are terrified of them. They snarl at everyone. Suger had a fit because Angelique has limited contact with me, therefore he has no access to his sister's lies. Louis cannot get in either, though he probably has no intentions of doing so. What will happen when I go into labour, I know not. Should I not be so close to giving birth, I would take a horse and as many loyal guards as possible and gallop to Poitiers.

***

I cannot sit still. The dogs and I today have wandered all over the palace. I am now in the library. Brother Joachim has a natural rapport with my dogs. They love him. He always has some treats squirreled away in the pockets of his robe for them. I am uncomfortable though. The dear man has gone to fetch me a drink. He says ewe's milk is good for one in my condition. I hope he does not take too long; this baby has taken up residence between my legs which now ache. I am writing in haste. I must stand, but I cannot, I must sit. God in heaven, liquid has cascaded from my body. Surely, I cannot have wet myself like an infant. My journal I will leave for Brother Joachim with a note. I must return to my quarters to change.

***

It is unbelievable what has happened to me. I am trying to make sense of a life I know my Papa would find foreign to everything he ordained for me. All he wanted was my protection. He would be horrified if he knew what has transpired.

I have a daughter, born on the fourteenth day of April in the year of our Lord 1145. I have called her Marie. She was taken away; I know not where. She caused me unimaginable pain and distress. My screams and moans are said to have reverberated throughout the palace. The dog handler had to come to retrieve the mastiffs. They would not allow anyone in my chamber. I was alone and in labour. This would never have happened had Renée been with me. My breasts are hurting. They have been tightly bound but milk seeps from them. I cannot stop weeping. The only sweet surprise in this mess was the brief appearance of Colette, one of the beetles. She thrust into my hand a small golden locket, whispering that it contained a snippet of Marie's hair. She gave me a dimpled smile and scurried from my bedside. Collette comes from a convent where she was left as an infant. It is hinted she could be the bastard daughter of old King Louis. Who knows? Whatever her heritage, she is kind, but under Angelique's thumb like all the other beetles.

I was given some herbal mixture to help me sleep. It tasted vile, but I was desperate for relief. When I woke, the bells were tolling I know not what hour.

I have asked to see my baby. After she was born, she was whisked away, and I was too tired to react. I heard her cries but that was all. Strange things were happening to my body. When I questioned Angelique about my baby's whereabouts, she said Princess Marie was being looked after. I told her I would look after her, I wanted my baby. Angelique sneered.

Chapter 4. Marie the Unwanted Heir

'I think not. You are an unsuitable mother.'

Where is my cowardly husband? Oh, Papa, Papa. Why did you do this to me?

***

After I was well enough, I went back to the kennels. Albert, the senior dog handler, was pleased to see I had recovered from my travail. This time I thought two dogs would be enough to guard me. Albert suggested two younger animals. They would be easier for me to handle and train. So, Titan and Mars became my companions. Everywhere I go in the palace they obediently walk at my side. Both are creamy coloured with black muzzles. My only grumble is they slobber, and Titan has chewed the corner off one of my rugs, a small price to pay for my protection.

I am now in charge of my quarters. Angelique and her coven of beetles only enter my chamber at my command to perform their duties. I have set aside a chamber for their looms, sewing and embroidery. To give them their due, their work is outstanding.

But I miss Renée with all my heart. I have lost my little *Maman*, my mentor, imparter of knowledge, my mender of sore knees and bumped heads and all the thousands of things she has done for me since my mother died. Papa would be horrified and furious beyond belief if he knew how she was dismissed from my household. I miss my other maids as well. Now I must sing to myself when I play my lute, so I no longer play. I am becoming a recluse. Therefore, the news that Louis has pledged to go on crusade to the Holy Land is joy to my ears. I too will take up the Cross. I try not to think about my daughter.

Chapter 5. The Lure of the Crusade

There is much to be done to prepare for our journey to Jerusalem. Louis has found a new purpose in life, me also. Since Renée, my Aquitainian Court, and Petronilla, were no longer in my life, I have been forced to solve my own problems, to look to myself. I have discovered a strength from within. I asked myself how Papa would advise me. I have begun to use my God-given talents.

It was not until I became Louis' wife that the Eleanor I thought I was and proud to be was considered difficult. I am sick and tired of having to guard my tongue, regardless of how I horrify the French court and its clerics. My learning is a well of information not fully plumbed to its depths. Furthermore, I will continue to explore, to search for knowledge from whatever source is available.

What an unusual father Papa was. He did not remove us from his court as we grew to be sent to a convent as was usual in our society: he took us everywhere with him. We learned, we read, we wrote, we rode, and ran free; what Papa did, we did. Renée took charge of the womanly pursuits. Being trapped in the backwardness of the French court is stultifying. If they want to call me a witch, so be it. I should have spoken out when I have held back, like putting Nilla's happiness before affairs of state. I should have told Louis I thought his choice for the Archbishop of Bourges ill conceived. I continue to live with the guilt of the annihilation of the poor people of Vitry-sur-Marne. Will the crusade purge my soul? I know not.

***

I would prefer logic and argument, but I am going to have to use all my beauty and charm, not something I like to flaunt, to woo men to take up arms, to leave their families

Chapter 5. The Lure of the Crusade

and the familiarity of their homes to follow the Cross. I know many will lose their lives; will they be taken into the bosom of God like Papa at Compostela? And what of those left behind, the wives, the children. I must push these thoughts from my mind to concentrate on the task I have set myself. I will gather my army. We will take back the land of Christ.

The journey will be exciting, I am sure. I am looking forward to it. Suger, who has been appointed Louis' regent and his henchmen, will not be coming with us but will stay in France praying for our glorious victory.

The possibility of Louis and I not returning was at the back of my mind, which prompted me to search through my thoughts, to record my inner, deepest feelings. I have instructed Brother Joachim to keep my journals hidden and safe. Should the crusade go awry, and I not return, he is to give them to Marie when she is old enough, so she can learn about her mother. I have penned a special letter to her to let her know she is loved that she was taken away against my will. I have written how she is always in my heart and prayers. I folded the missive, pressed my seal in place and asked Brother Joachim to keep it safe.

***

Activity, activity, activity! What a difference from the dismal moods of guilt and gloom since Vitry-sur-Marne. Amid the preparations for Louis and me to progress throughout our kingdom to rally citizens to join our mighty crusade, Troubadours came to Île de France to entertain us. It seemed like eons since we heard music, poetry and laughter. Even Louis enjoyed some light-hearted revelry.

To my surprise and joy, it was Marcabru de Gascon, an old favourite of Papa's, who arrived with his troupe of musicians, mummers, and fools. Papa was his patron, something I must continue now we have become reacquainted.

Marcabru has a most mellifluous voice and is a clever composer of songs penned in the tradition of Courtly Love. I dusted off my lute and put it to good service even if my fingertips need to be toughened up. Together, we sang songs written by my clever, musical Grandfather William, but not the naughty ones.

Suger, Angelique and the beetles were all tut-tutting as would be expected, but it was good to laugh and be gay. I had buried my happy disposition so deeply I never thought it could resurface. Marcabru revitalised my love of the troubadour tradition. He penned some *chansons* in my honour. I felt flirtatious for the first time since I left home. Marcabru is a talented, handsome man with sparkling eyes; how could I not but enjoy his flattery and fine musicianship.

The fun and frivolity ended abruptly but not in the manner I would have expected. Louis threw Marcabru out in a jealous rage. To think my monkish husband mistook some harmless flirting to be love for another man was madness. As Louis has shown little sign of deep affection for me, I am amazed he cared.

Louis' unusual behaviour jolted me back to reality. I returned to my preparations. I am trying to formulate strategies to rally the men of the Aquitaine to join the crusade. I have scoured books written about ancient conflicts. I catch myself daydreaming as I aspire to be like Penthicilia leading her Amazons, or Britain's Boadicea leading her army against the might of Rome. At times, I worry if I am up to the task. But I do not have to go into battle myself; all I must do is raise an army and be there to lead.

I know I can speak with eloquence to nobles like Theodore and Alphonso, my enemies as such. If they are inspired to follow the Cross, I am sure my vassals will also be eager to join my army. They will not want to be seen to be lacking in valour. I can organise tournaments for knights to test themselves, archery contests, boar hunting so men can pit their courage against ferocious beasts. Have Troubadours write and perform *Chansons de Geste* to encourage their bravery. But there is much to be done rather than sitting here dreaming. I must act.

***

Chapter 5. The Lure of the Crusade

I arrived home in triumph. The last time I was in Poitiers was when Louis unsuccessfully attacked Toulouse. As I sit here in Papa's old library with ink and parchment, I am overwhelmed and cannot believe the reception I received. Yester morn, heralds proclaimed my approach. They exhorted the people to heed my desire to carry the Cross, to follow the example of Grandfather William who gave his life in the Holy Land leading the first crusade. The heralds announced, that with the people's help we can reclaim Jerusalem, and avenge Duke William IX for his granddaughter, Lady Eleanor, Duchess of Aquitaine (no mention of Queen of France). That Uncle Raymond was now Prince of Antioch was another incentive. Papa's younger brother was brought up with us and loved by my people, like Papa. The Aquitaine has a proud connection to the Holy Land. Wild cheers echoed along my route.

My detailed plans succeeded. I chose to ride a gallant steed, a white hispano caparisoned in purple to match my bejewelled gown. I rode unveiled, my hair loose. The crown of Aquitaine graced my temples. Drummers were followed by standard bearers from every corner of the duchy. With great skill, they tossed their flags high in the air to the gasps of the crowds. A cross of gold was carried by the Seneschal of Poitiers who strode in front of my horse. I rode by cheering crowds several rows deep whom I showered with gold coins. Their love, their appreciation, was all heartfelt. I had difficulty stemming my tears of joy and pride in the Poitivins.

***

Within the great cathedral, I addressed my people as Duchess of Aquitaine. I allowed my voice to soar, to motivate would-be crusaders to join God's Army. I appealed to them in the manner of the *Chansons de Geste*; God was their knight in shining armour. They were to serve Him, not those who were merely God's vassals on earth, the clergy. I stressed it was their duty to God to reclaim the Holy Land for His Son and stride the streets of His city on earth, Jerusalem. Voices full of fervour roared in unison to my words.

Bernard and Suger, I hear, were aghast when the contents of my oratory reached their ears. But they had to keep their mouths shut. Without my vast army and my treasury to pay for it, they know the crusade will not take place. For once I was in control.

***

I followed my discourse in the cathedral with a jousting tournament and archery contest which I entered myself. I was pitted against some most adept archers. Lord be praised I did not disgrace myself. When it came to splitting the arrow in the bull, however, I had to concede to a fine young knight whose eye and steady hand were more skilful than mine. I had fun; I must admit.

The greatest challenge was to travel to Champagne to face Theodore. I was greatly concerned he would ignore my overtures. The Archbishopric of Bourges was still a sore point: Nilla's marriage another. It is a comfort to know she and Raoul are happy after their infamous start. At least Theodore was too chivalrous to turn away my request to meet. I arranged it to take place on neutral territory at the opulent palace of Pierre de la Chatre after my audience with the archbishop.

The archbishop was charming. I found him more erudite than I expected. He treated me with greater respect than I anticipated or perhaps he realised I was not the foolish, impetuous young queen he assumed. He was impressed I wanted to take up the Cross and congratulated me on recruiting so many men from the Aquitaine under my banner. I noticed His Grace had a half-completed game of chess on a table near his chair. After our conference, I asked him if he was black or white. He answered he was both: he was playing himself for his own amusement. I said I often did the same. With a gleam in his eye, he suggested we play a game and reset the board. His Grace juggled the black and

Chapter 5. The Lure of the Crusade

white pawns behind his back. He asked me to choose his left or right fist. As it happened, I picked white.

His Grace was a skilful opponent. I had to use every tactic I knew to keep abreast with his moves. To my benefit, I have had plenty of practice with Brother Joachim, who for such a gentle character, is a monster when it comes to chess. His Grace was concentrating with all his might. He was surprised, I think, I was so competent. When a page entered with refreshments, he was waved away with impatience. I had a dilemma. I could see the archbishop had left me a possible chink in his defence with an ill-placed knight. Did I go in for the kill and perhaps destroy a new friendship, or play to let him win? I mulled this over letting him believe I was thinking of my next move. But no, the *'win at all costs Eleanor'* dominated. I checkmated him in my next few moves.

I waited for what seemed like an interminable length of time before he spoke, trying to appear modest. To my surprise, he uttered,

'God's teeth! You are a mighty competitor, Milady.'

With that he stood, walked to a table set with goblets and a flask of wine and poured us both a goodly portion to toast my victory. After a hefty swallow, he said he had heard I was clever; honoured to be beaten by a worthy opponent. I felt my face flush with pleasure. I thanked him for his kind words. But before I left, the archbishop said he had something for me. From a nearby chest, he surprised me with a beautiful, bejewelled crusader cross which he pinned to my gown.

'There now Eleanor of Aquitaine, you are a true soldier of Christ.'

He made the sign of the cross over my head.

'In nomine Patris et Filli et Spiritus Sancti.'

I felt mightily honoured and touched by the gesture. I told him I would wear the cross with pride.

My amiable prologue with the archbishop eased my meeting with the Count of Champagne. Theodore was reserved, but he showed me respect which I appreciated and listened to my plans for the crusade without disapproval. He was straightforward with me and said it was up to the men of Champagne to make their own decisions, not wanting to exhort them one way or the other. He did agree to allow his son Henry to join my army providing he could lead his own men. I promised this would be so. The ice was broken between us which should bode well for future conferences between our houses.

I would have liked to have apologised for the debacle of Vitry-sur-Marne from the bottom of my heart, but felt it was not appropriate to do so. Louis is the only one who can make such overtures.

***

I had time to visit Petronilla and Raoul. It has been over a year since I have seen my sister. She has a new baby as well, a son, Ralph. It was a joyous reunion. All formality dissolved as we flung ourselves into each other's arms. We hugged with tears running down our cheeks. Another joy was being reunited with Renée who had been brought to Raoul's estates to be with Nilla during her confinement. Raoul was overwhelmed, not knowing whether to be humble in front of the Queen of France or embrace me as a sister. I put the poor man out of his misery by allowing him to kiss my hand. I hugged him too.

Together we entered their beautiful chateau with its spectacular river views, verdant hills with deep forests to the north. Nilla took me to my quarters where she settled me in the most comfort I had encountered since leaving Poitiers. I was weary. The journey, having to encourage would be crusaders through towns and villages, along with the emotional toll of having to confront Theodore and Archbishop Pierre de la Chatre, had tired me more than I liked to admit. To find a tub of hot water, fresh linens, chemise and gown laid out was like entering heaven. Renée bless her, took charge as she has done forever. I was bathed, my hair lathered, and my body perfumed. Renée wrapped me in large linen towels to dry off in front of a warm fire as the air by late afternoon was growing chill. She rubbed my hair dry combed and brushed out the tangles and complained as she often has in the past, I was too thin. I was not going to argue with her; in fact, I almost nodded off as my body relaxed.

Nilla kept the evening a simple family affair, far preferable than being grandly entertained. I was introduced to her baby son. He was given to me to hold. The weight of him, the smell of him, his little mewing noises, his chubby cheeks and gummy smile broke my heart as I thought of Marie whom I had never held. I started to sob. I frightened Nilla, Renée and the nurse. I disturbed little Ralph who sensed my distress and howled with me. Ralph's nurse took him from my arms, rocked him and took him to his cradle, while Renée and Nilla did their best to sooth me. Renée suggested a physic to help calm me, but I managed to control my emotions.

Later in the evening, Nilla and I were left alone to talk. She apologised for being thoughtless about baby Ralph. I replied I was delighted to meet him; honoured to hold him. I told her how I struggled. The denial of motherhood caused me great anguish. Nilla admitted she was happier away from my oppressive French court and how much she and Raoul loved each other. She confessed she used to be jealous of me. She thought Papa spoiled me, and Renée loved me more than her, that I was always more clever; more beautiful. With a sheepish smile, she admitted she had let Simian into the audience chamber at L'Ombriere to upset my first meeting with Louis because she was so envious, I was going to become a Queen. I think the Simian episode was one of the funniest of my life. We hugged and laughed reminiscing about our lives when we played, bickered and teased each other as big and little sister.

As I look at Nilla so happy and content, I am the one now who is jealous. Silly girl, she is pretty. We are different, yes. I am taller, she is rounded in a curvaceous, womanly way. My features, I am told, are classical and she, bless her, does not have the haughty nose I inherited from Grandmother Dangerosa. As for intelligence, she is as smart, but she has chosen to use her wits in different ways. I am more scholarly with my reading and writing, she happier with her music, lacemaking, weaving and embroidery. Nilla is as clever as the nuns who stitched my trousseau. I told her I envied her happy marriage to Raoul and wished mine could be the same.

We changed the subject to the coming crusade. I was proud of my efforts in rallying an army. Nilla begged me to take care on my journey into the unknown, and not to let Louis do anything foolhardy. As Suger and Bernard were not coming, there was a chance he may heed my advice, but I was not confident. Nilla said he was a stupid fool and I was twice as clever. I had to agree.

***

I spent two blissful weeks with Petronilla relaxing and being pampered, I am now back in Poitiers soon to return to Paris. I must arrive before winter bites into the balmy autumn weather. I have been meeting with my trusted Poitivin justiciars, including Guile my Constable, Geoffrey de Rançon, Hugh de Lusignan and Guy de Thouars, as well as others to finalise arrangements for the crusade. They will take over the task of preparing the men who have pledged to join our army. They will organise equipment, the armour required, weapons, siege engines and so forth, as well as scouring stables for the best horses along with procuring the hundreds of other items needed to send my men on their way.

Theodore's son Henry is young but enthusiastic and I think capable of the onus placed upon him. All of them, by the grace of God, will need to be formidable, resourceful leaders. They will never comprehend how deeply I honour and respect them. My words, I fear, will not do justice to these innermost thoughts. I am having a banquet prepared to thank these fine knights for their resolve to carry the Cross, not just for their own valour, but for mine and the Aquitaine too. I will not see them again till we all meet at

Rheims before our long journey. I hope to set out for the Holy Land next spring.

As much as I dread the thought, I must return to Île de France. My role in the Aquitaine was complete.

***

The ride back to Paris was tedious, with the weather being against us for the last leagues. Tired or no, I pushed on. Discomfort, I know, will be my companion from time to time next year as the crusade wends its way towards Jerusalem. But I hope the welcome at the various outposts where we will lodge *en route* will be better than the one I received on my return to Île de France. I arrived with chattering teeth, numb fingers and feet. Horse and I were dripping. I do not know which was more bedraggled, droopy headed animal or me. My dismount was more a slither to the ground in mud be-spattered boots and sodden miniver.

A miserable fire was lit in my grate. The first individual to receive the short end of my displeasure was a luckless churl who scuttled as fast as his bandy legs would carry him for more wood. Poor Colette received a tongue lashing as she fumbled with chilblained fingers to unlace my wet gown. Angelique, much to her hierarchical disgust, had to deal with my cape and filthy riding boots. There was no welcoming tub of steaming water. Dry linens, chemise and a warm gown had to be gathered while I shivered. They knew days ahead when I would be arriving. I reminded Angelique if she wanted to take the journey with me to the Holy Land, a desire I know she was desperate to fulfil, she had better improve her attitude, to heed her responsibilities. Tomorrow my first visit will be to the kennels to fetch Mars and Titan.

Louis at last deigned to show his face. He pulled a stool up to the hearth, warming his hands which were blue with cold. I asked him if he was saving the treasury by rationing wood. I rose and poured him some mulled wine. He looked more miserable than I felt. I should not have been so harsh on Colette, who produced it as a peace offering. Slowly, the wine and the built-up fire thawed me, but I was exhausted and needed to go to my bed. I suggested to Louis we continue our conversation on the morrow. He rose to leave. I gave him the remainder of the wine, insisting he get the churls to light his fire, for God's sake!

***

I had to take to my bed for more than a week. The day after my return I developed a fever brought on, no doubt, by having to sit around in wet clothing by a spluttering fire while Angelique and the beetles dawdled to get me warm and dry. Louis, I hear was furious. Brother Joachim informed me Louis told Suger that if his sister could not perform her duties to our satisfaction, she would be replaced. I would have loved to have seen Suger's face.

I was propped up on mountains of pillows with every physic known to the apothecary by my bedside. Most of them tasted as if they had been dredged from the bottom of the Seine with lemon and honey the only tolerable mixture. Louis sat by my bedside. At one stage, I hear he brought Suger to pray for me as I ranted with delirium. Heaven forefend, the prayers must have almost choked him. If he was after damning information from my raving lips, I am told it was all in Langue d'Oc. Brother Joachim had to take Titan and Mars back to the kennels. They were guarding me with fierce snarls. I am sorry I was too senseless to miss the hubbub.

I have recuperated. While still confined to bed, I had time to think about the legality of my marriage. Now back on my feet, I intend to look up Louis' and my dynasties. My unhappiness is grinding me down. At the first opportunity I intend to consider my future as Louis' wife.

***

Brother Joachim found our family trees in the library. Louis and I are fourth cousins. Why did I not know that? According to Canon Law, we should never have been

Chapter 5. The Lure of the Crusade

allowed to marry in the first place. It is obvious why our relationship was conveniently overlooked – my dowry! Anyway, I was far too young, in mourning and bewildered. During the haste of the events, the rule of consanguinity was not given one jot of attention by the Archbishop of Bordeaux or the Pope if it got that far.

I know I will not be able to pursue an annulment till after the crusade and who knows how long that will take, but later, if there is a chance, I will petition the Pope. I do not know which is worse, the atmosphere of Île de France or Louis himself. Even if Marie, poor child, had been a boy, I do not believe I can remain here, or find happiness. Seeing how full of love Raoul's and Nilla's marriage is, I know I want more than the cold isolation in which I live.

I know the worth of my political capabilities now. It was expedient of Suger to condescend to my return to the Aquitaine to rally an army. He knew Louis was incapable, nor had he the respect needed from my people to fulfil such a mission. Did Suger think I would fail, hoped I would return empty handed to Paris? Probably. I triumphed instead. Papa, after all, brought me up, educated me to lead. I have proved to Suger, Bernard and the Pope, I have the heritage, ability and power. Furthermore, I have proved it to myself. There will be no going back. I have prevailed, unwomanly or nay.

All I wish is to one day find love. My status, my wealth, I accept with pride. However, does this mean whatever destiny my life follows, my birthright will be a barrier to true love? I know not. I hope not. *Eh bien*.

***

Though well again, I was a little tired. Because my fever intervened, I had yet to relate to Louis the results of my journey to the Aquitaine. He would have been given some information about my successes from other sources, but until he heard from me and perused my written records there was every chance of distortion. I needed to let him know what transpired between Theodore and me as well as with Archbishop Pierre de la Chatre. Both men have become useful allies and have learnt of my capabilities after my meetings with them. My recruitment numbers for the crusade impressed them. The last thing I wanted was those still fragile diplomatic discourses sullied by misinformation. I had not mentioned that Alphonso of Toulouse refused to negotiate personally but had sworn a battalion anyhow. I was not sure of the trustworthiness of his men; except he is a seasoned campaigner who I hope they respect.

I sent a page with a request to meet in Louis' audience chamber. To think I must resort to such formality to see my husband! For once Louis was prompt with his reply. The dogs and I made our way. Suger was lurking. Mars and Titan greeted him in fine style with bared teeth and throaty growls. He shot out the door. Why did I not think to have mastiffs guard me from my first days? They looked at Louis with suspicion but obeyed my command to drop. I was pleased to see he had a decent fire lit in his hearth. No matter how warm my gowns and capes were, I was again not coping with the chill of this old, damp palace after the sun in Poitiers. Louis, thank God, had some mulled wine poured. I relaxed a little with the dogs disporting themselves on the hearth rug, albeit with one eye opened.

I gave Louis a detailed account of my journey: the numbers of men who have pledged to take up the Cross and the names of the knights already chosen to lead battalions. I explained some battalion leaders were yet to be finalised by Hugh de Lusignan, Geoffrey de Rançon, Guy of Thouars and other justiciars. Louis' only reservation was about the trustworthiness of Theodore's son Henry. I said I believed he was reliable; certainly, eager to take up the Cross. Young Henry had rallied a goodly number of crusaders from the county of Champagne and told me it was an honour to lead a battalion. Louis looked embarrassed when I said Archbishop Pierre de la Chatre had given his blessing.

Having exhausted my knowledge, I gave him the scrolls with the written details of my journey, recruitments and

Chapter 5. The Lure of the Crusade

discussions with nobles throughout my duchy. They listed the costs to my treasury so far, with estimates of future expenditure in armaments, horses, chain mail and all manner of necessities for the crusade. All were meticulous and under my signature as Duchess of Aquitaine. I told Louis he was welcome to share the information with his advisors. I think he was taken aback at the thoroughness of my discourse. I finished my wine and stood to go.

'Please, Eleanor, please! Do not leave.'

I paused. The dogs rumbled when Louis reached out his hand towards me. Again, I ordered them to drop, but he had stepped back. His eyes looked pitiful. Was this one of Louis' rare flares of interest, to gutter like candle dregs? My mind was telling me to be gracious, but my heart was like flint as I asked what he wanted.

'You.'

My eyes bored into his like basilisks. His voice was hoarse with emotion.

'You are so beautiful.'

If he had shown more appreciation for my success in the recruitment of my crusader army, praised my accomplishments in diplomacy with Theodore of Champagne and Pierre de la Chatre, I would have stayed. Instead I called Mars and Titan and left the wretched man. I am not proud of my reaction to Louis. I know it was cruel, but I have lost all warmth for my husband. All I do is endure.

***

The Christmas Court beckons along with the confirmation of Count Geoffrey of Anjou as Duke of Normandy, which will take place here in Paris. I must be present, of course, more decorative than anything else. Those who know the Duke say he is a handsome, charming man much adored by women far and wide. Maybe I will dress to impress.

The banquet went well. I wore one of my bejewelled gowns, a glowing scarlet, made of damask. It is embroidered with Fleur de Lis in gold thread. It takes six pages to manage the train. The beetles condescended to make sure I was bathed and perfumed. Angelique knows unless she complies with my wishes, there will be no Jerusalem for her. Collette did my hair beautifully, so it enhanced my neck and drew attention to my earrings. The only uncomfortable appendage was the heavy crown.

I made Louis gasp without intention. He grinned like an ape all the way down the great hall as he escorted me to my throne. After the formalities were over, the Duke was seated next to me at the banqueting table. He is one of those people who fix you in the eye and hang on to every word uttered. I agree the gossips are correct in their description. The Duke's gaze was intense, which enhanced his deep blue eyes. I heard he was an excellent jouster. He had certainly a strong muscular build.

We spoke with ease together. I found Lord Geoffrey had an interest in Greek literature and philosophy. We were soon conversing in the language. He was most fluent, but I am rusty, having not practised for some time. I discovered he had quite a sense of humour, was an amazing mimic and enjoyed my Grandfather's bawdy songs much to my embarrassment. As I turned red, he tossed his golden curls and roared with laughter. I could see why women from one end of our lands to the other are entranced by him. He is attractive, a change from most of the nobles I must impress for the sake of the French court. But by necessity, I had to observe protocol, look regal and behave with decorum. Even so, Louis thought I was having too much fun, so cut the evening short.

After the Christmas Festivities were over and we welcomed in the New Year, Louis and I began our individual preparations to journey to the Holy Land. Louis was to be presented with the Oriflamme of France at St Denis. I will have to attend the ceremony. I will wear my crusader cross to annoy Suger.

***

Chapter 5. The Lure of the Crusade

While I finalised my army in Poitiers, I had met with old friends who, with great excitement, expressed a desire to join my campaign. It was so good to see them all again; Mamille with her acerbic humour, little Sybilla, though not so little anymore, Florine and clever Torqueri, who once threatened to run away to join a troop of Troubadours, and serious Faydide. They were prepared to provision themselves and bring their own maids and escorts. I warned them about the beetles and Angelique, emphasising they were not the most pleasant of people. But I have little choice regarding my entourage, ruled by Suger as it is.

At our wonderful reunion last year, they were amazed at the restrictions I lived under. Faydide said she could not understand how I, as Queen of France or someone with my intelligence, played little to no role in the French court. Mamille jested she could not believe the 'precocious, outrageous brat' had had her wings clipped. They had fun jibing me about it in a friendly way until they realised how miserable I was. It made them more determined to come with me and to make my life fun again. We, too, will meet at Rheims. I must plan some excitement for us all. Louis and I will be travelling separately, so apart from the beetles who can try their pious best to keep to prayer schedules and the like, we will have an adventure. Angelique and her cohorts do not ride, so they will have to travel in the carriages and wagons. That will give them a dilemma for sure. I cannot wait to gallop off with them lurching behind.

In the meantime, I have started long lists of necessities to carry me through to the various posts. I have estimated the army will not be able to travel at the speed a few knights on horseback can. We do not want to injure the horses by pushing the animals beyond their endurance. Guile and the other knights have organised for fresh mounts to be available along our route. I will be riding with the men of Aquitaine: some are relatives, like my Chatellerault cousins from my mother's family, so I know we will be well protected.

When I was rallying my men, I made it clear to them they had to leave tendencies to squabble or be rebellious behind as they crossed their moats, a challenge for some. The people of the Aquitaine are famous for independent thought; some are too quick to argue at times.

We are a tall handsome people. I am certain we will impress wherever we go. I am proud to be at the head of such men and women.

My list has grown. I need to cross off some items. With great reluctance my quills, parchment and ink must go. I will have to store my experiences till I reach Constantinople, where we will be staying a while to regroup and to meet up with Louis. I will not have a chance to write while travelling anyhow. At the end of the day it will be food and bed, I think.

***

I have vowed to improve my Greek. This will be invaluable in lands where the language is common, even in parts of the Holy Land I am told. If I can find someone with whom I can converse, it should not take long to regain my fluency. I have asked Brother Joachim if he knows of a scholarly monk who speaks Greek. Papa taught us to begin with, and later employed tutors for Nilla and me. We learned the letters as well, but I read and write it most ill, something I must rectify.

Brother Joachim interrupted my arrangements. He has found me an elderly monk who is fluent in Greek. I have postponed my preparations to spend a few precious hours with him in the library. Brother Anselm is one of life's gems. He shuffled into my presence in a threadbare robe which appeared to be three sizes too large for him, his head turtle-like, disappearing into the cowl. Within his wrinkled face were two dark, currant eyes alive with wisdom and good humour. Brother Joachim told me Brother Anselm spent some time as a hermit. When I asked why he had given up his solitary life he grinned a toothless smile and said he had become tired of his own company. When he started talking to himself instead of God, he knew he was in trouble. I could not stop laughing, he is such a character.

His mother was from Athens, so he had spoken the language since childhood. Like Brother Joachim, he is truly likable. Not only was my Greek improving, but Brother Anselm made me laugh so much my days were a joy to behold. He also liked my dogs. He sneaked them little treats when he thought I was not looking. No wonder they loved him! I tried giving Brother Anselm a new, better fitting robe but he tut-tutted saying I was being extravagant, but he did accept a warm, woollen stole because I had woven it myself. I think he did not wish to hurt my feelings.

Some of his jests were bordering on being as naughty as Grandfather William's risqué poems. Coming out of the mouth of a man who appears to be naïvely innocent, was so contradictory, I had to shake my head. As I wiped my eyes after one of his jests, I told him if he ever tired of monastic life, he would make an excellent fool. He replied he was happy being foolish monk.

My Greek has improved. Again, I was thinking in the language and I was as prepared as I could be should I need to speak it on our journey.

I was eager to be on my way to Rheims. With a guard of chosen men already here from Poitiers, we leave Paris in four days. At Rheims we will join with the rest of my vast army from the Aquitaine, with Henry of Champagne, and with Alphonso of Toulouse, who will be waiting with their men. Alphonso's usurped title sticks in my craw but, for the sake of the crusade, I must put that upstart out of my mind.

I was impatient to be reunited with my crusader women, I had goose-pimples of excitement all over my body. I will not see Louis again till we arrive in Constantinople. I am not distressed.

Chapter 6. Unholy Holy Land

Stars and meteors, my friends and I were agog when we caught our first glimpse of Constantinople. Spires of gold with marble palaces pierced the horizon, dominated by the great dome of Saint Sophia, a shimmering mirage in the distance.

We were dressed in our gayest gowns, such a delight after months in drab riding garb. Only the beetles looked dowdy in their boring black robes. Even so, I detected a little twittering among them. If it were not for the dread of reuniting with Louis, I would have walked over the water to the shore. The last part of our route to Constantinople was via the Danube and the Black Sea.

As our craft docked, I scanned the pier. A colourful party with banners and fanfares awaited. My happy disposition plummeted – in their midst was Louis in his monkish robe with Odo de Deuil hovering Suger-like behind him. Suger had to keep his claws into Louis somehow by appointing Odo as his chaplain for the crusade, but I suspect he is there more to report back to Suger. Odo and the Abbé are close, one wonders just how close. Birds of a feather, I suspect.

I kept my countenance neutral, a practised, lifeless smile on my lips as we stepped ashore in a blaze of colour. Louis and I acknowledged each other, made awkward pleasantries, Louis eager and pink eared with I suppose, excitement, and I restrained. As Queen of France, I was welcomed by Emperor Manual and Empress Irene with the usual pomp. I had almost forgotten about protocol. Formalities over, to avoid Louis, I strode to my horse in a cloud of silk brocade followed by my joyous women. Louis trailed in our wake. A beautiful horse was awaiting me to mount. Louis heaved himself onto a similar animal. It looked like it would bolt from under him. We rode in silence.

Chapter 6. Unholy Holy Land

***

I am overawed by the beauty and sophistication of the imperial court. I will make good use of all those gowns I packed. My friends and I are housed with Louis in the Blachernae Palace with its panoramic views over the Golden Horn. It is full of light and beauty. The gardens splish-splash with a myriad of fountains. Roses and a climbing plant called jasmine tumble over bowers. Jasmine, I am told, was brought from the Orient by silk traders; its perfume is truly magnificent. I must have seeds sent to L'Ombriere and Poitiers.

Empress Irene was a joy to meet. She and I are enjoying each other's company. There is so much to behold. Anything we desire is at our disposal. As usual, I am a bit of an oddity. My request for quills, parchment and ink was a surprise. The women here, as most in France, are not educated. They are also secluded and rarely seen in public. The noblewomen have their own quarters and are tended by eunuchs, their own servants, many of them slaves. Slavery, I view with mixed feelings. Whereas the ones attending in our quarters appear happy and were treated well, I could not but wonder about their circumstances and how they came to this position.

My desire to find a quiet corner to catchup with my journal was accommodated. Empress Irene informed me she had much to show me and to entertain me; therefore, I must not bury myself away for too long. I will heed her by keeping this entry brief.

***

There was so much to record. I am writing at a desk inlaid with onyx and ivory and edged with gold. Before me are shimmering tapestries woven in silk. The work is so fine, one could presume they are paintings. The colours make stained glass appear dull. The floors throughout the palace are of marble or fashioned in exquisite mosaics like the ones in my chamber which depict handmaidens of Zeus feeding him grapes with Hebe carrying goblets of wine. They are so lifelike; I imagine if I reach out my hand, I will be given a cup. They are quite explicit. Zeus is naked, and Hebe is bare breasted with only a wisp of material about her waist. A sultry-looking Bacchus is leering at her. I wondered how Angelique and the beetles were coping with such works of art at their feet. There are many luxurious carpets throughout as well. In L'Ombriere and the palace at Poitiers, we have many beautiful rugs from Constantinople. They glow like precious jewels. Many were sent home to us by Grandfather William. It is sad he never saw them laid on the floors of our palaces.

Yesterday, Lady Irene escorted me and my friends to the palace hamam, which is a bath house. I must introduce one to the palace in Paris if I can persuade Louis it is not the work of the devil – like the fork, for God's sake. We were given several of these remarkable little devices for eating one's food. How civilised I thought, but Louis almost had a fit. He raved it was a devil's trident. But I intend to use one for the rest of my life. I will insist those who dine with me do the same. It was such a pleasure eating without having to use fingers.

The hamam was wonderful. After being steamed, bathed, massaged in scented oils and pampered beyond belief, I felt so relaxed. Gone were the aches and stiffness from long days in the saddle. I would love to stay longer but Louis, Odo and the wretched beetles have been muttering about decadence and wearing out their knees.

We were guests at a special service held in the vast, splendid Saint Sophia. With the mosaics of gold twinkling in the candlelight, it was truly moving. The architecture of this city is amazing; a mixture of many styles and influences, Eastern Orthodox, and dare I say minarets, which tower skywards like needles. Roman architecture was still prominent. Papa used to say it was a shame we had lost, even in the Aquitaine, much of the ingenuity of the Romans.

Constantinople was so civilised. This palace with its sculptures, gardens and fountains, and floors heated by hypocausts continue the Roman tradition. When I think of the ruins around L'Ombriere and the stories Papa used to tell, I can feel a connection with the history here. For instance, from the women's balcony, we saw chariot racing at the hippodrome as well as other sporting events involving beautifully formed young men, their oiled bodies gleaming. At least, Louis was not there to notice if I was enjoying the look of them too much. His jealousy was becoming overbearing. I must admit, however, that the young men did stir me in an unfamiliar way which was oddly disconcerting.

Tonight will be our last in this magnificent city and in this grand palace. I will be sorry to say goodbye to Lady Irene. She and Emperor Manuel have been the most welcoming and generous hosts. Only two weeks in this sophisticated atmosphere so akin to my childhood, was far too short. Lady Irene and I have enjoyed each other's company. Being older, I felt I could talk to her as a motherly figure. I was certain she detected Louis' and my marriage is strained. She did not say anything, but it would be obvious I find being in his presence disquieting. How I long to spread my wings to escape the suffocating atmosphere of the cloistered French court.

Emperor Manuel and Lady Irene have indulged us with many gifts; gold plate, jewellery, carpets and seeds from the gardens for me to plant. Louis has been less accepting, but Lady Irene wanted to spoil me, so my protestations fell on deaf ears. I will therefore treasure the luxury heaped upon me, humbled by such kindness.

A whole ship has been commissioned to carry my gifts to Saint Simeon in Northern Antioch. We will be guests in the principality before our final dash to Jerusalem. I cannot wait to see Uncle Raymond. We have not been together since I was a small child. I remember with fondness all the chess games, archery contests, poetry and music in which we partook. He used to tease us as well as playing with us; such patience, more like a big brother to Nilla and me. We adored him.

Before I prepared for the final banquet in our honour, I visited my men to wish them God speed. I gave them my blessings and let them know they will be in my thoughts and prayers. My friends and I leave early. Louis, the battalions and their knights will take to their horses at cockcrow. We will now be entering enemy territory. I wished them well with all my heart. Deep down, I do not believe Emperor Manual will be too sad to see the armies move on. Feeding them and their horses would be a strain on resources, I think. In the meantime, I will have to put my writing away till we arrive in Antioch.

***

After much trial, tragedy and unimaginable trauma, I am in Cyprus. It is hard to write down my recollections.

What folly, shades of another Vitry-sur-Marne! No planning equipped us for what occurred. Christmas gave us little to celebrate. With the weather most ill, we lost men, horses and equipment. Turkish raiding parties on swift rugged ponies attacked out of nowhere, firing their arrows with great accuracy from horseback. They knew every ravine, every chasm and mountainous rock while the crusaders blundered from one skirmish to another in unknown territory.

Some of Louis' army travelled south after crossing the Bosphorus and followed the coast, then rode inland to Nicaea. While Louis was camped at Nicaea, which was well fortified and protected, a courier from Emperor Manuel announced the German Emperor, Conrad, had been victorious against the Turks. Louis, in excitement, rode out to meet him only to discover this was incorrect: Conrad instead had suffered the loss of nine-tenths of his German crusaders, having been ensnared by the wily guerrilla tactics of our enemies. The remainder of Conrad's army, whom Louis encountered, were in a parlous state, in mighty travail. Conrad had been seriously wounded and had to return to Constantinople. Louis was warned by the survivors that a similar ambush

Chapter 6. Unholy Holy Land

awaited his men. Though it is hard to comprehend, some believed Manuel had deliberately mislead the crusaders.

As we were following Louis and his men, we came face to face with the horrors of the campaign; bloated dead horses, their legs stiffened skywards like grotesque branches, eyes pecked out by carrion-eating birds. Worse were the unburied bodies of their riders. Blood-blackened corpses, arrows still piercing their torsos or necks, many hacked beyond recognition as human, were so numerous we stopped counting. My men did their best to protect me and my women from the devastation. They could not. The stench and revulsion had me retching and gasping. I wept. Prayer was useless. I tried to give succour to a young German, a boy little more than thirteen or fourteen years, crying for his *Maman.* Guile begged me to leave him as he would soon be dead. But how could I. Pretending to be his mother, I held him till God took him.

To add to our despair, our food supplies dwindled. The Germans had raped the countryside. Nothing was left to forage. Horses were skeletal. Many we had to eat as our men were starving too. I called a stop. It was pointless continuing into the unknown without supplies to sustain us. I discussed our predicament with Alphonso, Guile, Guy and my other knights. Alphonso bluntly said we women were slowing them down with carts and wagons full of what he called our finery.

'Our finery!'

I snapped. Fear wracked me day and night. We too were hungry, filthy, and as dishevelled as the men.

At the next village where we made camp, I had my chests unloaded. Keeping the woollen practical gowns and some fur-lined capes, I bundled the silk, samite, brocade and damask into piles. I sorted my jewellery. I announced I was going to sell my possessions in the villages for food. I insisted the women travelling with me do likewise. God's teeth, I was determined to prove to damned Alphonso that I was not a burden.

With heartfelt thanks to Brother Anselm, I was pleased I had improved my Greek. It was put to good use. I was able to converse in the towns and villages we passed through, to sell our belongings and barter for basic food for ourselves and fodder for the horses. Traders were impressed a foreigner – and a woman, what is more – was so fluent in the language.

I am grateful my men were disciplined. I exhorted them to treat villagers and others not armed with respect, unlike Conrad who showed no thought for the innocent and as a result paid for his brutality. Louis lost control over his men, if ever he had any.

The weather worsened, forcing me and my women into carriages. I praised God for the heavy leather curtains which kept out most of the wind. But we were cold. Geoffrey de Rançon and his men were sent ahead to accompany us. Louis insisted our vanguard make camp on a high, windswept plateau where he said he would rendezvous with us. However, we could not pitch a tent. The wind, like a scythe, ripped them to shreds. Our horses were whinnying with hunger and cold. There was naught for the poor beasts to eat on the stony terrain and fodder had run out. A scout was sent onward to see if he could find shelter. He returned in great excitement having found a protected valley bearing good water, grass aplenty and protection from the howling wind and sleety rain.

Guile, Geoffrey and I decided to leave. We could not stay exposed on that bleak plateau as the weather deteriorated. Snow was mixed with the sleet. We had to seek shelter before more men and horses perished. It was a slow, treacherous descent down a narrow track just wide enough to take the carts and wagons of equipment. I rode with Geoffrey and Guile. I was freezing. There was no feeling in my feet. Even gloved, my hands could barely hold the reins. My skin felt chapped; the cold penetrated through every gap in my miniver cape. Frost had built up on my lashes.

Inch by inch we edged our way down the icy slope till we reached the protection of the surrounding hillsides where the

Chapter 6. Unholy Holy Land

wind eased. Before anyone could dismount, the poor horses wrenched the reins from their rider's hands to eat the grass around them. What was left of the tents were pitched, cooking fires lit, and gruels and broths were made from our meagre supplies. Never had a simple porridge tasted so delicious, so warming. My friends and I at last could attempt to dry off. My feet were like ice; never have I felt so exhausted. We piled in together, trying to warm ourselves in our remaining furs and whatever blankets we had to put around us. Angelique and the beetles were praying for salvation.

Of course, Louis could not find us. I had sent the scout back to warn him, to tell him the weather had compelled us to find shelter, but the poor man was forced to return. Snow on the plateau was knee deep. Later we discovered, we had been observed by the Turks, but like us, they too had taken refuge.

The next day we basked in wintry sunshine. We took stock of our dwindling supplies, gave our thin animals a chance to recuperate and attended to our own ills. Many of the men could not go on. I was in despair. I tried to keep a hopeful countenance even though we were being overwhelmed by events never imagined. Louis, because he could not find us on the plateau, panicked, thinking we had all perished.

He was furious with me when he caught up with us a few days later. They were attacked by the Turks who had let us proceed. They slaughtered hundreds of Louis' men snared in their ambush. I was horrified by his appearance when he arrived in our camp, his clothes rent and blood-stained, on a nag that looked like it would collapse under him. Louis would not listen that had we not moved on; he would have found us dead, frozen stiff from cold. He was now ranting we were vulnerable to another ambush cradled as we were in this lush valley. He commanded we break camp to leave for the nearest port to travel the rest of the way to Antioch by sea.

***

When we reached Attalia, it was an answer to a prayer. We all looked like ragged waifs. We were reduced to what we stood up in. My filthy, rent gown flapped around my aching body, but the relief in filling my lungs with the salty ocean air, and to have sea breezes flutter through my unveiled hair, was heaven sent, even if the next puff could have blown me away; my friends likewise. We thanked God we had reached safety.

It was a relief to be away from the misfortunes of the land, to put the bloody horrors of the previous weeks behind us though my nights are haunted. Anything that resembles the sound of a distressed horse sends me into a shuddering panic.

Our fleet set off with billowing sails towards Antioch. I managed to beg some writing materials from our captain. I wedged an ink pot between two heavy coils of rope as I tried to write on the deck. But the barque was heeling as it beat down the coast, so I had to stop the exercise before ink spilled over my words or soaked my already stained gown. I decided to continue when my floor was more stable.

***

The large flotilla of barques and other vessels looked grand as we beat down the coast. Louis, thank God, sailed with his men. My friends were in a ship behind mine. I would have preferred to be with them instead of confined with the beetles, but Louis would not hear of it. So I was with my elite knights, 'my Praetorian Guard,' as everyone calls them in jest, and Angelique and her coven. At least I could speak with the guards in my native tongue. Angelique was mightily annoyed because she had no idea what we were saying.

The beetles and Angelique were terrified of the sea and not good sailors. I wished for a severe storm. My wish was answered. We picked up speed further out to sea as we made good progress, but around noon the sun disappeared from the sky. Thunder clouds darkened overhead. In the distance,

Chapter 6. Unholy Holy Land

white-capped waves marched in serried rows towards the faraway shore. Our barques began to pitch and yaw as they heaved through the blowing spume. Sails were reefed. God be praised, I do not suffer from *mal-de-mere*. Angelique and the beetles, much to my delight, were as sick as dogs, and petrified as the sea sprayed over the decks. I hoped and prayed those aft of us were not suffering too badly. Their crafts were only shadowy outlines as they ploughed through the grey-green gloom.

Although I became very wet, I preferred to stay on deck, away from the odours and groans below. In fact, I quite enjoyed the rolling craft. But we were blown off course, so we headed for the safety of Cyprus. A half day later the final barque limped into the harbour with torn sails and damaged rigging. Except for Sybilla and Tarquiri, who were not severely affected by the stormy seas, Florine, Mamille, and Faydide said they wished to die, they felt so ill. A week in Cyprus will allow us to dry out while the weather abates. I am trying to catch up with my writing, but I have only a few quills left, which I must cherish.

We were afforded the hospitable company of the local governor and his charming wife. But all was not well with my travelling companions. Florine, who suffered sorely during the storm, was still ailing. She put on a brave countenance, but she has succumbed to an ague, that is not the result of *mal-de-mere*. I summoned a physician and apothecary. These knowledgeable men are concerned she may have contracted a disease, possibly measles, seeing she has developed a rash and a fever. We were all afraid. If it is measles, it was serious because the disease is often deadly. Measles, like typhus has been known to wipe out whole townships, like Jerome's poor family all those years ago. The deprivations of our journey, the bone-chilling cold weakened the most able of our men, so it is little wonder one of us has fallen ill. Much to my chagrin, Louis had me isolated. No matter how I much I grumbled, it has not done one jot of good. Angelique and the beetles agreed with Louis (of course they would!) so I have been removed from my friend's company. I am quarantined and watched like a hawk for possible symptoms. I am praying for Florine who, they tell me, is stoic. But I am no longer the free sea nymph. Back to reality Eleanor!

I was prevented from communing with any of the others also in case they too were infected. Sybilla, Mamille, Tarquiri and Faydide were showing no signs of illness, but I was considered too precious, no matter how much I protested. Sybilla managed to pen me a note. I am bereft – they have decided to return home as soon as Florine is well enough to travel. They fear passing the disease to the Queen of France. It is not fair!

I kicked my table in fury only to hurt my toe. I limped around my quarters, cursing in Langue d'Oc. It was no use begging them to stay. They are women of the Aquitaine. God's teeth, they are like me, pigheaded and stubborn. Their loyalty to me and my health may be noble, but I am devastated. They have been a buffer between me and the cursed black beetles. They kept me sane through thick and thin during our arduous journey. We laughed; we sang. Before Constantinople, for fun, they dressed as Amazons with me as Penthesilea. They suffered in silence when we staggered though the ravages of war, never complaining about the lack of food or when I made them sell their belongings. Oh, how I will miss them!

Chapter 7. Antioch Discovered

With a leaden heart I set sail again, our destination at last the port of Antioch, St Simeon. It was an uneventful voyage. I stayed alone in my cabin or kept to the prow of the vessel. Angelique and the beetles were still too afraid of the sea to chase after me. I almost wished for another storm, but nothing eventuated. We glided through smooth waters as gentle winds filled our sails in the wake of Louis' galley.

As we approached St Simeon my excitement grew. I could not wait to be re-united with Uncle Raymond after all these years. I was eager to meet his wife, Constance. I had been told she had her own troubles over the rule of Antioch, which was her inheritance. It was through their marriage Uncle Raymond was acknowledged the ruler of the principality. I hope Constance and I will like each other.

We slipped into the harbour as the midday sun sparkled on the water. A gentle bump against the dock announced our arrival. The sailors called to each other as they moored the barque fore and aft. A rattle of chains and a splash plunged the anchor to the deep. We disembarked.

Angelique and the beetles had dressed me in a plain woollen gown, one of the remaining ones left. My cape they had darned and cleaned. My face had suffered from the ravages of the ride no matter how I had tried to protect it with veiling. Collette found a half pot of lanolin at the bottom of a bag. Her rationed application improved my skin a little.

The temperature was balmy, such bliss. I wished I did not have to wear the damn crown of France: I had had to restrain myself from selling it! At least my feet were warm. My last pair of fur-trimmed boots were stitched by one of the sailors. The soles were falling off.

Louis and I made our way along a pathway flanked either side by my Praetorian Guard and Louis' men, followed by the beetles and Angelique who looked like a phalanx of moulting crows. (To be honest I did not look much better.) All manner of people working on the dock stopped as the captains and sailors from the fleet gave us a rousing farewell. Gallant destriers awaited us. How glossy these horses looked after the poor scarecrows we had ridden to Attalia. We mounted for the league or two to Uncle Raymond's citadel on the slopes of Mount Silpius, the seat of the Princes of Antioch. I was excited but nervous.

***

We dismounted after crossing a moat and a drawbridge. A ramp led through a towering stone wall flanked with huge gates bearing heavy, vicious, iron spikes. They looked like they could withstand Hannibal's elephants. The gates swung open on heavy hinges as a fanfare echoed from trumpeters lined along our path. They welcomed us into a high-walled palace surrounded by gardens, date palms and fountains.

We reached a colonnade where, in its shade, were Uncle Raymond and his wife. It was all I could do not to run into Raymond's arms. He stepped forward and took my thin hands in his. I looked like a scarecrow. His eyes betrayed shock at my appearance; his voice was hoarse with emotion.

'Look at you, look at you! Little Elea, all grown up!'

I could not utter a word as tears of joy tumbled down my cheeks. He had grown up too, tall, handsome and so resembling Papa I struggled with my emotions. I just wanted a hug.

Before Louis could step forward, Uncle Raymond introduced me to Constance who is about my age, small in stature, attractive with steady grey eyes. Her face was a study as she welcomed me. I think she was trying not to gasp in horror at my parlous state.

Louis' face was going red. His priority as King of France was being ignored by a babble of family excitement in

Chapter 7. Antioch Discovered

Langue d'Oc and I did not want a scene. I introduced him to Raymond in Latin. Raymond's Aquitaine charm saved the situation as he bowed over Louis' hand. I put my hand on his arm as Raymond escorted us to his reception hall.

I asked Louis about his welfare after the sea voyage and when would he hear if the remainder of his army had arrived in Antioch. He said he would discuss events later after we had refreshments. He said Angelique and the beetles looked tired. There was no mention about my state of health.

Food! Such abundance after weeks with so little. We were spoiled with spice-laden sweetmeats, some made with dates and an interesting textured concoction called coconut, a large, strange woody fruit. Louis amused me by looking at the little delicacy with suspicion, so I popped one in his mouth regardless of his protestations. Lord be praised, he liked it! But it was the cordial I really enjoyed. It is made from the juice of lemons, added spring water and sweetened with honey, so refreshing.

Uncle Raymond and I could not keep our eyes off each other. There was much I wanted to talk about after all these years. None of this attention was missed by my husband. Before we were whisked away to our quarters Uncle Raymond and I arranged to meet privately as soon as possible. I was twelve years old when we were last together.

***

Louis told me his chambers were cavernous. As in Constantinople the palace here is opulent. The floors are either marble or mosaic. The temperature is pleasant, but I am informed hot winds blow in from the desert in summer. After the freezing temperatures encountered on our journey from Constantinople, those winds sounded heavenly.

Summer heat is tempered by an amazing invention within the palace: the windows are of ornately carved grills instead of glass. They are covered with blinds made of a fine cane-like material called bamboo. From above, copper pipes pierced with tiny holes allow water to trickle down.

This dampens the bamboo. The breezes blowing through cool the room. So clever! Rooms also have their own tinkling fountains.

***

The relief of getting the crown off was bliss. Collette gave my head a good massage before plaiting my hair which needs to be bathed. Pages brought bowls of warm water scented with essence of roses. I could have dived in to splash among the floating petals. How I long for the hamam, also used here I am told.

On a table in my chamber were missives from my leading knights – Guile, young Henry of Champagne and one from Alphonso. They continued by land after we left for Attalia. Alphonso's screed was poorly penned but to the point. He was blunt. He wanted to know if the French army under Louis was going to show any discipline and would I intervene with the king to prevent his soldiers absconding like cowards when faced with battle. My heart sank. I may not like that upstart Alphonso of Toulouse, but he is a good campaigner. He did have the decency, for which I am grateful, to thank me for the sacrifices we women made to purchase food along the way.

Next, I read young Henry's letter. He and his men discovered French soldiers from Louis' crusaders hiding in caves, half-starved and freezing in inadequate clothing. These men had deserted. They said they could not go on under Louis' leadership. Henry says he prevented his men from taking the law into their own hands and murdering them for being traitors to the king and the crusade.

They begged for mercy. Those he questioned gave him harrowing tales. Conrad, as we knew, had failed. Louis, who was travelling after Conrad, came across a group of Turks in a small oasis and decided to attack. The encampment consisted of a small clan of mostly old men, women and children who begged for mercy, but Louis' men rampaged through them, slaughtering them all. Louis punished the

Chapter 7. Antioch Discovered

men who committed the outrage by having their hands, noses or ears cut off. How cruel!

As it happened, the vicious raid against Louis and his men was in retaliation for the assault on the oasis, not because Geoffrey, Guile and I led our men off the plateau to shelter from the elements.

Henry continues, his men did not consider the king's punishment fair because the French crusaders claimed they were obeying orders. Louis had urged his men into the oasis before ascertaining who the group were. To add to the chaos, Conrad's men, as I knew, had plundered the countryside and burned what was left of crops and other food sources, leaving the French with little to forage. Henry, although not condoning the desertions, says he can understand why the men did so. He asks if I can influence the Lord King before all his army abandoned the crusade. Anger churned my stomach as the turmoil of the last weeks resurfaced. I hung my head in despair.

***

I could not put off speaking to Louis any longer. Odo de Deuil opened the door. A familiar lurch of dread swirled around me as he hovered. I stiffened my spine. I told him I wished to speak to my husband in private. Louis dismissed him.

Our exchange relived the nightmare. Louis took my hand but dropped it again when he saw my displeasure, no matter how I tried to look impassive. He offered me a seat, I remained standing. I gave the letters I had received to Louis to read. He erupted in fury and flung them to the floor. He screamed what would my men know when they had avoided fighting, avoided doing what they were here for.

'Like killing innocent women and children and the old? Or raping and pillaging, leaving a scorched earth behind them, like Conrad? We came here to reclaim the Holy Land in the name of God, in case you have forgotten, Louis, to put the Saracens to heel, not attack the innocent population.'

Odo, who must have had his ear to the door, re-entered. Venom dripped from my lips as I told him to get out. With Louis, I tried a different tack. I said I was pleased he was safe and had arrived in Antioch with most of his immediate army. I attempted to sound sympathetic. I asked if any of his men needed to have injuries treated or had enough to eat. He calmed a little, saying the windburn and frostbite from the harsh weather was painful. I examined his face. His prominent nose was peeling and red, his countenance was weather-worn, lips cracked: his tanned face gave him a rugged appearance. Like me he is thin.

'My mail chafes.'

I told him I would enquire about a balm to sooth his abrasions and would he show me the areas affected. That stunned him. It meant he had to, maybe, remove his gown. He looked at me in a most peculiar way. He blushed under his browned face as I undid the lacing round his neckline and eased the gown to one side. The skin on his right shoulder is healing but still raw in places. I asked him if the other shoulder was the same. He said it was. I winced. To have chaffing rubbed daily would be painful. I eased his gown back over his shoulder. By now his demeanour had changed. Grabbing my wrist, he pulled me towards him. For the first time in our married life in the middle of the day Louis attempted to embrace me. I pushed him away with all my might almost toppling him backwards. I hissed 'no.' I said I would organise the balm and suggested he pad his mail with sheepskin as I gathered my missives. I left before he tried to kiss me again, or worse.

***

Uncle Raymond has given me the use of this splendid library. He had a desk installed, with quills, ink and parchment. We have agreed to have a long conversation on the morrow.

What to do? My life is dragging me down. I look around at the handsome, tall men of the Aquitaine and I know I want more than the restrictions imposed on me by my status and joyless marriage. I have been fantasising what it must be like to have a handsome man's arms around me. Not that Louis is plain – he is quite good-looking – but he does not desire me the way I think he should. I am aware men find me attractive. It would not take much on my behalf to go further than a little flirting, but this is where I run into the wall beyond the moat. I recognise there is more than courtly love. It is something I have yet to explore, let alone experience. For now, though, the drawbridge has not been lowered. Also, I have no idea what to expect of myself. The only man I know is fumbling, useless Louis.

***

The palace is built around many courtyards with cooling fountains. The gardens are vibrant with flowers, a haven for bees and bird life. Peacocks strut and display their shimmering magnificence. Breezes waft through the bamboo curtains with the tinkling sound of water adding to the peaceful effect.

Raymond and I sat together, looking out towards the garden through the elegant pillars of the assembly hall designed to make full use of any zephyr during the hot months. We were both shy to begin with, not knowing where to start with our 'catching up.' Raymond began with his life in England as a young squire. The loss of Toulouse we glossed over. Neither of us really wanted to discuss it, though I did mention Louis' fruitless attempt to win it back for our family. I skirted over Vitry-sur-Marne which he had heard about. I said at least it had brought us together because it determined the crusade.

I mentioned I noticed Greek was readily spoken in his palace and beyond. I told him about Brother Anselm and how I wished I could improve my writing and reading skills. He thought I should do it. If only it was that easy.

We talked about Petronilla. I told him how happy she was and how I envied hers and Raoul's love for one another, and about their dear little son, Ralph. But Ralph brought Marie to the forefront of my mind and the rawness in my heart. Uncle Raymond noticed I was unsettled so changed the subject.

He explained how his plans to capture Aleppo were progressing; his voice conveyed his excitement. I knew the seizure of Aleppo was strategic for the capture of Edessa. Both will strengthen Antioch against attack by a powerful Saracen Governor, Nureddin, who has his eyes on the city because of its position and wealth. Furthermore, our ride to Jerusalem will be safer if these two cities are controlled by Raymond's forces. These military tactics had been discussed before we left Paris with Louis agreeing to help by providing men and equipment for both assaults. Raymond was eager to discuss his preparations with Louis.

My heart sank. I was now in an embarrassing position because I heard Louis had since changed his mind or had it changed for him. I overheard Odo criticising Raymond's campaigns. Odo denounced them as self-interest, a waste of time for the French. I passed this information on to Raymond.

Raymond's face fell. He reminded me, he thought he and Louis had an understanding, an agreement. I sympathised with Uncle Raymond's predicament. I was ashamed Louis had backed out of his commitment. Why he allows himself to be led by religious zealots I know not. I would not be surprised if Odo was out to spite me by encouraging Louis to betray my Uncle. Like Suger, he despises me. I promised Uncle Raymond I would try to change Louis' mind, to make him honour his word, but in my gut, I feared my attempts would be ignored. Odo's influence is all encompassing.

We sat together in silence. It became too much. Misery engulfed me. Raymond detected I was struggling and stood to pour a cup of cordial. I thanked him. I tried not to make eye contact because I could feel myself losing control. The cordial was delicious but no matter how tightly I shut my eyes, tears seeped through my lashes. Raymond knelt before me and took my hands in his like he did when we were

Chapter 7. Antioch Discovered

children, when it was only a banged head, or an imaginary slight.

'Elea.'

One gentle word undid me. A torrent poured out; Papa dying; the removal of Marie, how I could not fight for my daughter against the black-hearted swarm who ruled Louis and Île de France. Then came the horrors I had experienced after leaving Constantinople. I sobbed about my sham of a marriage, raved on and on, ranted about Vitry-sur-Marne, Suger's and Bernard's malignant treatment of me, Angelique and the dreaded beetles, Renée's banishment, the spurning of my intelligence and education, being called a witch. I became hysterical.

'I am at my wit's end Raymond! I cannot go on. I want to escape, to be free! Sometimes I want to die.'

Raymond wrapped his arms around my shaking body, kissed my forehead.

'Poor little Cuz, poor little Cuz.'

He sent a page for Constance who arrived, concerned. Raymond sat next to me. Constance took over. She ordered a cloth and cool water as I tried to catch my breath. They took me to Raymond's bed chamber nearby. Both sat with me till I calmed. Constance bathed my face and massaged my temples with lavender oil, Raymond poured more cordial. Both realised how alone I was and understood my devastation.

***

But no matter how bad I felt, I had to drag myself out of this pit. I had to endure. My men had arrived in Antioch with disturbing information: the Saracens were planning an ambush along the route where Louis planned to ride. Raymond called an assembly of all concerned in the great hall. I had no choice but to find the strength to attend. Maps were rolled out on a long banqueting table. I looked a bit dishevelled and puffy-eyed, but no one was looking at me, except Louis. Guile, Alphonso Henry, Guy and all the others pored over the route. Raymond was too polite in their company, for my sake, to mention Louis had reneged on his agreement over Aleppo.

Guile sent for the man who had provided the information about the Saracen's plans. He conveyed his knowledge to the group. The only person who ignored him was Louis; he was fuming about something. After many exchanges of opinion, we believed it was necessary to alter the route to prevent more bloodshed. I asked for two chess boards and set them up to demonstrate the tactics formulating in my head.

Without warning, Louis' fist crashed down, scattering the pieces.

'Are you going to stand there like dumb mules, to be dictated to by a woman – this woman!'

Guile pointed out I was no fool and had read about more military campaigns than most in the room, emphasising I was a fine tactician.

'Tactics!' Louis' shrill voice echoed around the room.

'She disobeys orders to remain on a strategic plateau to run away to a valley to keep warm, exposing the rest of us to the murderous Turks!'

Louis turned on his heel.

My heart thudded. At the door he stopped.

'You will attend me now!'

His lisping voice hit the ceiling, higher than usual.

An embarrassed silence hung in the air.

Before I left, I addressed the silent men.

'This is an order from your duchess. You will not march through this mountain pass where you will be open to ambush.'

I pointed to the map.

'Please find an alternate route.'

Alphonso, I said, I wanted in the rear to protect those ahead, because his men were valiant, disciplined and seasoned; also, he knew what to expect.

With a deferring nod he replied, 'Aye, Milady'.

Geoffrey de Rançon was to lead. He was still under a

cloud like me because of our decision to abandon the plateau and needed to prove himself. Henry was to take the central position with his battalion, meaning no disrespect for his bravery or capabilities, but he is the youngest and does not yet have the experience needed against a cunning foe; also, I wanted him protected. Guile I ordered with Alphonso. Guy de Thouars and the rest of the Aquitaine battalions could decide with Guile the best order in which to march, depending on their strengths and weaponry.

A heavy silence followed me from the room. Words cannot explain the humiliation I felt.

***

How often do I find refuge in libraries? The aroma of books usually has a calming effect, but not today. I recorded what took place between Louis and me. It was difficult. My hand trembled. I dripped ink, my scrawl, most ill. My head ached.

Louis' eyes bulged and spittle flew from his lips as he loomed over me. Was I afraid? No, I was too enraged. When he struck me before in Paris, I retaliated, but this time I thought with calm logic, it would not be a slight sting, he could hurt me. Yet I stood my ground. I let him rave and roar. I waited for the blow.

He ranted about me being in Raymond's bed, about being shamefully embraced and kissed in the full view of minions, screamed about the crimes of adultery and incest.

I demanded to know where he had heard these ridiculous, outrageous accusations. He said I had been observed. I had no idea what he was talking about. The only people who saw what transpired between Raymond and me, as far as I knew, were his wife and two pages. I said Constance had suggested taking me to Raymond's chamber, which was close by, so I could lie down because I was upset. They both ministered to my needs. Should Louis not believe my words, he could consult my aunt. I left the room with as much dignity as possible.

The door I closed as gently as I could, but Louis almost wrenched it off its hinges.

'How dare you walk out on me! I have not finished speaking to you.'

I turned.

'How dare you betray my relative, to whom you had promised aid for his assaults on Aleppo and Edessa. You, who cannot control your troops, who takes ill advice from religious fanatics, you who have no conception of military tactics other than to burn innocent people alive in their church!'

I thought Louis was going to erupt like boiling pitch. With outward, ice-like calm and inner turmoil, I left.

'When you calm down, I will return.'

I strode towards my quarters. Heads ducked back into doorways as I passed. Impotent rage followed my passage. Dust showered down as the door to Louis' chamber slammed shut, shaking the ancient walls like an earthquake.

***

Aunt Constance found me some time later after a frantic search when I was not in my chamber. I was asleep from exhaustion with my head on my arms at the desk. Louis was distraught, she told me, after he was given the facts about what took place between Raymond and me. One of the pages saw Angelique when both aunt and uncle were trying to comfort me. She will be the one who has fabricated the tale about my so-called incestuous relationship with Raymond. It was obvious she wasted no time tittle-tattling to Louis, even though she could see Aunt Constance and the pages by my side. I can imagine a scorching missive hurtling across lands and seas to Suger – anything to discredit me.

Raymond told me, regardless of the warnings about the route to Jerusalem, Louis was ignoring advice and intended to take it. Nor had Louis changed his mind about Aleppo and Edessa. Raymond insisted I remain in Antioch for my personal safety. He made it clear I would be a prime target for

Chapter 7. Antioch Discovered

capture and ransom, if not worse. It was common knowledge, he said, amongst our enemies the Queen of France planned to lead her crusaders. Neither do my men want me placed in danger. The trek from Constantinople was bad enough. Raymond said he spoke to Louis who shame-faced agreed I should stay here. I am saddened I cannot fulfil my mission.

I was feeling superfluous. How was I to occupy my time in Antioch? I did not want to spend the many weeks to come worrying about my men and the outcome of our quest. Uncle Raymond reminded me of my wish to improve reading and writing in Greek and said he knows of a tutor who could fulfil my desire. He suggested I should put it to Louis, who is now so full of guilt and remorse he will agree to anything to make me happy.

As the Greek tutor Raymond knows is a young man, I think Louis' jealousy will colour any decision he makes, guilt or no. I could wait till he sets off for Jerusalem, but that would be foolish, with Angelique here to run to him with glee at the first opportunity. I wrestled with approaching Louis. I was keeping well out of his way except formally. I will be happy to exploit his guilty conscience but, knowing Louis' beliefs about the education of woman, I held out little hope.

***

My final consultations with my crusader army were bitter-sweet. Alphonso, Guile, and Henry with Geoffrey and the rest of the leading knights were leaving ahead of Louis. They have chosen more open terrain. The route was longer, but they cannot be trapped. Alphonso, seasoned knight that he is, knows how to live off the land, light cooking fires using the driest wood to avoid, as much as possible, tell-tale smoke, and to camp blending with the landscape, as well protected as possible. He will also ride at a speed less likely to create columns of give-away dust. His study of the ancient Roman legions and their military skills was admirable. I discovered we had read the same books. He gave all the men from the

Aquitaine and Champagne tactical advice, for which I was grateful. I spoke to the men about loyalty, not just to me and their leaders but to each other. I asked them to care for one another like brothers. I wished them God speed. It was hard. I felt like a mother farewelling her children and longed to give each a loving hug.

Conrad, though still unwell, had returned and was on his way determined to be the first to reach Jerusalem. Our informant thinks the Saracens will let him almost through the pass before attacking where the pass enters the plain. I feared they will also wait till Louis enters behind Conrad and will trap him from the rear. Louis ignored Raymond and any other advice. *'Deus Vult,'* 'God Wills It', was his zealous chant. He said God would protect him because he carries the cross and the Oriflamme of France.

Chapter 8. Love and Prophesy

Raymond spoke to Louis on my behalf and introduced him to the young tutor whose name is Abraham. Constance said he is a very pleasant person, the grandson of Raymond's physician. Raymond refused to tell me what transpired between the three, but Louis, much to my amazement agreed, providing I liked Abraham. I meet him today.

I was nervous. I wanted to look my best, but I was afraid Louis would have a fit if I looked too attractive. Thanks to Constance, material had been purchased and the beetles have been busily stitching me new gowns to replace the ones I sold. I selected an indigo brocade. It was a warm gown, even though spring was approaching. The neckline was high and the train not long. I made certain I was veiled. Louis insisted I wear my crown. To please myself however, I put kohl around my eyes. Praise God I no longer look like I have been starved.

Louis escorted me to Uncle Raymond's assembly chamber to meet Master Abraham. Raymond came forward to introduce me. I kept my eyes demurely on the floor, but in time I had to look up. I do not know what I was expecting in a tutor, perhaps someone a little older. In front of me was the most beautiful man I had ever seen. My mouth dropped. I think I turned scarlet. He gave a courteous bow of his head as we met. I managed to mutter in Greek I was delighted to meet him.

The afternoon was a success. Louis was quiet, much more his usual shy self. I put on a modest demeanour, speaking only when I was spoken to. For Louis' benefit we switched to Latin, in which Master Abraham was equally fluent.

After he left, Louis, Raymond and Constance asked what I thought of the young master. I said I thought he was very scholarly; his Greek was perfect, and he seemed to have a pleasant disposition. Louis asked me if I liked him. I replied it was not for me to like the tutor, it was for me to learn from him. I said I hoped to respect him. Raymond spluttered into his wine. I glared at him; I recognised the naughty twinkle in his eye.

We departed to our various tasks after Master Abraham left. After I rid myself of the crown and veil, I bolted to the library. Abraham has set my heart fluttering. He has large, dark eyes; almond shaped with the longest eyelashes I have ever seen on a man. His hair is a mass of black curls, he has a dark beard; both were neatly trimmed. His skin is the colour of creamy honey. I think he would be taller than Papa, who was considered a giant even for an Aquitainian. Abraham was dressed in the local garb; a long crisp white gown called a *jilaabiyah*. I noticed he had long slender fingers. I am having fantasies about how they would feel on one's skin. I will have to be very disciplined in my classes with him. If Louis found out I was attracted to him, a mighty eruption would take place. Also, Angelique and the beetles will be humming about like a swarm of bees ready to report so much as a flutter of an eyelid. I am stunned Abraham was allowed anywhere near me.

***

Louis left with his army of crusaders. All I can do is pray God will watch over them as I wished all good luck and to take care. I told Louis I still thought it was folly travelling through the mountains, but he would not heed me. Fanaticism was driving him to be first into Jerusalem in front of Conrad.

I have had my first lesson with Abraham surrounded by the beetles who I suspected were all agog. Angelique understands a little Greek, but only if it is spoken simply, slowly and deliberately. I will not be accommodating her.

The lesson went well. Abraham has a delightful baritone voice. I kept to one side of the table, indicating he sit on the other. He used a slate and a type of chalk to write simple words and sentences. He brought with him a copy of the Bible in Greek and asked if I had one in Latin, which I do. My homework was to translate the Latin to Greek. I will do my best – anything to please him.

***

Each day has been a joy. It is almost three weeks since my lessons started. I have had little time to write in my journal, so busy am I with my Greek, which is coming along in large leaps. Abraham is not only handsome but has an agreeable personality, a sense of humour and a wealth of knowledge in many areas. His grandfather wants him to become a physician or an apothecary. His knowledge of herbs, spices and other plants is vast. I have learned a little of his family. His mother sadly died when he was born, he has an older sister, Judith, who is blind but has remarkable powers of insight and can foresee the future, which I find fascinating. I hope to meet her. He does not speak much of his father who lives some leagues away further in the mountains with his wives. I may have misheard, but I did not wish to appear rude by questioning whether it was singular or plural. He said his father is a poet and a dreamer. Abraham and Judith live in a house provided by their father here in Antioch. His grandfather moves around to where he is needed. He was his mother's father.

Sometimes we walked in the palace gardens before it got too hot. The spring weather is far more akin to a Parisian summer. The beetles hate it because they do not like going outside in the sun. Angelique has threatened me with everything from freckles to sunstroke to try to keep me inside. Today, I told them to stay undercover as I wandered the gardens and courtyards alone with Abraham – such a pleasure. There was a special rose I had found. It was heavenly. I think it is called a damask. They were abundant in Empress Irene's garden, too. Another plant's seeds to take back. I would like to have the essence blended with jasmine. I love its scent.

We found the rose. As I was bending the stem towards me to inhale the perfumed petals, I was suddenly stung by a bee on my palm. I let out a howl of pain; God's teeth it hurt! Poor Abraham was startled. I yelled I had been stung.

'Wait,' he said.

He hoisted up his *jilaabiyah*, tore down the path, and leapt over a garden bed. He hurried back with an onion. He demanded I give him my stiletto – how did he know I had one? I pulled it from my belt and gave it to him. He cut the onion in half, rubbing the cut section on my hand. It was a miracle – the pain immediately stopped.

'Always works,' he grinned.

He said he would have to remove the little black sting the bee had left behind.

Abraham suggested the herbarium where he was certain the herbalist would have tweezers and alcohol to dab on the wound. With mock homage he gave me back my stiletto. When I asked him how he knew I had one, he said with a naughty grin that he was very observant.

The herbalist was not there but Abraham knew where he kept the key. His grandfather and this man worked together on remedies for the sick with support from Raymond. Inside, the air was redolent with mint, drying rosemary, thyme and other fragrances. After searching around for a few minutes, he found the plant tweezers. Abraham removed the tiny sting and poured some alcohol on my hand.

'An interesting perfume, Lady Eleanor, a heady mixture of onion and bad wine.'

He made me laugh. I am pleased he does not grovel to my status.

He replaced the tweezers.

'Better?'

In a mad flirtatious moment, for a reason I know not, I said,

'When I had hurts, my nurse always kissed them better'.

Without hesitating, he took my palm to his lips.

I cannot explain the sensations that filled my body. My

Chapter 8. Love and Prophesy

heart was racing with my breath. It was confusing but overpowering; something I could not control or had any wish to do so. The drawbridge was down, our eyes would have melted a portcullis. Gently, he drew me to him.

He led me to another room, the perfumery. Within, there was an old couch with some cushions. I had shed my veil in the herbarium because of the heat. Now Abraham loosened the laces on my gown. His long fingers caressed my breasts. Never have I felt such sensations as my nipples hardened under his touch. Eventually the gown slipped to the floor followed by my shift. Abraham's *jilaabiyah* joined my garments. He laid me down, saying he wanted to kiss me in five places. By now I would have died for him. Raw instinct as old as humanity took over as our bodies became one. A spasm of such intensity pulsated through my body. I moaned in pleasure; my back arched. My life reached another dimension.

Time seemed to stand still as we kissed and explored each other's bodies. He said my skin was as smooth as alabaster, his was silky to my touch, covering hard muscles on his arms, legs and torso. He is as beautiful as a Greek god. Both of us, we discovered, had been attracted from the first, struggling to keep our feelings in check.

In the distance a bell tolled. I was jolted back to reality. We bathed in cool well water. How delicious it would have been to keep that yeasty odour about me, but I could not return to the palace smelling of sex. We parted with tender kisses, he to a back entrance of the palace walls, I to the library where I bumped into Angelique. She questioned my whereabouts. I told her we must have missed each other.

My mind was a gale of emotions as I tried to comprehend, to believe what had happened was not a dream. This was the first time I had ever seen a naked man or lain naked with one. It was the first time I had experienced unrestrained desire, sensual pleasure I had no wish to control. Unlike Louis, when I lie rigid and unresponsive waiting with disgust for his bungling efforts to end; when he grunts and groans and flees in the dark, I felt fulfilled. I had no idea the joining of a man and a woman could be so tender, an act of tactile beauty, a throbbing sensation of bliss.

I now write in Greek.

***

It was not easy finding moments or places to be alone with Abraham. During his tutoring, we kept to our chosen sides of the table as if nothing had taken place between us. He was beginning to teach me Aramaic and Hebrew. The Aramaic script is beautiful to look at but reading backwards was most odd. My grasp of the language was rather childlike. Both Hebrew and Aramaic have a throaty sound to them which I found difficult. Abraham said I had a definite Greek accent in my efforts.

I can now read my favourite Greek authors in their native tongue, quite a revelation in some respects because not all the translations I have read in Latin catch the nuances of the Greek language. Abraham is mightily knowledgeable. We can spend hours arguing the merits of Plato's *Republic*, followed by debates on Socrates and Aristotle. We have also laughed ourselves into stitches over such plays as *The Birds* or *The Frogs*. *The Lysistrata* initiated an interesting discussion! I had never read it until I found a copy in Raymond's library.

At last, I have found someone who does not regard my education as unwomanly or considers my intelligence a gift from Satan because of my sex. He loves my mind as much as my body.

Today we found a few precious moments together in the perfumery while everyone was resting during the midday heat. I am a willing student of sensual delights as I learned about my body and Abraham's. Dear God, I had no idea how naïve I was. I am eager for his lips, his touch, his tender caresses, my body's readiness for his penetration. I cannot get enough. Oh, how we love each other. Never have I been so blissfully happy.

I asked Abraham if I could meet his sister. Reality is

Chapter 8. Love and Prophesy

niggling at the back of my mind and on my desk. Abraham told me she has the skills of a seer. I am curious to discover what my future holds. In the meantime, I am trying to find courage to open three missives in front of me. The letters arrived at great haste this morning by a sweat-drenched courier. They bear the seals of Toulouse, the Aquitaine and Champagne; therefore, I know the authors. I think I would prefer Raymond to be present in case they carry bad news. There is nothing from Louis.

***

To recall this day has been most difficult. I did not want to write it down nor want to remember. But in the end, I thought it might calm the swirling thoughts in my head.

Raymond was busy with affairs of state for most of the morning. A page arrived with a note from him permitting me to travel to visit Judith, accompanied by Aunt Constance. So, I pushed the missives to one side to prepare to leave the palace. I dispensed with my maids, no matter how much Angelique grumbled. There was not enough room in the covered *araba* for them, even if I wanted their attendance. We had the Praetorian Guards, though. I would have preferred to have gone alone, to have a few glorious moments with Abraham, but I had to be chaperoned and guarded. Even so, I was excited to exit the palace to experience the township below its base.

The enclosed carriage was hot and stuffy, cutting out any view of the town. I was eager to see the streets and people, but Constance stopped me from peeking. She warned me this was Antioch, not Paris. Women of our rank must not be seen. So, I had to make do with the tantalising cries of street vendors, the bray of donkeys, laughter, and the odd angry shout. I could pick up some words in Aramaic. We must have passed someone selling spices. Not only did the words for cloves and cinnamon filter through our curtains but their heady aromas, as well as others like bread baking.

Abraham greeted us as we alighted within the walls of his house. He told us it was a typical design, built around courtyards with high outer walls. It has stairs leading up to the flat roof, where on hot evenings they sit or sometimes sleep to keep cool. We were shown into a beautiful courtyard with gardens and fountains. He took us along a colonnade through shuttered rooms, another courtyard, more like an atrium and into a chamber with beautiful, geometric patterned floor tiles in blue and white. It was furnished with low couches scattered with brightly coloured cushions. Although not large, it was cool and comfortable.

Seated before us was a lovely woman dressed in flowing robes.

'Lady Eleanor and Lady Constance, allow me to introduce you to my sister, Judith.'

Judith stood with ease bowing her head in greeting. She said it was the first time she had been honoured to welcome a queen and a princess to her humble home. I said in Greek we were delighted to accept her hospitality and honoured to meet her too.

She called for a servant to serve us drinks and sweetmeats. The drink was most refreshing. When I asked what it was, Judith explained to me it was made from a bright red fruit called a pomegranate. She had the servant fetch one. Abraham cut it open to display a multitude of glistening red seeds like sparkling rubies. Judith said the juice, which is slightly tart, was mixed with ginger and lime juice and sweetened with a little honey – delicious as well as thirst quenching. The little syrupy pastries melted in the mouth. They had the subtle fragrances of rose or orange blossom water.

If I had not been told, I would not have known Judith was blind. She was most adept in all her actions. After the servant had removed the dishes, Judith asked whether we minded if she could 'see' what we looked like. I was puzzled till Abraham explained: Judith's fingertips were so sensitive she could discern a person's features by running her fingers across a face.

Chapter 8. Love and Prophesy

'— except for the colour of your eyes and hair, Milady, but I already know which of you is which by your voices.'

Removing her veil, Constance offered to go first. I was fascinated as Judith knelt before my aunt, who was perched on a low ottoman. Judith's fingers fluttered across her pretty face and explored her hair which was plaited and pinned round her head to keep her neck cool. She described Constance with amazing accuracy as she traced her oval face, her lips, her retroussé nose, eyebrows and ears, which made Constance giggle.

When it was my turn, my eyes caught Abraham's. Judith seemed to detect the slight movement, pausing with an almost miniscule change of pressure on my skin. Where her delicate touch over Constance's face was swift and deft, with me she seemed to be searching. My hair was loose, which I had done deliberately for Abraham's benefit as he adores my tresses. Judith gave a slight sigh with a hint of sadness. I felt it. Abraham looked away as if he did not want to acknowledge something he could read in his sister's expression. I tried to lighten the situation by asking if she could improve the shape of my nose. She replied my nose was important to my status in life, giving my face a regal bearing. My levity seemed inappropriate. Constance sensed the air was tense for some reason and asked if she could visit the herb garden Abraham's grandfather had told her so much about after she had heard Judith's description of my features. Judith described my face as being classical, with high cheekbones, a straight nose, large eyes with long lashes, pouty lips (I did not appreciate that!), a firm chin, delicate ears and a thick mane of hair.

'How right and clever you are, Judith. Now, the herb garden.'

I remarked we would be leaving Judith alone, therefore I should stay. Abraham sent for his steward and a maid to escort my laughing aunt to the garden.

My eyes found Abraham's. Silence fell. Judith suddenly broke it.

'Your life is turbulent, Lady Eleanor.'

Had Abraham discussed my circumstances with his sister? As if reading my mind, she said she detected tension and sadness in my face as well as some great happiness. I replied the crusade had put an enormous onus on my life. The suffering I had witnessed was horrifying, incomprehensible, but I had managed to counter the pain with the education I was receiving from her brother, which I found stimulating as well as a great joy. However, I knew not what the future held. Again, a deep silence fell between us.

From out of nowhere, Judith, Cassandra-like, pronounced in Greek that one day I would *'marry the love of my life, I would bear him many sons, but my life would be tumultuous.'* How could this be? Did she mean Abraham? For a second, my heart skipped. My eyes sought Abraham's, but he was looking bereft. Tears slid down his cheeks into his beard.

'Who do you mean?'

Judith intoned, 'All will be clear in the future'.

I reached my hand out to Abraham.

'Ibby, take care,' Judith warned as she stood. As if one with sight, she moved to her brother. I stood to one side, bewildered. He pushed past his sister.

'Do you mind if I give Her Ladyship a guided tour?'

'Is it already too late, Ibby?'

What was Judith implying? Too late for what?

Abraham grabbed my hand, pulling me towards an archway at the back of the room.

'I will not be long.'

We hurried down a dim passage and into a small bed chamber. There was little time. We did not undress. It was too swift to be truly pleasurable, but it fulfilled a desperate need for each other. As I adjusted my gown, I voiced my suspicion.

'Judith knows, does she not?'

Abraham sighed. He explained Judith may lack sight, but she has an ability to detect nuances between people along with an almost supernatural sense of the future. As I kissed

Chapter 8. Love and Prophesy

him, I told him he was the love of my life. His voice was thick. No, it was not him to whom she was referring. A hand of ice clutched my heart.

'Please, I want to go home.'

We returned to Judith who was sitting back in her chair. Her nostrils flared, her expression said everything. The air around her vibrated with what Abraham and I had done. She shook her head.

'Oh, my poor darling Ibby.'

In a saddened tone and change of language, Judith continued. My Aramaic was still too new and green to understand most of what she said. But Abraham's jagged breath translated our impossible love. The reality I had been trying to keep out of my mind was now staring at me like a giant ugly ogre. Regardless if ours was the greatest love in all the world, we could never remain together.

***

The missives from Guile, Henry, Hugh and Alphonso were still unopened in front of me. No matter how hard I have tried to push the reality of my love affair with Abraham into the deepest recesses of my mind, I must accept there has to be a finality to my joy. Whatever fantasy world I have been inhabiting, the truth is I am still Louis' wife. I remain the reluctant Queen of France.

After what transpired at his home, I wondered if Abraham would want to continue tutoring me? Will he still desire me? I ripped open the seals. Whatever was contained in the letters could never be as bad as my broken dreams, so I did not bother Raymond to hold my hand, irrespective of how I dreaded the contents.

What a disaster!

Louis has escaped with his life but much of his force was routed in the predicted ambush. Alphonso, Guile, Henry and the other battalions who came to their aid have lost men. Guy was wounded and died days later of infection; how will I be able to face his wife and children? What a debacle! They did reach Jerusalem from where these missives have been couriered, but at what price? Louis at least was able to place the Oriflamme of France on the altar of the Church of the Holy Sepulchre. I will have to join him in Jerusalem after all.

I swallowed my pride and sent a letter to Abraham. I must see him. I need him.

***

He came, bearing a book of sensual poems written in Aramaic. We must face the reality of what will befall us soon. Past Louis' empty chamber – I cannot defile his bed – there was a distant room off a courtyard I had seen churls entering from time to time. It looked like it was not in use. I found there were odds and ends stored in there, some piles of carpets and a few cushions woven of the same material. Abraham said they are used by cameleers.

It was late. Most of the palace were preparing for, or in bed. I dismissed my maids. I said I had a headache and did not wish to be disturbed. Within deep shadows, I made my way to this little nook wearing nothing, but a shift covered by a cape. Our love making reached a frantic level.

Raymond and Constance were worried about my demeanour. I have little appetite. In bed at night, I cry myself to sleep. It often eludes me altogether. Puffy eyes and listlessness are constant companions.

The crush of the crusader armies did not help my lack of spirits, guilt ravished as I am for the loss of life. My fool of a husband who ignored all advice, who would not heed the warnings of ambush, enrages me to screaming point. Most of the failure was of his own doing: his reckless stupidity cost lives, *Deus Vult* indeed! All those brave men who went to his aid, along with those who have been maimed; all sacrificed for his zealotry and stubborn pride.

As we sat overlooking the mountains beyond the palace, a rare hour to talk alone, poor Abraham had to put up with me ranting about everything from the crusaders' fate, to me being Louis' wife. With hope in my heart and a tremor in my voice, I told him how I intended to petition the Pope. All I did was upset him. Taking my hands, he told me even if I were successful, which he sincerely hoped I would be, no one in my society was going to let me marry the Jewish bastard son of a Saracen prince.

It all came out, his unique heritage. His mother, also a Judith, as a young girl often accompanied his grandfather Isaac who was physician to his father's family. Jewish physicians were favoured because of their training and skill. His parents fell in love, like us, from the moment they met. His mother was never surpassed by any of his father's wives or concubines; the only love he had was for his Judith. Her death after Abraham's birth devastated him. He never fully recovered, becoming a recluse. For most of their lives, Abraham and Judith were brought up in their father's court and harem before moving to Antioch. They were well cared for, loved and educated. Abraham's mother was a clever woman, taught by her father, like I was by mine. How similar our backgrounds are, with me never knowing my mother either. Abraham sees his father from time to time and loves him. He tells me he is a good man.

His sister Judith became blind as a little girl after a sickness thought to be measles. Nothing their grandfather could do could save her sight. I was curious as to why Judith called him Ibby. Simple, really – to his father, he is Ibrahim.

This information did not make me any happier; I am still shackled to Louis and I have no choice but to join him in Jerusalem.

***

I asked to visit Judith again. This time I went alone. Angelique, as usual, was not happy, but I said I would be well guarded.

Judith and I sat together as before, sipping the pomegranate tea. But I could only nibble at the delicate sweetmeats. At the back of my mind niggled Judith's prophesy. There was no point in pretending there was nothing between Abraham and me. I told her I could not imagine loving anyone as I loved her brother. I begged her to tell me more. Did this mean I was going to escape this hell of a marriage? If it could not be Abraham, who was it? She said she did not know, but she predicted I would follow a long winding road. It would have some dead ends and deep chasms. There would be storms to navigate. Sometimes, I would feel I was lost. She told me I had the will, the inner strength and, above all, the intelligence to overcome adversity, regardless of the despair I felt now and will feel again in the future. She finished her prophesy by saying I was destined to be a great queen. I answered, that being a queen was anything but great. I was queen only because of my dower. Abraham joined us. He was being discreet so Judith and I could talk together.

A heavy silence filled the room. Judith was tired, no doubt she felt my resentment. I was close to voicing my welling anger but, with respect for Abraham, I held my tongue. I was about to take my leave when Judith surprised me by telling 'Ibby' to take me to his chamber, to make the most of the afternoon. I blushed, unable to look Abraham in the eye. He needed no more encouragement, but she called after us.

'I hope, Ibrahim, you are being cautious,' is what I think she said in Aramaic.

I realised she was referring to preventions for conception. My face was scarlet. Early in our affair, Abraham had introduced me to these beeswax balls, as small as beads, mixed with a special, ground herb. He told me it was used in the harem where he was brought up as a child, when some of the women did not want to conceive. He explained it was an old remedy from a rare plant called silphion used extensively in the ancient world of the Greeks, Etruscans and Romans for the same purpose. It was considered more effective than a douche of vinegar or lemon juice.

Abraham gently closed the bed chamber door. Once enclosed in his arms, I lost all embarrassment. This time, we slowed our desire, drawing our passion out to a delicacy of

Chapter 8. Love and Prophesy

touch, taste and precious fulfilment. In the warmth of the air and our loving, he licked the perspiration between my breasts, indulging in the silkiness between my legs as his hard-thrusting manhood was welcomed within. I wanted time to stand still.

Later as we bathed and dressed, I again told him I did not know how I was going to live without him.

'Nor I without you.'

'You have a loving sister who will do everything in her power to help you through your pain. Who is going to hold me to their bosom?'

Abraham held me as if in a vice. Unable to speak, my body shook.

***

With a heavy sigh I lay back in the cushioned comfort of the *araba* and pushed Judith's prophesies from my mind. I needed to have a plan of how best to approach Louis in Jerusalem. Louis and I are to be guests of the Pope in Rome during our return to Paris and I must get clear in my mind how to broach the subject of having my marriage annulled. I was mulling this over when angry voices and shrieks of pain invaded my cocoon of curtains. My guards cursed, the horses shied at something, side-stepping to a halt. Regardless of protocol, I yanked the curtains aside. Several burly men were dragging a bloodied bundle along the ground. The bundle was screaming as they flayed it with whips. The high-pitched wails indicated a female or child. I have no idea what came over me except outrage.

Before my guards and coachman could move on, I was out of the *araba*, stiletto in hand. The men with the whips stopped in their tracks. My dress, mode of transport and guards alerted them they were being confronted by no ordinary woman. What they did not expect was a torrent of Greek in a voice that rang with authority. I demanded what in God's Name they thought they were doing. They stepped away from the bundle. I ordered one of my guards to carry it to the *araba*. By now, the other five were by my side, broadswords drawn. The men with the whips raised their hands, swearing with rage. I backed towards my transport, stiletto in hand, reboarding as the horses plunged forward followed by my guards.

I drew the curtains. We moved at speed, leaving the assailants cursing behind. As gently as I could, I mopped the bloodied face of the bundle of rags with my veil. It was indeed a girl. The poor thing was so beaten her swollen face was almost unrecognisable as human. All I could do was cradle her in my arms as she whimpered.

When we arrived within the palace walls, I had the girl taken to my quarters. I ordered pages to fetch me warm water. I sent for Constance. When she arrived, she panicked at the sight of my blood-stained gown, fearing I had been attacked. It took me a few minutes to explain what had taken place. The beetles, too, lent a hand. We sponged the poor girl's features. She could not speak. Her lips were split and swollen, her eyes almost shut and blackened, she was covered in bruises, her hair caked in blood. After we had administered to her, we awaited Abraham's grandfather, Isaac, who had been summoned. By now, she realised she was safe, and we were not going to hurt her.

After Isaac examined her, he thought she may have broken ribs. He said the bruises and abrasions would heal in time with tender care, as she was young. He prescribed various balms and potions to ease the pain and to aid sleep. As she was in my bed, I chose to spend the night on a trundle at the foot.

Instead of dwelling on parting from Abraham, and all my other woes, I concentrated on the battered bundle. In a funny way, this was the best thing that could have happened to me.

***

Today our guest was able to speak. I had been trying to communicate with her from the day we brought her to the palace. I attempted my rudimentary Aramaic, as well

Chapter 8. Love and Prophesy

as Hebrew and Latin. In the end, I discovered there was a glimmer of recognition for Greek, so I have been addressing her in that language, impatient for a response.

We managed to get her to eat a little chicken broth. She is healing, the bruises on her face and blackened eyes are changing from purple to greenish yellow. But she still looks beaten. We had to cut her hair to remove the caked blood from the nasty gash in her scalp. However, today she whispered, 'Thank you.'

I was so excited I had to rush out to tell Constance and Raymond.

Now I can leave her bedside for short periods. Colette and Jeanne, two of the more accommodating beetles, sat with her while I was away. Some of Constance's maids also took turns to stay by her bedside. I hoped soon she would be able to tell us her name.

I had been neglecting Abraham because of my nursing, though he was not complaining; he is the most understanding of men. We had not lain together since my visit to his house. Tonight, I think I can sneak to our little storeroom of carpets.

Deep in the seclusion of the orchard, we held hands, looking into each other's eyes. He was pleased I was being kept busy; my mind occupied. As we kissed, I told him I was longing for tonight.

I wished I knew her name, but so far, she remained anonymous. Before I slipped away to Abraham, I told her I would not be long, that I had responsibilities to attend to, and she was to ring the little bell by her bedside should she need anything. As I stroked her forehead and kissed her, much like Renée would have done to me, she whispered her name was 'Amaris.' I was delighted. I told her it was a pretty name. I asked if she wanted to tell me more, but she appeared to have fallen asleep, exhausted. It was hard leaving her, but I needed Abraham.

I slipped through the shadows of the darkened corridors. I was late for our secret tryst because of the extra time spent with Amaris.

I tapped on the door, but he did not let me in. My heart thudded fearful he had not come. I tapped a little harder, not wanting to make too much noise, but still the door remained shut. As silent as a mouse, I tried the handle, and it opened. To my surprise, Abraham was there, perched on a cameleer cushion, dressed, with his head on his knees. A flask of wine was by his side, with two goblets, one half full of wine. Something was amiss.

'You are late.'

I explained Amaris had at last told me her name; I could not leave as planned. I sat beside Abraham, taking those beautiful sensual fingers to my lips. In the candlelight, his dark eyes were as fathomless as a well. He felt bereft; he said he feared I was not going to come. Abraham stood. His body was shaking. Was it anger? I was not that late. I tried to make light of it.

'I am here now. Please, Ibby, what is it?'

'Do not call me that!'

His words hung in the air like the *Sword of Damocles*.

My instinct was to remind him who he was addressing. Rank, status and love battled within me. My mind was roaring.

If I uttered a word, I knew I would regret it, so I fought to remain silent as he turned to face me. Before him stood the Queen of France, ingloriously robed but wearing a metaphorical crown, a barrier between us.

Abraham's voice registered our turmoil.

'One minute is an eternity, one minute gone, one less to share before we must part forever.'

We faced each other like two snarling dogs instead of lovers. With eyes blazing, he took two strides, flinging off his *jilaabiyah*. The room was filled with the renting scream of silk. I buckled under his weight.

***

I left my quarters early this morning. Amaris, I left in the care of two of Constance's maids. I was trying to make sense

Chapter 8. Love and Prophesy

of what took place between Abraham and me. He did not leave unscathed, bearing bites and scratches. Our love fight was as exciting as it was brutal. I cannot call it rape because I was an eager participant. We ended up weeping in a tangle of arms and legs. Words were of no use. Maybe in the light of day, if he ever wanted to see me again, we can explain ourselves.

I knew we were both suffering in different ways. I must go to Jerusalem, which I dread. Some remnants of my Aquitaine army are limping back towards Antioch on drooping horses, no doubt. Others remain in the Holy City to await my arrival. Alphonso, who, I am told, fought like ten knights, and who had little respect for Louis in the past, now has none. Young Henry is in shock from what I glean from his sad epistles. Guy's death haunts me.

***

I have learnt much since I have been in Antioch. I have found the community lives in harmony together, even though a crusade is being fought around them. Raymond has many respected acquaintances among both the Jewish and Musselman inhabitants. They get along. It was hard for me to fathom, considering outside we are at war in the name of Christ and not doing well.

Raymond and I have discussed, ruminated, questioned and prayed to God, as to why the army of Christ has been forsaken. The crusade is a disaster. We have been outmanoeuvred and outwitted, defeated by a superior foe. Raymond no longer mentioned Aleppo or Edessa though I know he is preparing his forces for the assaults which my darling uncle must face without the additional troops he was promised. I am enraged and disappointed with the way Louis has let him down.

A page knocked. He told me Master Abraham begged my attention. In haste I flung down my quill and scrabbled together sheets of parchment. I had forgotten my Aramaic lesson. God's teeth, I want not another argument!

Abraham had a bruise forming on his cheek. Did I hit him? I felt like a naughty child. I muttered an apology and received a curt nod of acceptance as I sat opposite. I stared at an ink blot on my work with my head in my hands. I apologised again. Abraham pushed a page of Aramaic in front of me to read. It was elegantly written in the beautiful, flowing script. It was on vellum. With my finger, I traced the words from right to left, struggling a little with the translation.

> ELEANOR
> *All the stars in the heavens cannot number the ways I love you.*
> *Look to the heavens when you leave me; there, you will see my infinite love.*
> *Honey does not taste as sweet as your lips,*
> *Silk a poor cousin to your alabaster skin.*
> *Your rounded breasts that cushioned my head and inflamed my fingertips*
> *Will never be mine again.*
> *Your sensual welcome to my animal lust*
> *Will be another's.*
> *But every night in the starry orb of heaven, my love will shine on you*
> *my Angel,*
> *Where 're you may be.*

I needed fresh air. The beetles were gossiping and stitching. Angelique fortunately had her back to me, unable to read my face. I asked Abraham to accompany me.

I strode ahead towards some unguarded ramparts and raced up the stone steps. Abraham caught up with me. He grabbed me by the waist as I leant out into the breeze. I looked at him with soulful eyes, shaking my head. Backing me into a secluded corner, he cradled me in his arms. Words were impossible for both of us. His poem overwhelms me with its love. Dear God, why must this be, this unbearable cruelty. Never have I felt so powerless. How can I live without him? I raved,

'Any day now, I will have to leave for Jerusalem after I have met with what is left of my army. The whole crusade has been a rout. What fools we are. Why did we think we were

Chapter 8. Love and Prophesy

doing God's will? If we were heeding the word of God, why were we defeated? Louis believed he was invincible because he carried the Oriflamme of France blessed by bishops and the Pope – all those holy blessings for nothing! I used every word of God-fearing rhetoric to cajole, to exhort, to inflame the passions of my subjects to leave the safety of their homes to be slaughtered. I must now face the wives and children of the dead. I can barely look at my reflection. This is no Holy Land. Jesus, Mary and Joseph, this is the gate of hell!'

I was pounding my chest. Abraham grabbed my wrists. I wrenched my arms, trying to break from his grip. He sat me down on a low stone plinth and knelt in front of me.

'Do not blame yourself for doing what you thought was divinely right as a Christian. What you did not know, your men are warring against people who are of this land, have been for thousands of years. My mother's ancestors, the tribes of Israel, have wandered as nomads over every rock, through every wadi and oasis since before Moses. Those who follow Mohammed, the Saracens, also. This is their land. They do not see it as you do, they see it as home, like you, the Aquitaine.'

'This is the land of Christ, too, our Saviour.'

'Eleanor, your Saviour was a Jew.'

Twang! An arrow between the eyes. I had no more words or argument. I felt I knew too much. The horror of the realisation, *we* were the infidel, this was something I would have to erase from my consciousness. This was heresy.

Below the fortifications, the turbulent water swished its gurgling timeless presence. I looked again at the piece of vellum in my hand, crumpled from my grip. Like a scraped knee, I wanted to kiss it better, to smooth it out again. I reread the beautiful words. At least this folly has brought me unexpected love. I stood. I allowed myself to be kissed as a butterfly alights on a petal. Words could not convey the depth of my feelings for this beautiful, gentle, intelligent man. As for his sister's prophesy, it will have to be a most remarkable love to ever surpass what I carried in my heart at that moment.

***

Time in Antioch was coming to an end. I must go. To farewell my nearest family, Uncle Raymond and Aunt Constance will be hard. My heart was heavy. But worse, there was Abraham.

I was destined to leave libraries as well. Uncle Raymond's books housed a haven of solace. Each library has its own odour; this one, a dry mustiness. Here, as on Île de France or in Poitiers, I find refuge to express myself, to unburden my heart and mind. But not only have I practised writing in Greek or Aramaic, I have come to question notions beyond reason, to question what I have held sacred. Maybe the scales have fallen from my eyes? I know not. I am fearful about this terrible realisation; the realisation others are as fervent about their beliefs as I am. Who is right and who is wrong – or is there no right or wrong? Are we all blundering fools? We have fought a war because we believed our God of Christendom is supreme, that His Blessed Son is our Saviour. Yet I have discovered it is the same God worshipped by my Jewish lover, his Jewish grandfather, and his Saracen father. I must keep my bizarre thoughts to myself. But the bejewelled red cross pinned to my gown, which I have worn with pride, is now a burden.

***

When they returned – Alphonso, young Henry and Geoffrey, and their men – I was horrified by how their features had altered. Guile remained with some of my knights in Jerusalem to await my arrival. Those before me looked like they had been whipped. When young Henry uttered it was so joyous to see beauty before him, I knew it was not me to whom he was referring, it was his surroundings of peace and tranquillity. The poor boy had aged past the years of his father, his eyes hollow, lines around his mouth, his face gaunt. Alphonso's visage looked like it had been hacked out

Chapter 8. Love and Prophesy

of rock.

Alphonso was first to dismount. He strode from his horse with a limping gait. As usual he did not waste words nor wait for me to invite him to speak. In blunt tones he told me my men fought with valour.

'They did not shame you, Eleanor of Aquitaine.'

With a nod, he left for his encampment. I was touched by his forthrightness.

Geoffrey, Robert, Will, Hugh, Emile, Pierre, so many of my knights of the Aquitaine came forward, surrounding me in homage, bending one knee, heads bowed. Words deserted me as I struggled with the lump in my throat. The pride in my heart almost undid my resolve not to cry. I asked them to stand. Each one in turn I addressed. Like a mother, I embraced them one by one. I told these brave survivors I was honoured to know them.

I asked Geoffrey de Rançon if anyone had any special requirements; injured soldiers who may need attention, food, anything at all, including their horses. He said Raymond had pre-empted my concerns. Necessities had been taken care of and should there be anything else he would let me know. As they were tired and travel worn, I dismissed them so they could bathe and break bread.

***

Today my mind is running in circles. I must see Judith again; her prophesy haunts me. If it is true, logic tells me I will be free of Louis. I know I cannot remain with Abraham, though God in heaven, I wish I could. But I keep asking myself, how can I love another? Out in the world somewhere is a man I will love – 'the love of my life' – but will he love me? I needed to know. Judith has said nothing about that. My suspicious nature made me wary.

I asked Abraham, while he was correcting my Aramaic exercise, if I could speak to Judith again. He surprised me by telling me Judith also wished to see me. A prickling between my shoulder blades lead me to think this was mighty odd.

Are we, Judith and I, connecting in some uncanny way or am I letting my imagination take hold of logic?

I must go unchaperoned: I want this visit discreet. Abraham uses a secret way out of the palace, but we would have to find a time when I would not be missed. There were not many days left for me as time galloped towards my departure. Abraham suggested we go in two days, either after dark or noon when everyone rests during the heat of the day. I chose noon. Planning my strategy involved Amaris, who is now up and about. Apart from her growing loyalty, not just because of my involvement in her rescue, we have a genuine rapport. At last, I have someone who is on my side.

The day I was to visit Judith was quite warm. I told Amaris I did not want to be disturbed while I rested. She obeyed my wishes, saying she would insist the beetles keep to their quarters. I blessed the heat.

Time was of the essence. I only had about three hours to get out and back. Abraham and I arranged to meet in the herbarium. He gave me a veil, and a voluminous robe as worn by the local women. It was wonderfully comfortable, unlike the restrictive, fitted gowns I wear. We stowed mine in the perfumery.

Nearby is a stepwell which has always intrigued me. About halfway down its cool interior is a little used passage leading to the left; dark and dank. Water dripped somewhere. Abraham had a flaming torch to lead the way. Taking my hand, he led me under the walls of the palace citadel till we emerged near a *suq*. I recognised the sounds and the spicy aromas from riding by in the *araba*. They lingered in a tantalising way. We pressed on. Outside the confines of the *suq*, Abraham helped me into a cart drawn by two mules. It was only a short bumpy ride to his house, which I saw from the outside for the first time, surrounded by tall sandstone walls with its flat roof. Lofty palms rose above and creepers with vivid flowers tumbled down, a colourful cascade. We entered by rear gates near the stables where my Praetorian Guards had played backgammon with the household ostlers.

Chapter 8. Love and Prophesy

Judith was pleased to 'see' me. I did not have the privilege on this final visit to waste time on small talk. I hoped I was not too abrupt when I asked if I were to wed the 'love of my life' as she predicted, would he return my love? To my annoyance, instead of answering directly, she said she had a gift for me. I replied the only gift I wanted was her answer. She said it was connected and reached to the bronze table next to her chair, handing me an ornate, square wooden chest. With an impatient sigh, I opened it. Inside was a girdle, the likes of which I had never seen. Glittering gold thread dazzled in a cradle of purple silk smelling of sandalwood.

'Take it out.'

It was heavy, magnificently woven, encrusted at each end with a jewelled fringe. Rubies were stitched at intervals down its length. Oddly, it was knotted.

Judith, with uncanny sense, instructed me.

'To wear it, you loosen it and step into it, or it goes over your head. It must not be untied except by your husband.'

I recognised what it was – the *'Knot of Hercules'* – worn in Greek mythology by a bride on her wedding day, with her husband ceremoniously untying the knot and consummating the marriage.

'Will he love me?'

'Yes. But it will be a tumultuous love. It will not be easy or straightforward.'

'Then why in God's name, would I want to enter into such an arrangement?'

'Because he will be the love of your life.'

I looked at the glittering girdle, so heavy in my hands. I tried to imagine it around my waist, any waist. My head was abuzz as I attempted to make sense of the unknown. This was no knot of love, I thought. All I could envisage was a tangled, mangled future. I wished I had never come. This thing of beauty was an intractable *'Gordian Knot.'* I told Judith I could not accept her gift. Abraham intervened.

'You must – it is ordained.'

I have never contemplated he should defer to my rank. But now? I stood, silencing him with an imperious gesture.

'It was ordained I marry Louis of France, a miserable disaster. Nothing decreed for my future could be worse. What you prophesise, Judith, gives me little confidence. I cannot foresee happiness, or love.'

An unknown voice from behind me, deep and resonant, made me turn. In flowing robes stood a turbaned figure who stepped out of the dimness of the archway. Before me was another beautiful man, tall, with an elegance of bearing. He approached and addressed me in Greek.

'I am Hamid Abdullah, Your Highness. Do not insult my children by refusing their gift.'

The hairs prickled on my neck. I was on edge. No one, not even Amaris, knew where I had gone. There was no doubting who stood before me – the Saracen prince, Judith's and Abraham's father.

I said I was honoured to meet him, that I did not wish to insult Judith or Abraham, but as the girdle seemed to have a deep significance, I felt I did not deserve it. Nor could I foresee or understand its connection to my future life back in France or the Aquitaine.

Abraham interrupted. He informed me the girdle had been their mother's. Hamid Abdullah, with deep sadness in his voice, said Ibrahim's and Judith's mother had been the love of his life. They had never married, so the knot has remained tied. Judith begged me to take it because she would never marry. But Abraham perhaps? As if reading my mind, he said he would not either. He intended to follow in his grandfather Isaac's footsteps to become a physician and apothecary. It was enough to know the love of his life would wear the girdle, even if the *'Knot of Hercules'* was to be undone by another.

Control was deserting me. I clenched my fists.

'Do you think I could ever wear this girdle, to have another man untie the *'Knot of Hercules,'* knowing from whence it came? Have you no respect for me or my love for you, Abraham?'

Cassandra-like Judith intoned, 'It is because of that love you must accept it'.

'It was your mother's! How can you give it away?'

Hamid Abdullah took the girdle from my hands: with tenderness he placed it back in the folds of silk. He indicated I should sit. A click of his fingers brought a servant with pomegranate tea along and those delicious pastries dripping with honey. He placed the chest back on the low table of beaten bronze. My head was spinning. As charming as this man was, he was my enemy. Should my whereabouts be discovered, I would be in serious trouble. I did not want to appear hasty as I sipped the tea, but I had to leave. Amaris could only protect my chamber for so long.

I stood.

'I apologise, but I must leave before I am missed from the palace. My visit will not be approved.'

Prince Hamid Abdullah said he understood. I repeated it was an honour to meet him. He placed the chest in my arms again, closing the lid.

'Enchanté, Your Highness.'

There was no way I was going to be able to refuse the gift. I thrust it into Abraham's arms. I muttered he must carry it. From my shaking hands, I yanked two rings from a finger and thumb, both too precious to be sold for food for my troops. I gave my mother's gold and amethyst wedding ring to Judith and the other, my father's signet ring, to Abraham.

'Prince Hamid Abdullah, I have nothing on me I can give you. However, I believe you like poetry. Do you read Latin?'

He nodded.

'Good. Abraham will return with a copy of *The Aeneid* for you.'

In one impetuous moment, I had given away my three most valued possessions. With a nod of his head, he said I would not regret taking the girdle because my fate was written in the stars. God in Heaven, I thought, another seer. I shook my head in disbelief.

***

Abraham and I returned in silence, a chasm a league wide between us. The palace was coming to life. I was not missed, praise heaven.

I went to the library to write and to try to make sense of what happened. In the musty quietness I opened the chest. The afternoon sun streamed in, making the gold dance and glitter in its nest of purple. My fingers felt bare, my heart heavy. *The Aeneid* stared at me like a basilisk. It is not my only copy; in Paris I have old King Louis' tome. But Papa's has always been at my bedside. On the long journey here, it has not left my side. Stupid, stupid Eleanor! Rings can be replaced by others of my parents, but not this dog-eared, much-loved poem from my childhood. I could hear Papa's voice: *'And you thought your impulsiveness had improved, Elea!'* In a blind rage I swept the items onto the floor.

How long I stood bawling, I know not. A tentative page squeaked open the door, only to be roared at to get out. I dug my nails into my palms. Ink soaked my gown from waist to hem, ruining my gown. Quills were everywhere. The contents of the upside-down chest lay askew in an array of purple and gold by a bookshelf. *The Aeneid* had split its ancient linen bindings, stained like my gown. I retrieved my journal, hugging it to my chest. I crumpled in the middle of the debris.

***

Amaris came to collect me for dinner with my aunt and uncle. Before the poor girl could open her mouth, I barked at her not to utter a word. She ignored me, and her even voice suggested a clean gown. I stormed after her, slamming the door, flinging the key at her to lock it. Over dinner I stewed in an uneasy world of my own. I ate little but drank too much wine. Raymond coughed and suggested an early night.

The tempest has abated. I have cleaned up. With a candle, I searched the bookshelves for a copy of *The Aeneid*. Mine,

Chapter 8. Love and Prophesy

back on the desk, resembled blue-tinted autumn leaves, the broken bindings detached from its old, tooled leather cover. At least I am prevented from giving it to Prince Hamid Abdullah. I was sure Raymond would have a copy that I could ask for or steal if necessary. I needed Brother Joachim; he would know exactly where to find one on the shelves. As penance, I promised myself I would stay till I found it.

I was down to the butt of the candle late into the night before my search was successful. In fact, there were two tomes, one a Greek translation, the other in Latin. I carried both to the desk. I was tired. From the candle stub, I lit another.

At least the chest with its *'Gordian knot'* did not break. I had stuffed its contents back and shut the lid. But I felt guilty the girdle could have been damaged because I did not place it back with any care. I was forced to look at it again. In the candlelight it glittered and twinkled, tempting me to look at it closely. The craftmanship was exquisite. The woven strands of gold are almost four fingers wide, and the long fringes are threaded with tiny seed pearls. Along its length, graduating in size, are rubies, the largest as big as a quail's egg. They too are edged with seed pearls. The rubies are placed geometrically in a curious eastern pattern. Only the intricate knot is devoid of gems.

I gently this time, replaced it in its beautiful chest which is inlaid in gold, lapis and silver as well as pink stones. The pattern depicts lotus flowers.

Bed – I needed sleep.

***

I tossed and turned like a twig in rapids before I fell into a heavy slumber. I was like a dullard when I awoke. My mouth felt like it had been stuffed with wool. Angelique asked me, to my surprise, if I was unwell. Uncle Raymond wanted a word. He must wait. I needed to bathe and clean my teeth. The action of rubbing the linen strips across and between them hurt my head.

Raymond was a little annoyed at my tardiness. He looked at my pasty face and hollow eyes without sympathy and grunted that the cause was self-inflicted. I could not argue. But he did not know I was up half the night searching for a copy of *The Aeneid*. I asked him if I could please have one of his copies of the epic because mine had fallen apart. He said to go ahead; he had little time for reading these days. I thanked him. He will never know how fervently! Raymond sat opposite me wearing an expression like a confessor. My conscience was doing circuits of my brain with my hangover. Had he discovered my affair? I held my breath.

'Elea, you are worrying Constance and me. You have become introspective. Is there anything giving you concern?'

I breathed out.

'Concern? God's teeth! This whole crusade has been damned from the start. What a fool I was to ever think we could destroy the Saracen armies. The Saracens are superior in every way. And I am married to the weakest fool in Christendom. I live in a nightmare!'

I spat like a cat, raged how I loathed Louis. To travel to Jerusalem was the last thing I wanted to do; I would prefer to stay here or go back to France where I could petition to have my marriage annulled. I filled my lungs and gave a heavy sigh, relieved I did not have to confess the other turmoils in my life – Abraham, Judith's prophesy and that damn girdle.

Constance appeared with a page bearing fresh and dried fruits. My stomach churned in circles. She poured a sweet-scented tisane. I was grateful. I nibbled a date. Raymond and Constance sat in silence. The Saracen victories were an open wound, facts all had been avoiding. Raymond declared with determination they would be defeated.

'This is God's land,' he said.

'Yes,' I thought *'but whose God: Yahweh, Allah, or the God of Christ?'*

I stared at him with blank eyes. They said they understood the regrets about my marriage but despite my frustrations, Louis appeared to love me very much.

Chapter 8. Love and Prophesy

'Whose side are you on?!'

Raymond told me to calm down. It was just an observation. Gently poking me in my ribs, he suggested I rest before Abraham came for my lesson.

'Maybe you will get rid of the hangover.'

I glared at Raymond and wondered if Abraham would appear. To be honest, after yesterday, I was not sure I wanted to see him.

***

Abraham did come. On my side of the table, with my inky fingers, I tried to write the Aramaic he had prepared for me to copy and translate. My hand shook. I must have looked like a hobgoblin, all puffy-eyed and ashen faced. Abraham kept to the task in hand but noticed the script was ill formed. He came around to my side of the table, put his hand over mine like Papa used to do, to guide my hand over my letters when he was teaching me to write. As if I was a child, Abraham gently pushed the quill in the right direction.

'You seem unwell. Would you prefer a lesson in apothecary? It will take you into the fresh air.'

I glanced at the beetles, deep in their embroidery. I told them I was going into the garden with Master Abraham. Did they wish to accompany me? Not really. Amaris, bless her, opted to remain too, saying she was trying to learn some French.

We walked in silence. The air was refreshing on my face, the sun warmed my body. Both of us were sensing strain, minstrels playing out of tune. We started to speak together. An awkward moment followed. Abraham asked if the presence of his father yesterday had upset me. He said they did not know he was coming. Hamid Abdullah was in Antioch on an unexpected visit and wanted to see them. I shook my sore head, wincing. It was full of spiked balls. I had to admit to over-imbibing in wine the night before. So, had he. He grinned, lopsided, as if his face hurt. The coolness between us dissolved in mutual queasiness. We walked to the ramparts that overlooked the moat. The water swirled below. We sat in the sun. Much I wanted to say to him sloshed around my brain with last night's dregs. In the end, I said I was more muddled than ever about Judith's predictions. I could be stuck with Louis. There was no guarantee the Pope would annul our marriage. Abraham picked up the innuendo behind my words,

'You do not have to wear it.'

'But it is what Judith wants.'

'She will never know; nor will I.'

'But I will.'

'The floor of the step well is hard. Can you manage, do you think?'

'Desire feels no pain.'

Afterwards, as we dressed, Abraham asked when I had to leave for Jerusalem. In three days, in three short days, my wild desire, my beautiful pleasure will end. My love...!

The next evenings in the carpet room were bitter-sweet. I gave him Raymond's copy of *The Aeneid* for his father. What it would have been to have lain together for one whole night, to be entwined in each other's arms till morning. Dear God, how I longed to bear him a child. What a beautiful child it would be.

Chapter 9. Raging Queen

The barque glided from St Simeon. I had soaked Abraham's *jilaabiyah* with my tears as he buried his head in my hair, wracked with sobs. The song he sang to me rings in my ears. If it were not a sin, I would throw myself overboard.

We docked at Acre which was a blur of activity to mount horses to ride to Jerusalem. Despite my melancholy, my arrival was uplifting as I gazed at the Holy City. Suitably dressed (an ornament again), my entourage and I crossed a narrow bridge they called the Pilgrim's Ladder through the Jaffa Gate into Jerusalem. There I was met by Louis, Queen Melisande, her son Baldwin and Foulques, Patriarch of Jerusalem. For reasons unbeknown to me, I felt my welcome was polite but cool. Even Louis seemed remote. Maybe he had retreated into his shell again, ignoring his wife. He was probably immersed in some religious fervour though I cared not one jot. I was only there for diplomacy, after all. The Knights Templar formed a guard of honour, the fanfares echoed around the age-old walls. Ancient stones surrounded buildings of antiquity, domes shaped the horizon, alleyways wandered in many directions. A dry odour mixed with animals, spices and humanity permeated the air. I could imagine Christ and His disciples bustling along these ancient streets. Ah, the history, if these stones could only relate their tales.

I caught sight of Guile and my men, part of the guard of honour. He looked weary; worn by the travail he has suffered. I hoped to speak with him as soon as possible.

***

After the official greetings were over, I rode with Louis to the palace where he was housed. Dusty and as sweaty as my horse, I wanted to bathe. Angelique and the beetles had gowns ready for me. They probably imagined I wanted to look special for my 'personal' reunion with my husband. I chose a wine-coloured brocade with little adornment except for the golden girdle about my waist. My veil was whisper-fine silk in the same colour accompanied by, of course, the head-aching crown. I probably looked like a raspberry. I insisted my hair was in a single plait. Except for the crown, I wore no jewellery, seeing the veil covered most of my neck. Heaven forbid I should look seductive!

The page at Louis' door announced my arrival. I told Odo to get out. Louis heaved himself out of his chair. He looked gaunt. His gown hung on him like a sack on a scarecrow. One of Louis' finest features was his golden curly hair; now it looked thin as if he were balding and his beard was scraggly. Both were streaked with grey. He must have aged ten haggard years. He limped towards me. I felt my gut tighten, knowing he was going to embrace me. I braced myself. His arms, once soft from his life as a monk, were now hard and bony, his hug was wooden. I was as stiff as a pikestaff.

'Would you like some wine?'

I told him to sit, that I would pour it before he fell over. I handed him a goblet. I stared at my reflexion in the wine. It matched my gown. Louis told me about his glorious entry into Jerusalem, how he felt uplifted and one with God when he placed the Oriflamme on the altar of the Holy Sepulchre. With sarcasm dripping from my lips, I asked if the thousands of dead crusaders rose around him to also give thanks. He looked at me like a wounded animal.

'Are you cruel by nature Eleanor, or do you cultivate it from your books?'

My eyes drilled through him; my lips curled with disdain. Once he would have run from my presence, but now he stared back. I am not proud of my heartlessness and I question if I have the fortitude to rise above what I have become – embittered.

Chapter 9. Raging Queen

Louis spilt his wine, his hands shaking so much with anger, or was it despair? I took the goblet from him. I walked to the door. I asked the page to fetch me a cloth. I returned to Louis. He was hunched over as if someone had punched the air out of him, head in his hands. I felt no sympathy, only resentment – resentment I became his wife, resentment even for my beloved father who condemned me to this fate. Yet I stayed. I mopped up the wine from the floor. The page had also brought a bowl of warm water – was he listening at the door to Louis' outburst, for I asked for none. I fetched a stool, sat before Louis and tried to remove the stain from his gown.

I have never had to do this. Others tend spills. I made it worse. Louis was weeping. I felt nothing, but I put my arms around him anyway. He clung to me like I clung to Renée when they told me Papa had died. Sobs shook his bony body, guilt-ridden perhaps. His gown slipped off one skinny shoulder, exposing the scars where his chainmail had bitten into his flesh. What was the point of this crusade? Nothing. We achieved naught. Would victory have soothed the scars or the futility of fighting men who call the same God, Allah? You, too, are a fool Eleanor. You are no better than this thwarted, warrior monk.

After sitting in silence by Louis my mind wandered back to Abraham. My head drooped with the overwhelming sadness caused by our separation. I sniffed back my tears, gulped my wine and rose to pour Louis and I another. I wiped my eyes on the end of my veil; sat again after I helped Louis take a sip. I placed his goblet on the table beside him where I noticed some sealed missives, one with the familiar mark of St Denis. Suger! The seal turned my stomach. I would love to know what the letter contained. But I will be the last to find out.

As there was no more conversation between Louis and me, I begged to take my leave. It was pointless sitting there with ice between us. Or that is what I thought till he suggested I come to his bed.

'NOW!'

I was aghast, shaken, revolted. He dragged me to my feet. The man who I thought would blow over in a gentle breeze had surprising strength, the power of Hercules. I struggled. The crown dislodged, bouncing on the floor, rolling away. I fought like a tigress only to inflame him further.

'Leave me alone!'

I screamed as he dragged me towards his bed. My gown tore. I slipped from his grip and pushed him away with all my might. My stiletto was in my hand. Louis reined to a halt; his lips stretched across his teeth as he stared at the finely-honed knife.

'My God, Eleanor, you would, would you not? You would run me through?'

My breath came in gasps. I backed to the door, reaching behind me for the handle. I was out before he could utter another word almost falling over two pages who were alight with expectation. I slapped one and shoved the other out of the way. Malevolence dripped from my lips. I hissed, if one word circulated from this passageway, I would know who to string up by his manhood. They got the message. I hitched my torn gown around me and stalked away with as much dignity as I could muster. Around the next corner I took to my heels and ran.

***

Back at my desk, I calmed down. I needed to change my gown but wanted to record what took place. What came over Louis? He has never been interested in my body, except when forced to procreate. And the violence, where did that come from? Could it be he has seen so much bloodshed, this monkish, timid man has become an animal?

Lord, where were my maids when I needed them? I had to summon a page. I walked to the door. God's teeth, I could not believe it – the door was locked! I rattled and shook it, but it would not budge. Pride would not permit me to call out. I picked up a stool to throw it with all my might but

Chapter 9. Raging Queen

smashing a stool against the door was not going to open it. I sat back at my desk to think. Who had locked me in? It could only be on Louis' orders, spurred on by Odo, I would think.

I explored my cage. The windows overlooked a courtyard, with my quarters on the first floor. I could see churls and other servants passing below going about their chores. Louis' chamber was across the far end of the wing; my maids on a third side of the rectangle. I tried the door again, but I am jailed. I must admit Louis worked quickly.

I peered through the keyhole. The key was in the lock. I considered using my stiletto to push it out, but all that would achieve would be a key on the floor on the opposite side of the door. Rage, frustration and swearing did not help. I had to wait. Surely one of my maids would appear soon. But what if Louis had ordered them to keep out? Amaris was my only hope. Angelique and her coven would keep me locked up forever.

To while away the time, I took out my destroyed copy of *The Aeneid*. I reassembled the pages in order. At least none were missing. The snapped and frayed linen bindings will have to be replaced. If I ever get out of here and back to France, I am sure Brother Joachim will be able to repair it. The old leather cover has seen better days, but knowing how clever he is, he will know how to mend it too or to tool another one.

Now what? I had nought, I thought to further record in my journal. I could write to Raymond, or Abraham, but I fear anything I pen will be scrutinised, so I dare not. I stared at the stiletto. Would it turn the lock if I pushed the key out? The blade is fine, it could break. I returned to the door. Exasperated rage grew into violence as I tried to shake the door off its hinges. I cursed Louis to hell and back, vindictive beast. Had I succumbed to his attempted rape I would now be as free as the spirit of Simian. I flung myself onto my bed. Exhausted I fell asleep.

***

The sound of someone unlocking the door woke me. Amaris slipped in, key in hand, locking the door again from this side. She put her arms around me and asked if I was all right. I wanted to know what had happened. Why was I locked in? She said it was the king's orders. I told her about Louis' attack and my escape.

'I cannot take him to my bed. It is too revolting to contemplate.'

She understood my predicament.

She had to be quick because the beetles would notice she was missing,

'I thought you could be interested in these.'

From the bodice of her gown she produced two missives. She had found a bewildered courier trying to find Angelique, so she offered to deliver them. For a small gold coin, he was only too happy to be on his way. The seals were Suger's. One was addressed to Angelique, the other to Louis.

I did not need any persuasion to break the seals. The one to Louis addressed my supposed adultery and incestuous relationship with Uncle Raymond. There may be other men, it went on to say. I had no concerns about Uncle Raymond. Louis knew the tale was false, but could have someone discovered my affair with Abraham as careful as we were? But what surprised me was Suger mentioning a 'rancorous letter' to him from Louis regarding a request from me to annul our marriage. No human could be as unhappy as I am, but I have never spoken to Louis about my desire to divorce him. Raymond knew, so did Constance and Abraham, but I have said naught to anyone else. I have been biding my time. Angelique was prowling the day I poured out my pain to Raymond. The purveyor of lies and innuendo, she could not possibly know, or could she?

Suger advised Louis to be patient, to wait till we returned to France to discuss the matter – interesting! He reminded Louis of my dowry, impressing upon him he still has no heir. There will have been other epistles between Louis and Suger. Has the old crow been hammering Louis about his

Chapter 9. Raging Queen

duty to France? Could that be the reason for his attack on me this morning? Am I locked up so Louis can exploit me, sully my bed? He can damn well try! I will sleep with my stiletto by my side.

I read Suger's letter to his sister. I should have guessed she would have elaborated on the lies she told Louis about my so-called incestuous affair with Raymond. Abbé Suger was suitably horrified, but 'not surprised at my perfidy.' He again said it would be dealt with in goodly time when the king and his treasonous, treacherous queen returned to France. He exhorts Angelique to keep her eyes and ears open. France will have the Aquitaine yet.

I crushed the parchment into a ball and flung it to the floor. So, they were planning to build a case against me, to have me accused of adulterous treason, punishable by death for one of my rank. I am not afraid, because Raymond and I are innocent – and Louis knows it – but lies can be piled upon lies. I will need a counter plan. Dear Amaris, I have thanked from the bottom of my heart for bringing these letters to me.

I have mulled over their contents. My spirits have been low, but now they are fired up! There was no way I was going to be tried and put to death for Angelique's untruths. Regardless of how abhorrent it will be, I am going to have to lay with Louis. A child may be my only salvation, my annulment for now a distant dream.

***

I carefully hid Suger's letters after smoothing out the creases. I was going to destroy them, but I thought two can play this game. I may not get Suger, but I can condemn Angelique for her lies.

Later in the day, Amaris was able to come back into my bed chamber with food and drink, Angelique accompanied her with the dreaded crown. I snatched it off her, flung it on the bed, and told her to get out, I had no need for her services. But I let her hear me ask Amaris to carry a sealed letter to the Lord King, conveying my contriteness to a disagreement between us. In the letter, I apologised to Louis for my part in this morning's misunderstanding. I wanted to see him as soon as possible. No doubt he will think a half-day of being locked up has brought me to my senses. I called for Colette to brush out my hair. As Amaris found one of my fine chemises, I whispered I would explain the reason for my madness and sacrifice in due course.

***

I could only hope and pray, Louis would arrive, when I heard the key in the door. I was playing my lute – the haunting tune of Abraham's beautiful love song. I had positioned myself so when I stood, the candlelight would shine in such a way through my chemise that it would look as if I were naked. I ran the risk of Louis running off like a startled hare, but I was hoping this morning's hunger would keep him eager, or more likely Suger's nagging. I managed to put on a fine act of contrition, begging his forgiveness, saying he was so rough, so frightening, so unlike his usual self I was terrified.

'I thought you were going to rape me.'

He said he was sorry he had caused such apprehension.

I managed to wrap myself around him. I hoped he would not wonder how, suddenly, I seemed more experienced. His wooden attempt to kiss me lacked true desire. His breath was unpleasant. As nauseated as I felt, I had to get it over and done with.

'Come,' I whispered, leading him to my bed.

I used a little of the scented oil from my bath to make penetration less painful and hoped for the best. As usual, it was over within minutes. Our bodies remained covered. I was hoping he would run off as usual, but this time he did not. Instead he fell asleep. I lay on my back beside him, repulsed. Silent tears ran down either side of my face into my hair with unfulfilled yearning. I longed for Abraham.

***

Chapter 9. Raging Queen

I am disgusted with myself for crawling back to Louis to save my sordid soul. In the short term, it released me from 'chamber arrest', but I cannot leave the palace or the floor of the palace where my quarters are. Like a caged animal, I run in circles. I have asked if I can visit the Holy Sites of Jerusalem, but my cutting remark about Louis' exultation over the Oriflamme and dead crusaders prohibited that.

So, we have fought and raged again, or to be honest, I did the shouting while Louis did the sulking. I reminded him, he would never have crossed the Seine if it had not been for my treasury and manpower. What is more, most of the debacles of the crusade were caused by his stupidity and refusal to take wise, tactical advice. Odo must have been eavesdropping during this argument. He stormed into Louis' chamber and roared at me to leave. I turned, taking two steps, so we were eyeball to eyeball, and reminded him who he was addressing. As Queen of France, I told him, he had no right or privilege to order me anywhere, but I would return to France with pleasure – via Rome.

They could make what they liked from that statement.

***

I have mapped every inch of my bed chamber, from my bed with its filmy, curtains in white at one end, to the door at the side. The bed is carved in scented sandalwood with lace embroidered linen. There is a row of narrow, shuttered windows overlooking the courtyard below. My chests and desk are at the other end of the room. The marble floor is adorned with magnificent rugs, one in as many shades of blue as can be conjured. It comes from Persia, I think. Papa was given a rug like it once. Nilla has it now. The door was of a carved, dark wood. Another doorway near my desk lead to a dressing room that houses my gowns, linens, other clothing and my dwindled array of jewellery, the damned crown and the exotic Knot!

I am confined again and bored. In the courtyard below there was a mulberry tree, much loved by silkworms, casting a cool shadow. There were many mulberry trees growing in Antioch in Raymond's gardens, but until Abraham explained, I did not know about the connection between the trees and the little spinners of the silken thread. Over many years, I have worn silk. I love the way it glimmers and rustles when I move. If ever I am allowed out, I must make enquiries about getting the seeds of the mulberry home to Poitiers or Bordeaux. If I can grow them, we may be able to weave our own silk from these little worms and their cocoons. I hope they can emigrate to the Aquitaine with the other exotic seeds I have been collecting.

***

Today, Louis let me loose. I could not go far without an escort of guards, but I could let the breeze blow through my hair while in the beautiful courtyards of fountains with colourful shrubs around the ancient walls. I recalled what Abraham told me about the tribes of his mother's ancestors, the oases, camel trains and caravanserai. Amaris and I had brought some embroidery into the sunshine. We were working away like tranquil bees when, to my delight, I recognised a familiar voice – Guile. Only propriety, with the beetles gossiping nearby, prevented me from throwing myself into his arms. I introduced him to Amaris. He had heard about my dramatic rescue, but his reason to talk with me now was political.

Aided by a few gold coins, he managed to bypass Louis' guard and come to this courtyard. Angelique will be quick to report, but she could hardly jump up and dash off without drawing attention to herself. Lord be praised, she does not understand the dialect of the Aquitaine so Guile and I could talk.

He came with a warning. Guile told me there was talk of an assault on Damascus, a powerful Turkish stronghold. The hierarchy of Jerusalem aided by Louis and backed by the Knights Templar were planning an attack. Guile thought it was reckless and no good could come of it.

Chapter 9. Raging Queen

The Emir of Damascus is a formidable enemy and will have the support of the infamous Nureddin, who as I know from Uncle Raymond's description is not to be taken lightly. Guile asked if I could persuade King Louis to change his mind; because the offensive was doomed to failure and will lead to more loss of life. What is the point of this attack? None! We have already been defeated and I can see no tactical advantage when we should be going home.

I had to explain to Guile the king had confined me to the palace and refused to speak to me, that all we did was argue. I said I had no influence over him whatsoever.

'I am sorry, Milady. Lord King Louis is treating you most ill. With no disrespect, if it were not for the manpower of the Aquitaine, he would not be here, nor may I be so bold to say, alive!'

Red faced with suppressed anger, I nodded and bade Guile farewell. I had promised him I would try to dissuade the king (if Odo will let me through the door). I was guessing that Louis believed if he could take Damascus, he could redeem himself for his failures. An ugly thought he could be killed sped through my brain and out the other side. I stared at the embroidery in my hand. How low have you descended, Eleanor?

***

I entered Louis' chamber without waiting to be ushered in. He was reading a missive and Odo was scratching his quill across a page of parchment like a peasant ploughing a field. Both looked up, surprised at my audacity. I told Odo what I had to say was for the king's ears alone and would he have the grace to leave us. He did not move till Louis nodded for him to go. I reminded him not to stay with his ear plastered to the door.

I did not waste words. I stressed to Louis his intention to attack Damascus would end in a bloody massacre, also he could lose his own life. He wanted to know how I knew of his intentions and who was my informant. As Angelique would be in his chamber faster than a bolt from a bow, I told him about my visit from Guile and his warning.

Louis did not bother to enquire how he got past his guards. Instead, he answered it was none of my business. I reminded him, as I was Queen of France and his wife, I believed his life was my business. He snorted he was amazed I cared. I felt like yelling he was right. I did not give a damn about his life, but I did care about the men in his army and their wives and children. I suggested he reconsider.

I repeated what I had heard from Uncle Raymond about the Emir of Damascus and his ally, Nureddin.

'Louis, Damascus is considered impenetrable, even if by the slimmest chance, the city can be attacked.'

'And from whose bed did you glean this information?'

That was the last straw. Rage engulfed me, igniting a fire.

'Wherever you go, Louis, whatever you touch, chaos and mayhem follow in your wake. Your army is in disarray, your military tactics an inferno of hell on earth. I would have thought the disaster of Vitry-sur-Marne could not have been surpassed but no, your failures during this crusade have transcended even that tragedy. You have placed the Oriflamme of France on the altar, steeped in blood.'

I ripped the crusader cross from my gown and flung it at Louis' feet. As I stormed through the door Angelique and Odo jumped aside. With authority she dared not question, I ordered Angelique back to her chamber. I barked at Odo to stop Louis' madness before hundreds more died.

The siege of Damascus lasted four days. Louis, like a cur with its tail between its legs, crept back to Jerusalem, the butt of every jibe from every Mussulman between Jerusalem and Constantinople. At least the failure of his campaign saved lives.

Morale was at rock bottom. Funds were running out and I will be damned if he gets another sou from me. He knows I have some jewellery left which could help, but God help him if he dares to ask.

***

Chapter 9. Raging Queen

I have packed my belongings. I no longer care what Louis does or says. While he was gone, I made sure I could get out. A few gold coins in the right quarters had me unlocked. I have given Angelique the tongue lashing of her life. I have threatened her with treason. I informed her I had received letters exposing her lies which I will air to the Pope and the court when I return. Angelique realises she has been caught out, for once her acid, lying tongue has been silenced.

Amaris is now my full-time companion and has elected to come with me. Bit by bit her story has emerged. On a fateful journey, when her father, a wealthy merchant from Constantinople, and his family were travelling to Ephesus, their barque was overrun by pirates. They all perished except Amaris. She became a prize to be bartered, enslaved and abused. What this poor woman has endured is beyond comprehension. I was reduced to tears, pleading she continue her tragic tale at another time. I put my arms around her. I told her from now on, I would do everything in my power to keep her safe, that her future would be with me, if she can bear my fiery temper and a life I can no longer predict.

I have organised my return via Antioch to bid farewell to Uncle Raymond and, I hope, see Abraham one last time. Guile and the remainder of the men from the Aquitaine will travel with me to St Simeon from where they will return home. My Praetorian Guards will continue in my service. I have ships ready to take me to Sicily and Ostia, thence to Rome on horseback where I will petition the Pope to have my marriage annulled. What Louis does from now on I care not.

***

The day arrived for my departure. Out of politeness, I farewelled Louis and told him of my plans. He said he too, and what was left of the French crusaders, will leave soon.

With little fanfare, we rode out of Jerusalem the way we rode in. In Antioch, I was met by my uncle and aunt. My set mouth and stony visage alerted them all was not well. Over a light meal, I enlightened them on the state of my marriage and plans for my future. I said I would like to see Abraham to thank him again for his tutoring. Raymond said he would send a messenger to his house. I emphasised I wanted to set sail before Louis arrived. I refused to stay under the same roof with him. Constance reported she heard the coast near Acre was being lashed by storms, so I should be able to spend a few days without Louis because no-one would be leaving port in such conditions. My heart leapt, a few more days with Abraham.

***

A note was couriered to me from Abraham. He says he will come on the morrow. Words of love cover the page.

In the morning, I bathed carefully and had Colette brush my hair, leaving it unplaited under my veil. The weather is chilly, so I have chosen a heavier gown with the help of Amaris who has an eye for occasion; a voluptuous, sensual velvet in scarlet. It is trimmed with miniver, so it will be warm.

The library would provide a haven, so I raced there after I asked a page to fetch me the moment Abraham arrived. I paced like a tigress. I heard a gentle tap on the door and flung it open. There he was. The door shut. He enveloped me in his arms, backing me against the desk. Our lips crushed together. I could feel his manhood through the thickness of the velvet.

'Not here, not here. The carpet storeroom – I will be with you directly.'

We fell into each other's arms. There was a frantic removal of clothing. My legs entwined his waist as I clasped his manhood, guiding it into its silky chasm. Magic took over. We said not a word till the last erotic moan.

'I love you!'

I licked the tears from his face and he mine.

We had two glorious weeks before the sea abated, and I heard Louis was on his way. I told Abraham about selling

Chapter 9. Raging Queen

my soul to the devil to try to save my reputation from the allegations, sent to Suger, accusing me of an affair with my uncle. My duty was to protect the Aquitaine. I explained to Abraham what would happen to me if I was found guilty of adultery.

'It is a good thing then, my Angel, you are leaving.'

I said I was still amazed Louis allowed him to tutor me when plainer men are not permitted in my company.

'That is because your uncle said I was a eunuch. Prince Raymond told members of your court I was brought up in the women's quarters.'

I laughed till I cried.

Our last night together was heartbreaking. I had begged an early night after dining with Raymond and Constance. Abraham and I said our final goodbyes in the small hours. I cried myself to sleep.

In the morning, we sailed from the port at St Simeon. I felt wretched, apprehensive about my future as the shoreline faded from the horizon, leaving me steeped in sadness. I have been trying to formulate my petition to the Pope, but so far, suitable words have escaped me. I pray with all my heart one day I will be free to feel the sun of the Aquitaine on my face, smell the waving wheat and cuvees of wine, wander under fruit trees and hear and speak the tongue of my birth.

Tonight, looking at the stars, my heart yearned for Abraham. I keep his poem close, his poignant love song rings in my ears. I pushed Judith's prophesy into the recesses of my mind.

Chapter 10. Shipwrecked Marriage

Imagine my surprise when we docked at Rhodes to find Louis' ship, a Sicilian galley, only half a day's sailing behind us. I was told Sicily and Constantinople were in conflict. My captain wanted to set sail as soon as possible to avoid any skirmishes at sea – our barques were not heavily armed and could easily be attacked – but he said he would like to wait for the Sicilians because they will offer greater protection, being a larger, more capable, fleet. I could see the merit in being within a larger flotilla, even if I would prefer to sail without Louis nearby. After Jerusalem, we were no longer on speaking terms.

Louis' vessel docked late yesterday. After all were loaded with supplies, our much larger armada was ready. Anchors were weighed. A brisk wind caught our sails and our bows sliced into gentle waves to head for Palermo, skirting around the Peloponnese and its islands' coasts.

Our progress was steady, with some tacking from cross winds. The sails billowed; the rigging creaked. My maids and I were now used to the drowsy, rocking comfort of our barque. I have a nook in the bows where I can read or daydream. Raymond allowed me to rummage through his library before I left Antioch. I have chosen a selection of favourite books: Plato, Socrates, Cicero, Ovid and some of the Greek comedies for light relief and thanks to my foul temper, the loose pages of The Aeneid.

I was in a half-awake, half-asleep reverie when I was bolted into consciousness as the barque heeled over at an alarming angle. As I tried to scramble to my feet, it lurched on an opposite tack, flattening me on a pile of ropes. There was a roar. A ball of iron thundered into the sea, missing our bows by several yards but terrifying all on board. We were under attack. Sailors ran in all directions. A burly fellow

Chapter 10. Shipwrecked Marriage

yelled at me to get below, the last thing I wished to do. If we were hit, I wanted to be able to get out, not be engulfed in a cabin. Instead, I wedged myself between two tied barrels riding the plunging, zig-zagging craft like a bucking horse.

Our sails swelled as we ran before the wind. Speed was our saviour, along with the skilled seamanship of our captain who outran whoever was firing cannon at us. We were forced to retreat from whence we came, but this way the wind was full behind us. Peeping over the bows of the vessel, I could see little but the sea ahead, but I could hear the battle behind us.

We found a haven within a group of small islands. There, after we praised God and our captain's skill for bringing us to safety, we decided to keep out of sight till it was safe to leave these moorings. The captain requested an interview with me in his cabin. Over maps, he pointed out a new route he intended to take to avoid the battles continuing between the Sicilian and Byzantium navies. It will take us further out into the Mediterranean. The voyage will be lengthened by a week, less if we have good winds. My safety, he said, was paramount. And everyone else on board I hoped.

Shortly after, Louis' ship sailed into view, Fleur-de-lis emblazoned from the masthead of his galley. They moored alongside our vessel, looming over our smaller craft. I could see him on the deck. I disappeared with all speed into my cabin. I paced about, disturbing Amaris who was taking time repairing a small rent in the train of one of my gowns. Frugal! I have accumulated more gowns to replace the ones I sold, but she has taken it upon herself to repair them, even if I intend to pass them on or never wear them again. As I am taller than every woman I know, whoever receives them will have to alter the length. She put down her needle, aware I had something on my mind. (I think she can read it!) I explained Louis' ship had docked and, although I was pleased he was safe, I did not want contact with him. She reminded me the feeling was probably mutual. I snorted. Amaris went back to stitching. I am now recording events.

An hour or so later there was a tap on the cabin door. A young sailor brought a scroll for my attention. I recognised the seal at once. I delayed opening it. My heavy sigh sent Amaris into the fresh air. But it was no use procrastinating. I slid my stiletto under the seal.

To the Queen of France, Duchess of Aquitaine, my beloved wife, Eleanor,

To God, the Blessed Virgin and all the heavenly host I give my humble thanks that you, my beloved Eleanor, is safe from the adversity faced by forces beyond our control. When I witnessed your small craft fleeing the warmongering Byzantium navy, their cannons balls with thunderous roar plummeting in fearful plumes of spray around your vessel, my heart was being torn from my body in fear for your life. I prayed as I have never prayed before to Our Lord God, the Virgin Mary and all the Saints that you be spared.

I know we have had our differences. Harsh words have been spoken. I have never had any desire to hurt you, but I know I have, and beg your forgiveness. I know you wish our marriage to end. For a short time, I too believed there was no possibility of reconciliation, but when I thought I was going to lose you to a watery grave, I was filled with overwhelming grief.

Please consider my plea. The thought of living without you fills me with despair.

He signed the letter, simply 'Louis.' I sent back a reply. I penned nothing to give him false hope that I would reconsider.

But I have mixed emotions, his words have made me weep. I know not what to think.

***

I insisted we fly the standard of the Aquitaine when we left our moorings. What Louis made of my gesture as we sailed past his galley, I care not. He looked like a lonely monk in his usual white woollen robe. I know he would have seen me in my red velvet cape, my unfettered hair blowing as the wind filled our sails. He probably thought I was offering myself up for ransom, the wealthy Duchess of Aquitaine out on the high seas, so I ordered the Fleur-de-lis to accompany my flag, not because of fear but because my father would have been disappointed in me if I had desisted. But it flew below mine. I feel disquiet again. Sympathy has deserted me.

Chapter 10. Shipwrecked Marriage

After we left the protection of the islands, the sails billowed in the stronger wind. The barque sailed well under our experienced captain. It was expected to take us about five to seven days to arrive in Palermo because of the extra distance we now needed to cover. We headed south for most of the day. The wind was not in our favour, so the journey was slow with the barque having to tack. By nightfall, we turned to harbour on a small island. On the morrow, we will be in open sea, with enough distance between us and the warring parties to proceed without further ado.

***

We woke to grey skies and scurrying rain. The sea had little white caps on the horizon. It looked as if we could be heading into rougher weather. I consulted the captain, knowing my maids and some of my guard do not travel well if the sea is little more than a pond. His craggy face showed little emotion, so I presumed it would be nothing but a squall. I returned to a rather grim-looking Amaris. I smiled, telling her not to be concerned. But for her, of course, there would be the memories of her abduction at sea. I kept her company. I hoped my presence was comforting.

While I have been writing, I have noticed the ink slopping around. I have had to wedge myself to stop my chair from moving. A light knock on my door brought a young sailor who asked with all politeness if he could batten down anything loose in the cabin. He suggested I dispense with writing unless I wanted ink everywhere. He insisted all our belongings be stowed securely in chests and lockers. He advised Amaris and I to wedge ourselves together in one bunk with as many pillows and blankets available so we would not be thrown around should the sea and wind pick up. The cabin now looked as if nothing could move, even if we heeled right over – which I sincerely hoped we would not!

***

I am trying to piece together my memory of events. We were caught in rough weather, I know, but Amaris tells me that was weeks ago. During the storm, I remembered leaving my cabin to give instructions to Angelique and the beetles who were in hysterics and praying like they were going to die. Everything was surreal. One minute I was crawling on the wall, next the floor. I recall insisting the beetles wedge themselves in their bunks as Amaris and I had been instructed to do. It was my duty to reassure them, to make certain they were safe. I had to scramble along as I returned to my cabin, zigzagging and being flung against the bulkheads when the barque lurched upright or sideways. The crescendo of roaring wind, thrashing sails and grinding rigging was terrifying.

Amaris said I was stupefied when I returned. I recall someone slapping my face and yelling at me to stay awake. Amaris said I had a lump above my left eye as big as a hen's egg. I had also banged the back of my head on the cabin floor when tossed backwards like a rag doll. Bruises covered my body and I had skin off my knees and elbows. Was it a nightmare? As I tried to write, I felt most unwell and shaky.

***

The storm blew us into a harbour, we knew not where. They told me one of the beetles, Jeanne, was washed overboard when she panicked and ran onto the deck, along with a young sailor who tried to save her. I feel ill. I know not what ails me. Everything revolves in circles. My forehead is damp with fever.

Angelique has a broken arm. It was set by the ship's surgeon. I do not like her much, but it caused her so much pain she fainted, which I wish upon no-one. Her arm is now in a splint. She looks most pale. Watching her trying to say her rosary with her sinistral hand is amusing. The beetles were bereft at the loss of Jeanne. I pray to God He took her quickly, that she and the boy are now in His Bosom.

Our barque and two others of our fleet managed to dock, listing half full of water, into this tiny port. Amaris has found

Chapter 10. Shipwrecked Marriage

us accommodation in an old fort on a peninsula jutting into the harbour. Amaris, Colette and the other beetles have managed to clean it out, making it quite comfortable. Amaris could communicate in a mixture of basic Aramaic and Greek with the people who are a Berber clan. The Romans she said, called the town Rusuca.

Today, I am sitting in the sun. My head seems disconnected from my body. I can barely concentrate and keep forgetting where I am. I am tearful. When I try to walk, I feel the world wants to swallow me up. Writing helps but I tire quickly. When I re-read my words, some are nonsensical. I know not what is going on in my brain. Sometimes I can barely move from my bed. The ship's surgeon thinks the bangs to my head may have caused my problems. I am experiencing a weird panic. I asked one of the beetles to find Amaris. I must stop writing.

***

Amaris now has more time to spend with me. She informs me our ships are being repaired. The riggings were sorely damaged, sails ripped and so forth. The beetles' personal belongings were saturated and had to be dried out. Thanks to the diligence of the young sailor who stowed our possessions, Amaris and I were luckier – none of our chests were water-damaged. When I asked Amaris about my journal, she smiled and said it was in front of me. I feel embarrassed: my usually sharp wits I think, have also been waterlogged.

Collette and Amaris managed to haggle with traders in a small market for food and beverages. Where was my gold coin? I panicked because I could not recall where I had stowed it. My gentle maid calmed me by taking my hands. She insisted I rest, and not to worry. Everything she assured me was safe. She took my jewellery, coin, the crown of France and the other beautiful chest and secured them in a safe place.

'What beautiful chest?'

***

The repair of my senses was frustrating. My bumps and bruises have long healed. This morning I sat in my bed chamber, a tiny nook with sand-stone walls, and stared at my stowed treasure. I found the mystery chest. With all my might, I tried to remember what was inside. I lifted the lid. The flash of gold couched in royal purple told me it was more than special. Gently, I removed an exquisite bejewelled girdle. It was heavy. My fingers traced over its intricately woven gold thread, pearls and rubies. The chest exuded a sweet perfume that filled my nostrils. Memory hovered; a will-o'-the-wisp I could not grasp. Panic made my heart race. What was wrong with me? I breathed deeply to control the anxiety as the wave of familiar scent awoke something in my brain. Then like a flash of lightning illuminating darkness, it all came back. Just like that! The *Knot of Hercules*, Abraham, Judith, Hamid Abdullah, emerged from my dulled mind. God be praised, my wits had returned!

Before I placed it back, I buried my nose in the folds of its purple nest. I inhaled the perfume of my love, spicy sandalwood. Oh, Abraham! I have hated the girdle, resented it and vowed I would never wear it. Beside the joy of my restored memory lay the sadness of my lost love. I curled the girdle back into the chest and tucked in its pearled fringes. Shall I ever open it again? Who knows?

***

Days became weeks. The measured tempo of village life was enjoyable. The women gossiped around the pump, ground grains for the delicious bread they make, spun wool from their goats, and dyed it in brilliant colours to weave into cloth. They knotted rugs and made cushions like the ones in the room where Abraham and I lay together. For sentimental reasons, I asked if I could buy one or more. Cheeky boys herd goats, looking for pasture in the surrounding barren land. Near the fort, there are ancient olive trees with twisted

Chapter 10. Shipwrecked Marriage

gnarled trunks so reminiscent of L'Ombriere. Within the compound were some grape arbours. Hens ran everywhere. The young girls collected the eggs. The whole village had a timeless ambience, a relaxed charm so opposite to my life.

Our ships were almost ready to sail, repairs completed. Angelique's arm has mended. It was bliss not having her disapproving sneer hovering over me. Maybe I should break the other one. I cannot thank Amaris enough for all she has done during the weeks I grappled in the misty fog of amnesia. I hope the relief I feel since the return of my memory will help me look at my life in a more balanced manner. I cannot but admire Amaris. She has overcome such adversity since she lost her family. The pirates who captured her sold her to a slave merchant who decided to take her for his wife. His family treated her most ill, but one day she managed to escape only to find she was with child. She tried to reach her mother's home in Ephesus but was forced to stay in Bodrum. There, her child was born but died shortly afterwards. Again, she was captured by other slavers and ended up in Antioch where I found her being beaten for attempting to escape. Her fortitude gave me courage to fight for my future.

My determination to annul my marriage has not disappeared, but I am confident I can now confront Louis without wanting to strangle him. When we sailed from the Greek Islands he looked like a kicked dog, desperate for his master's approval but terrified of another beating. Once I was so angry, I would not have cared one jot about his feelings. Now, I know not. What was it he said in Jerusalem – 'Are you naturally cruel?' I do not know if he is still alive. It has been two months since we left the islands. He probably thinks I have perished. There has been no way to inform him of our plight.

I still have his letter.

***

The village fishermen tell us the winds should be fair for our departure in the morning, followed by a swift journey to the coast of Sicily. We aim to dock at Syracuse in the south before sailing on to Salerno and Ostia. At Salerno, I will arrange for couriers to ride with all haste to Rome to give Louis the news, if he is still there; that we are safe and proceeding to Ostia. Should I find he has returned to France, I will still go ahead to beg the Pope's indulgence to put forward my petition.

Before leaving our little haven, we all gave thanks to God and our kind hosts. It was a pleasure to give alms to Georgius, the headman of the village. Underground water is plentiful, so a new well could be completed. There was coin for strengthening the sea wall and to buy a camel to take produce to distant inland markets. The hard-working women gave me a vivid shawl. The brilliant red comes from the madder root, they tell me. Indigo I know well. It is one of my favourite hues. All my maids received pieces of embroidered fabric. Such kindness from those who have so little! I bought two of the cameleer cushions. I had pleasure talking to Georgius. He is a good man. He is well respected by his people for his wisdom and fairness. I have learned much from him by observing the way he handles disputes between villagers. He is patient and listens carefully before giving advice or meting out justice and, although not educated in a scholarly way, one perceives he is not without intelligence. I know of several people in our court who could learn from this honest man.

I have praised God for our survival and for the skilled seamanship of our gallant captains who steered our limping barques to safety. Introspection tells me I need to look at myself. I am so privileged. So much I take for granted. Nilla is right, I have been spoiled. I know when to use my title for my advantage, to make people bend to my will. Even kind Georgius' demeanour changed when he was told by our Captain who I am. I had to beg him to judge me as a person, not by a title.

Chapter 10. Shipwrecked Marriage

As we farewelled these good people, I wondered if I would ever be able to rein in my impetuosity, my lack of discipline, my temper? Dear God, I still have much to learn.

***

It was indeed a fast trip to Syracuse. The bustling activity on the wharf when we docked was almost overwhelming. People were rushing hither and yon, donkeys were braying, merchants calling in many tongues, surrounded by all manner of enterprise.

Our Captain told me we will stay a few days in port to replace some of the rigging and sails he could not purchase in Rusuca. Although the village fishermen were able to provide timbers and pitch to make our barques seaworthy, we could not leave them without gear for their own maintenance. Our captains and sailors had to improvise repairs, using bits and pieces from each of our vessels. The ships have become a patched combination of each other.

With the Praetorian Guard, Amaris, Angelique and the beetles, we did a little shopping of our own in a nearby market in Syracuse. To me this was such a treat for I rarely get to take part in such frivolous activity. I found a scribe from whom I purchased ink, parchment and quills. Amaris' nose discovered some heavenly perfumed oils – and soap! Now that was a luxury. I bought the beetles some lovely embroidered handkerchiefs. By the noon day bells we repaired to the ship, giggling like milkmaids.

***

Salerno came and went. However, it was there I learned Pope Eugenius was residing at Tusculum, not Rome, due to an ongoing dispute with Arnold of Brescia. It appears it is not only our nobles who try to usurp each other's powers; holy clerics can do the same. I care not where Eugenius resides so long as I can petition him regarding the annulment of my marriage. I recall Cicero once lived in Tusculum. I may need to call on his ghostly legal argument when I draft my plea. Whether Louis is there, I know not.

Docking in Ostia was a relief. I must admit my love of sailing has diminished a little after the storm which tossed us onto the Barbary coast. I found the old port fascinating. Some of the ancient town still functioned but much of it was crumbling into ruins. I would have loved to have explored but there was no time for such occupation as I was eager to press on to Tusculum. Horses were waiting. As I had not been on horseback since I left Jerusalem for Acre, I will probably be stiff and sore on arrival, a small price to pay seeing I am alive and well after our travail at sea.

Soon after I dismounted at Tusculum, I was ushered into the Pope's audience chamber. There was Louis. My feelings were mixed; relief he was still in Italy but sickened by his presence. Louis threw himself on his knees, wrapped his arms around my waist and sobbed into my gown. God, he wailed, had answered his prayers and returned me to his bosom. One would think I had risen from the dead. I was mightily embarrassed. Worse, Pope Eugenius stood there with a benign expression on his puffy face, nodding as if we were reunited lovers.

'Louis, I cannot draw breath. Please let me go.'

In the end, Eugenius managed to persuade him I needed to sit and have some refreshments. As it happened, Louis had been caught in the same storm we struck, but his vessel, being larger, was able to limp into Brindisi where it was so delayed by repairs, they took to horses to ride to the Pope's palace. He was not that far ahead of me after all.

Louis babbled he had almost lost hope of ever seeing me again. Pope Eugenius agreed. My husband, he said, had spent his time prostrate in fervent prayer before the altar in his quarters. Also, the whole church had sung a special mass on the king's behalf that my life be spared from a watery grave.

I was at a loss for words. My plans for annulment were becoming awkward. Eugenius ordered Louis to take me to my chamber. With a lewd twinkle in his eye, he insisted I be welcomed in an appropriate manner.

Chapter 10. Shipwrecked Marriage

My chamber was vast. Tapestries, Byzantium carpets, an altar and all manner of exquisite drapery were overwhelming after the cramped cabin on the barque and the simple stone chamber in the old fort at Rusuca. I had a dilemma, how to get rid of an ardent Louis? Wherever I moved he hovered behind me. He raved he had lived in despair, not knowing if I was alive or dead. His life over the last months had been hell on earth. He thought he was being punished for every sin he had ever committed and the failed crusade. My taciturn husband had become more garrulous than a mummer. I begged him to hush, which he perceived as me wanting something more physical. In two strides, he crushed me to him in an uncomfortable embrace. My veil hampered his awkward attempt to kiss me. I shoved him away and stumbled into a chair, head in hands.

'Louis, I am not well.'

He panicked. He said he would fetch the Pope's physician, a most learned man. Tears of frustration filled my eyes. Not once had he asked what had happened to our fleet, to me, or anyone else, not even the beetles. I told him I needed to bathe, to go to my bed, to sleep. I did not need a physician. The tortured dog left me to my misery. God's teeth, what a mess.

***

I wrote my petition to Pope Eugenius. Surely rumours about the state of our marriage had reached his ears, or had Louis' pathetic display on my arrival make him think there was something still between us? I awaited the Pope's reply. In the meantime, I spoke with Louis. He kept away from me, believing my tale. But Angelique would soon put paid to my so-called illness unless I confronted Louis.

My good intentions to become more conciliatory flew off faster than migrating swallows. My meeting with Louis was a screaming fit on my part, with him retreating into his kennel. I reminded him although he had spent a lot of time praying for me, he had shown no interest whatsoever in what transpired at sea or where we found shelter. I roared at him I had found more kindness and care among a simple Berber tribe than from him. Prayers were all very well, but thoughtfulness was a greater remedy. Horrified, he accused me of blasphemy; he had prayed for me because he loved me. I yelled back, asking why he had shown no interest in what had befallen me.

Silence! I thundered I was lucky to be alive and stormed out. As I write this, I am still fuming.

***

I was summoned to present myself to Eugenius. Louis stood beside the Pope. Eugenius waffled on about the sanctity of marriage. He said King Louis' recent prayers and prostrations proved how much my husband loved me, verified by what Eugenius had witnessed himself. I know I should not have rolled my eyes. The Pope asked me to translate my gesture. My reply was too blunt; it did me no good. The dressing down I received was humiliating. Eugenius reminded me, as a woman, it was my duty to obey my husband: as Queen of France, it was my duty to produce an heir to the throne to continue a noble dynasty. I was told to curb my tongue, I was far too outspoken, which was not flattering in one of my sex and status. (Now where have I heard that before?) He dismissed my petition; ordered me into Louis' bed to fulfil my husband's needs and to do my duty.

'You are far too learned, Eleanor of Aquitaine, Queen of France. I suggest you keep away from books and leave them to your superiors.'

If a woman has ever torn into a Pope before now, I know not. As Louis stepped to escort me, I yanked my arm from Louis' grip. I told Eugenius I would burn in hell before learning was denied to me, nor could I, in God's name, unlearn the knowledge I had already gained, any more than he could. Furthermore, books were as much my God-given right as any man's. He was speechless. Louis nearly had a fit, hauling me out of the Pope's throne room before I could add more fuel to the flames.

My reputation was in tatters. The clergy avoided me in case I crossed their path like a black cat. I do not think I will ever be allowed to set foot in Tusculum or Rome again. All haste was being made for our return to France. I was suffering Louis' grunting and groaning. The only person who hoisted me onto a pedestal was Amaris, who has not stopped grinning since my outburst. Needless to say, the Pope did not see us off. Louis ranted I should thank God none of us has been excommunicated, and an interdict put on all of France denying the population the sacraments. I told him to stop nagging if he wanted access to my bed. It was going to be a long trip.

Chapter 11. Reluctant Return

Louis and I have arrived in Bourges. I was reacquainted with Archbishop Pierre de la Chatre. He had heard about my infamous outburst in Rome. He told me, with a raised eyebrow, most men would not dare to take on a Pope.

'But, of course, Lady Eleanor, you are an excellent chess player. Quite a checkmate, methinks.'

I am not sure if he was flattering me or saying, *'do not try it again.'* Louis found our friendship hard to fathom.

The Archbishop had not forgotten Louis had had him locked out of Bourges and the failure of the crusade did not endear him further. Much to his embarrassment, the Archbishop reminded him that if it were not for the Duchess of Aquitaine's army, the crusade would have been a greater disaster. Pierre de la Chatre was gruff,

'Lord Louis, King of the Franks you have much to learn!'

Louis, I think, was relieved we were to leave on the morrow for Paris. The Archbishop did not comment that I was no longer wearing the crusader cross.

***

I am with child. The tell-tale morning nausea was making its presence felt. My feelings were jumbled. I do not know whether to be happy or full of despair. Forced to copulate with a man I have no feelings for whatsoever – it might as well have been rape. I think of Abraham. My heart aches for him. If he had made this child, it would have been with love, joyous, sensually satisfying, a delight.

I have escaped to the library. Louis was not speaking to me, but I cared not. He is yet to know he is to be a father again. I will let him know when I feel like it.

I am as popular as the pox, having vented my spleen

Chapter 11. Reluctant Return

on Suger. When he tried to blame me for the failure of the crusade, I bristled with indignation; no longer will I cower to this self-righteous hypocrite. I roared,

'Had the king kept his word, his promise, regarding Prince Raymond's campaigns and well considered plans, if he had heeded the warnings, he would not have found himself ambushed where he had to be rescued by my Aquitainian army, and whereby the loss of many good men would have been avoided. Abbé Suger, if you have a tincture of compassion or humility in your heart, if you have one, you should get down on your knees and pray for those brave men's immortal souls.'

I stormed out.

***

I have my dogs back. Titan and Mars remembered me and were delighted as they jumped to lick my face, then galloped in excited circles chasing their tails, their exuberance making me laugh. They have grown into huge monsters. I hope I can manage them, though Albert tells me they have not been allowed to forget their manners and will obey my commands. Angelique and the beetles were less than overjoyed by their return, muttering about the smell and fleas. Thank heavens Amaris was not scared of them. I have encouraged her to give them little treats so they will love her forever.

Brother Joachim was also excited to see me. Amaris and Joachim liked each other at once and have become good friends, for which I am grateful. They have similar senses of humour, which are needed in this place. Poor Amaris cannot believe any building can be so cold and dank. The fireplaces are working overtime, having, I think, been dormant during the two and a half years of my absence. Our fastidious natures to keep clean, to bathe regularly, is also something of concern. Unlike the French, whose hygiene is much to be desired, Amaris was brought up with hamams and soap.

The dull grey walls of the palace, the depressed atmosphere of Île de France surrounded by the sludge of the Seine and the stench of rot, has enveloped me. Louis has left on some self-flagellating pilgrimage with Suger. I am in turmoil over this baby. When I told Amaris what happened to Marie, she was appalled. She did not know I had another child because I had never mentioned her. I said I cannot bear the empty ache, so I do not talk about her. Amaris looked at me with haunted eyes. I may not have my daughter, but it is with heartfelt relief to know she is alive. I hugged Amaris to me.

***

Louis has returned. I requested to speak to him in the library. What occurred between us was painful, awkward. I did all the talking while Louis stared at the floor. I emphasised the hurtful facts, starting with his mother, the ongoing cold, heartless treatment meted out to me by Suger and his fellow clerics and the hurt and loneliness caused by the dismissal of my maids, particularly Renée, just before Marie's birth. All followed by the appointment of Angelique, who is still spying on me, who, as he knows, has no qualms about lying to have me dishonoured.

'To be blamed Louis, for everything from the conflagration of Vitry-sur-Marne to the failure of the crusade, I can no longer accept.'

He rose to bolt out the door saying naught. I screamed after him,

'Furthermore, I demand my life improve before this next child is born'.

That stopped him in his tracks.

He went scarlet, as it dawned, he had managed to impregnate his wife, again.

I told him he could check with Angelique to confirm dates so I could not be accused the child belonged to another.

***

The whole of Île de France is flagellating themselves into a frenzy, praying for a boy. Louis is annoying me by

Chapter 11. Reluctant Return

constantly checking on my health while as before, trying not to look at my middle. The little one has started to exercise with lots of kicks. But I seem to be in a veil of forgetfulness which is maddening. Never again will I show impatience for a woman who cannot concentrate one jot while carrying a child. I waddle around or sprawl staring into emptiness. I have neglected my journal for days on end. Reading is little better.

I am so tired today. I cannot find comfort in bed. I spend the nights rolling like a barque in a tempest. Unlike Jonah who was swallowed by the whale, I look as if *I* have swallowed the whale. I do not remember feeling quite so listless when I was awaiting Marie, or so large, but of course I was younger. Amaris said I look serene. She said I reminded her of the Madonna, which I find amusing. The thought of being compared with the Virgin was such a contradiction. I told Amaris she should mention her observations to Angelique to watch her face turn puce with horror.

Louis is certain this baby will be a boy. It should be if all his prostrated prayers to God and every saint in Christendom are answered. I share his optimism with divided hope. I am anxious as I await the arrival of this child. I am not looking forward to the birth, yet I also want it over. I have no idea if it can hear me, but I have been talking to my baby, telling it is making *Maman* uncomfortable and I am impatient to see who it looks like. I told the baby it has a sister.

'Little darling, I love you both with all my being.'

I lumbered into the library with little Marie on my mind. I wondered if she was ever curious about her mother, if one day we will meet. I pondered who she looked like, me or Louis. I pray she is happy. Her birthday is never forgotten. She would be more than five years old now. In a special chest, I have placed all the little gifts I have stitched for her, little trinkets I have found I think she might like. Will I ever be able to give them to her? Above all, I pray to God she is being taught to read and write. My most precious possession is the locket containing a snippet of her hair tied in a piece of silken thread. I was touched beyond belief when Colette gave it to me. Colette could be a closer friend to me if she were not so terrified of Angelique and the other black beetles. She is the only one who smiles. She has pretty dimples.

I have begged Louis not to send this baby away if it is a girl, but he is adamant it is a boy. I am gripped with a panic I will never know this child either. A premonition? Only God knows. (Stop this, Eleanor! You are becoming melancholy.) I should get up, but it is such an effort. It is even a trial to write. Earlier, I almost upset the ink pot stretching over my belly to dip my quill. I heard the bells of Notre Dame peal out the hours. Since the last strike, the base of my abdomen has tightened and there is a dull pain in my lower back. My vice-like fingers around my quill have left blots of ink. I should stop. My time is nearer than was predicted. Dear Mother of God, help me to endure, give me strength to fight on, regardless of my coming fate.

***

My body healed quickly enough after my daughter was born. My mind, however, was sorely afflicted. I have regained strength, but I am thin. I spent many weeks in Poitiers, which helped cure me. Now back on Île de France, I find Brother Joachim has left a row of quills and there is fresh ink, as if he knew one day I would return. When I read the last entry I made, I am shocked at the sight of the page. It was scored as if a thousand claws had torn through the parchment. Ink was spilled and smudged. Reading what I wrote in those moments, is difficult.

I have a daughter. She is called Alix. She was expelled from my body and taken away. I screamed, sobbed and pleaded with Angelique not to take her from me, to at least let me hold her. I flung myself from my bed, but I fainted. When I awoke, my chest was bound. Even so, milk seeped from my swollen, burning breasts while another suckled my child. I am in unbearable pain.

They gave me a bitter herbal mixture to drink, to make me sleep, but I spat it out when they turned away. I pretended to sleep but slipped from my bed when they left

Chapter 11. Reluctant Return

the chamber and the nurse dozed. The room revolved in circles, I almost crawled out. I have searched everywhere for Alix, listening for a crying infant, but all is silent. I cannot comprehend how my legs carried me to Louis' audience chamber. Were the various black-hearted clergy there aghast at my appearance; a wild apparition, hair dishevelled, my feet bare? I know not if the priests recoiled in horror because, with the last ounce of my strength, I flew at Louis. I implored him to give me back my baby. He had difficulty defending himself as I struck him, tore at his hair and face with my nails, I cursed him in dialect with every foul word I knew.

I have no recollection of what happened next or how I got to the library to scrawl these words. Amaris told me I had locked the door. They had to find Brother Joachim who had the other key. They found me unconscious, surrounded by leaves of parchment and smashed quills, with my chemise blood-stained and soaked in ink. All I remember; I woke in my bed.

***

Recalling these past events was helping my resolve to leave this hellhole as Judith's prediction hovers, a mirage over the desert of my life.

Following my attack on Louis, I was declared insane. My chamber was locked. I curled up like a child, weeping continuously. Maybe I had gone mad. I had no desire for food. Amaris, and Colette too, bless her, sympathised with my plight. They spent hours trying to tempt me to eat. The cooks produced all my favourite titbits. But I was in hell. Colette whispered Alix had been sent to the Duke and Duchess of Blois. Another locket appeared, containing a snip of her hair. Although knowing where she was eased my panic, it was of little comfort my melancholic prediction came true. Like Marie, Alix will never know her mother. Amaris told me she tried: implored Angelique to at least let me see my baby, but she was told if she wanted to remain in my employ, she was to mind her own business and to do as she was told.

So concerned were these good maids, Collette and Amaris, they petitioned Louis on my behalf, requested I be sent home to Poitiers where I could be cared for by darling Renée. I think Louis was so ashamed and plagued with guilt for having caused my grievous condition, he agreed. The journey helped to soothe the turmoil in my mind. The gentle rocking of the carriage lulled me. When we reached Poitiers, I was a little improved.

Renée, beloved nurse, comforted me. When the tears flowed silently down my cheeks, she would rock me in her arms like she did when I was a little girl. Whenever I left my bed to sit in the sun, Renée would find me staring at nothing, sometimes with some flowers in my lap. Surrounded by love and being cared for with tenderness by those who value me, I awoke from the nightmare. But there was a hollow. My womb was empty as were my arms.

Chapter 12. Determining the Future

Poitiers, as ever, was filled with light, music, poetry and provoking thought. How easy and relaxed it was without Louis and the pious French court. When a troop of troubadours arrived one day, so reminiscent of my childhood, I almost expected Papa's ghost to make an appearance to join in their songs. Their gaiety and music encouraged me to take up my lute again. I was so out of practice my playing was discordant, but I persevered. Instead of my usual ink-stained fingers, I redeveloped calluses on my fingertips. I pledged to myself to practise daily till I was adept again.

As the days became weeks, I began to leave the palace and gardens to wander further afield. I started to practise archery again, at which I was once most skilled. Although there were moments when I thought I would never be well, the sun came out in my wintry mind. Little by little I managed to control my tears and the cacophony in my head, that addled my brain.

***

Several weeks later, when I returned from the archery range, an unexpected visitor and his men were dismounting from their horses. I had not seen my dear friend Geoffrey, Duke of Normandy since before I left for the crusade. He had always raised my spirits with his wicked sense of humour. Geoffrey strode towards me greeting me with due homage, but with such a twinkle in his eye, I was disarmed. He is not called 'Geoffrey the Fair' for no reason. I blushed as we exchanged greetings. I invited him and his men to be my guests. I asked them to meet for a repast after they had removed their dusty tunics and bathed. I knew a few days in his company would be better than any physic.

We met again in the gallery off the great hall where a banquet was to be held in the evening. Lord Geoffrey and I were having a private joust about Socrates' philosophy (if surrounded by several knights and maids could be considered private) when he surprised me by mentioning he had heard I had been unwell. The heralds must have been busy, but then Louis having another daughter would have been proclaimed far and wide along with my supposed madness. Lord Geoffrey said he was delighted to find me well if a little 'skinny.' He continued to say he had heard I had been near to death and, had such misfortune taken place, he would have been devastated. My heart fluttered as he took my fingers to his lips, his eyes gentle, full of concern.

My lonely empty life spread before me, a bleak landscape. I was entranced, touched, by the endearment on this man's face. I suppose we have been attracted for some years but have kept our feelings in check. But now they have been kindled; a spark struck from flint. He cannot be the love of my life. He is married and so am I, but with that gesture, I knew I desired Geoffrey Plantagenet with all my being. My mind raced to think of a place where we could be alone. I suggested we take a stroll around the gallery, breaking into Greek to keep our conversation private. I began by showing Geoffrey the beautiful tapestries that lined the walls. Thank heavens my maids and the Plantagenet knights were more interested in each other than me taking Lord Geoffrey on a guided tour. I suggested we visit the Maubergeonne Tower which contained greater works of art.

What took place is etched in my memory like an inscription in stone. We climbed the tower's many steps, tiring me a little, but I cared not one iota. My infamous grandparent's old bed chamber was my destination. On entering, our bodies entwined. For such a rugged, barrel-chested man, his lips were soft and tender. With expertise I did not question, he unlaced my gown. This man was no monk, he knew how to caress. Each exploring touch made my body hum in harmony as his strong fingers slid between my

Chapter 12. Determining the Future

thighs, stroking, arousing, till I was ready for his manhood. Outrageous Grandmother Dangerosa, I like to think, would have given me her blessing as would I hope Grandfather William. Their love was legendary within this tower. My mother's mother and my father's father, the joining, if unwed of the houses of Chatellerault and Aquitaine.

A week's visit flew past too quickly. My newly discovered love was better than any herbal remedy. I was the happiest I have been since leaving Antioch. Abraham no longer haunted my mind but fell into a special recess in my heart. I told Geoffrey how I yearned to escape my marriage, how I was unsuccessful with my petition to the Pope to have it annulled. He encouraged me to try again. I resolved to return to Île de France to confront Louis. After Geoffrey left for Normandy, I made my way to Paris, only this time I rode a powerful destrier instead of travelling in a covered carriage in a stupor.

***

I was greeted by stony-faced Angelique. She was annoyed to find Colette had preferred to remain in Poitiers; she would have forced the poor maid to relate every minute of my convalescence. Colette is kind and good. I can never repay her for her gentle care during my darkest days. She deserves every ounce of happiness and freedom from this miserable court. It was heart-warming to see her blossom, and to find a man in her life. I hope she marries.

At least Brother Joachim was pleased to see me, happy I am well again. He returned me my key. He took possession of it and locked the library when he found prying eyes attempting to search for my writing after I had left for Poitiers. I have looked to see if anything is amiss, but all seems in order. The concealed closet containing all my journals has not been disturbed. Only Amaris and Brother Joachim know where it is or how to open it.

Since my return, I have not seen Louis except for a brief embarrassing meeting when I insisted on giving him a copy of the petition I had penned to the Pope. I knew Suger was doing his best to make sure I remained where I was. Deep in my gut, I feared he would try anything to keep my dowry.

How right I was. Within my chamber, I was embroidering with Amaris when our peaceful activity was shattered. Two burly guards placed themselves inside my chamber by the door and I was commanded in a rude manner to attend His Lordship the King in his audience chamber. Angelique was with them, looking like a cat that had lapped from the cream pail. I stepped out of my chamber with a guard on either side followed by the smirking black crow and her entourage of beetles. Amaris was ordered to stay where she was.

I was led to stand in front of Louis, Abbé Suger and a panel of clergy. I noticed Suger had a thin booklet of parchment open in front of him. Although it was upside down, I recognised my hand. It was written in Greek. Abbé Suger said he did not realise I was so religious. I had learned to read and write in Greek when in the Holy Land by copying excerpts from the Bible but Suger does not understand Greek, though he could find a scholar who could translate. I was puzzled. But his next gesture almost undid me. Between forefinger and thumb he held up a page of vellum as if it was contaminated filth. It was Abraham's love poem expressing his deep passion and pain of separation before I left Antioch. How did the Abbé come by it? Could our love affair have been discovered? My heart thudded.

As far as I knew, no one in Louis' court understood or could read the beautiful flowing Aramaic script. Yet, with a sinister sneer, Suger declared the script the work of Satanic influences. I said I was surprised a man of his learning did not recognise the language of Christ. That put him back. So as not to look foolish, he said, 'But you do, so enlighten us!'

I replied, although I was learning the language shortly before I left the Holy Land, I was not proficient. Now, almost two years later, I no longer had the skill to be able to translate what the Abbé had before him. He demanded to know if I had written it, and if not, who had. I shrugged. Suger had

Chapter 12. Determining the Future

no idea of the source of what he held. I felt confident to challenge him as to why I had been summoned in such a manner to stand before this panel of eminent persons as if I had committed some crime.

'Madam.'

His sneering insult in not addressing me by my title took my breath away and was noted by those present.

'Adultery by one of your rank is a treasonous crime, punishable by death.'

I took a deep breath, challenging Louis directly. Surely, he did not believe the charges based on a scrap of writing no one could read. Louis shocked me by asking again if I had had an affair with Uncle Raymond.

'I am stunned that you question again that accusation, My Lord, knowing full well it was proved by Prince Raymond's wife, Princess Constance, that nothing of a romantic nature took place between my uncle and me, ever! This lie was perpetrated by this man's sister. What is more, if you think Prince Raymond of Antioch was the author of the page you have in front of you, Abbé, it is baseless because, although my uncle can speak the language a little, he cannot write in Aramaic.'

Suger, fury shaking his bony body, ordered me to translate. I repeated I could not. He could put me on the rack; I would never translate Abraham's words to anyone. As if twisted by tremors, he wheezed to one of the guards to fetch Amaris. He knew she could read and write Aramaic, it being her second tongue through her late mother.

My heart pounded as she arrived in front of the panel. Terror ran across her face as she looked at me, beseeching me for help I could not give. Suger thrust the piece of vellum into her shaking hands. He ordered her to read the poem. Poor Amaris did her best to bide her time. She pointed out it was in Aramaic. Suger's patience deserted him. He threatened it was in her best interest to read it at once. Again, she halted; she told the panel she had not read Aramaic for some years and was no longer fluent in the script. Spittle foamed on the corners of Suger's thin lips, as he screeched at her to read.

Poor Amaris looked at me with fear on her pretty face. She started to read. Had the situation not been so dire it would have been amusing because no one at the table could understand a word. Suger demanded she translate the text, to which she replied her fluency in Langue d'Oeil was not good enough, but she could translate into Greek. Blessed Amaris, she was playing for time. She knew none of them spoke Greek either. Suger was not going to give in, insisting she translate into Latin. His eyes were bulging out of his head. I hoped he would suffer a fit.

Poor Amaris was cornered like a rabbit before dogs. She cleared her throat and, with her finger tracing the elegant script from right to left, she began. She hesitated, frowned. Amaris looked up at Suger and Louis: she said the piece was from the old Bible. With a rush in impeccable Latin, Amaris recited:

> I am very dark but lovely!
> O daughters of Jerusalem,
> Like the tents of Kedar.
> Like the curtains of Solomon,
> Do not gaze at me because I am dark,
> because the sun has looked upon me.
> My mother's sons were angry with me.
> they made me keeper of the vineyards.
> but my own vineyard I have not kept!
> Tell me, you whom my soul loves,
> where you pasture your flock,
> where you make it lie down at noon.
> for why, should I be like one who veils herself
> besides the flocks of her companions?

'That is all, Abbé.'

Before Suger could snatch it back, Amaris handed me the page. I thanked her for jogging my memory. I told the panel, I remembered being asked to copy the Songs of Solomon from an ancient edition of the Old Testament written in Aramaic as an exercise set down by my tutor.

Chapter 12. Determining the Future

Suger was speechless. Louis, for once in his life, came to my aid, roaring that enough was enough. He ordered Amaris and I be allowed to leave because I had been much maligned. He apologised for the inquisition and returned my little exercise book of Greek. I thanked him. Amaris and I left with as much dignity as we could muster.

Back in my chamber Amaris and I fell into each other's arms shaking with relief. Her clever recital had saved my life; how can I ever repay her? She replied, I had saved hers, therefore I owed her nothing. But I do. Over and over, this loyal, unassuming, pretty woman gives and gives to make my life bearable, putting up with my often-uneasy temperament. How could I go on without her?

***

I never saw Suger again. He died after returning to St Denis shortly after my confrontation. I felt little sympathy for Angelique's grief. She, I discovered, had found my old Greek exercise book in which I had carelessly tucked away Abraham's poem. I must have taken it out of the closet during the madness I suffered after Alix's birth. Her lies and innuendos would now be interred with Suger, having nowhere to go. To get rid of her, as she took her red-nosed, puffy-eyed presence from my chamber to travel to St Denis, was a pleasure.

Louis is bereaved by the death of his mentor and wants to leave with all haste for the funeral rites. I have 'taken ill', anything to have my attendance excused. Geoffrey sent me a letter. He will be passing through Île de France on his way to Tours, my reason to remain here.

Louis was too busy whipping himself into a frenzy of grief to think of our future. I wondered which sycophantic cleric will take Suger's place at Louis' right hand. Old Bernard de Clairvaux who has no time for me, or any educated woman for that matter, will be the favoured candidate. His appointment could work in my favour. He will be only too pleased to be rid of me to find Louis a more suitable wife, a woman who will 'know her place' and not question the status quo.

***

During Louis' absence, I was able to spend time in Geoffrey's arms. How precious I felt, how loved again. He housed himself outside the palace with the students on the Left Bank, a noisy crowd, he said, with their drinking and carousing, but it enabled him to move around without drawing attention to his comings and goings, so we could meet in secret. I had escaped one accusation of adultery, therefore I needed to be more than discreet.

Our last day together was bitter-sweet, with our bodies more in tune than ever. After a few hours of bliss, he was gone. I took solace in the library, but my heart was heavy. It will be some time before we will next see each other. He gave me a small gift, a gold trinket shaped like a heart cleft in two. Set in precious stones was the Greek letter Gamma. Geoffrey has the other half with Epsilon as its decoration. I put it on a chain and hung it round my neck.

***

Louis returned in mourning and, I am told, wearing a hair shirt under his tunic. In this mood of religious devotion, our marriage will be the last thing on his mind. Although I managed to avoid Suger's funeral, I am obliged to attend services at Notre Dame for the rest of his eternal soul. I hope he rots in hell. I instructed Amaris to lay out a gown I knew he would hate, one embossed with elaborate embroidery and stitched with precious gems and pearls. Gloomy-faced Angelique was fuming but, as she now had no one to run to with her tittle-tattle, she had to keep her mouth shut. The neckline enhanced my shoulders and neck and the long train needed to be carried by six pages. My veil was so fine a thousand spiders could have woven it from gossamer thread. The loathed crown of France crushed my temples. Between my breasts, on its long golden chain, was the cleft heart.

The gasps I received from all assembled when I made my way into Notre Dame made my heart sing. I was surprised Louis was not taken aback by my glamour. I did not need his admiration, was all I thought when I espied Geoffrey among the assembled knights and ladies. I was not expecting him, so my heart skipped with delight. He had managed to place himself on the aisle, so I passed within a breath of him, his eyes piercing, as he caught mine. Louis and I sat. As the pages fussed arranging my train, I searched the crowd for Geoffrey before we turned towards the altar. Somehow, he had managed to move closer to the transept where Louis and I were enthroned. He gave me a look of pure lust before bowing his head in prayer, though I do not believe he was praying for the safe journey of Abbé Suger's soul. With flaming cheeks, I bowed my head over my missal. My inner core longed for him in a manner no saint would approve.

Priests chanted and filled Notre Dame with plainsong. The filtered light from the stained-glass windows spread like jewels. At the end of the service, on our exit from the cathedral, I paused in mock surprise before the Duke of Normandy. I managed to relay in Greek to meet me under the rose arbour in my garden at the rising of the moon.

The great hall was filling for the sober banquet as Louis and I made our way to our thrones. I hesitated and gripped his arm. I told him the heavy crown was giving me a headache that I felt faint. He grasped my elbow; urged the pages to bear more of the weight of my train. I whispered I needed to lie down, or I would be ill. Louis became frantic. I managed to roll my eyes back, a trick from my childhood. A murmur ran around the hall: 'The queen was ill'.

Louis insisted I leave, he could manage without me, a relief! I was helped to my bed chamber where Amaris and the beetles undressed me. I lay down with a rather nasty-looking herbal mixture by my bedside. I told Amaris to draw the curtains around me and whispered she could go to her bed and the others could return to the hall. After a suitable interval, I peeped though the curtains. The rising moonlight was slanting though the windows of my chamber. I wore only my shift, slippers and a miniver cape to protect me from the evening chill. I held my nose and drank the ghastly mixture gagging as it went down; 'that is your penance, Eleanor.' My heart fluttered with anticipation as I slipped through the garden door.

A light cough alerted me to Geoffrey's presence in the dimness of the arbour. With a merry chuckle, he congratulated me on my acting skills, saying I could join a band of mummers should I tire of being Duchess of Aquitaine. I quieted his silly quips by kissing him as his hands made their way under my cape and shift.

Geoffrey left the following day. Why is it my fate to fall in love with men who can never be mine? Judith's prophesy haunts the recesses of my mind.

***

Abbé Bernard stepped into Suger's shoes to become Louis' mentor as I predicted. He was far more concerned about the effect our failed marriage was having on the future succession. He insisted Louis and I have an audience with him after he moved into his quarters in the palace.

I went into action to finalise my petition when Louis surprised me by coming to the library. I was suspicious. It has always been me who has instigated discourse between us. Before I could ask him to sit, he was begging me not to leave him, to think again because he loved me. I put down my quill, dusted the velum with the pounce to dry the ink and stood.

'Louis, it is too late! I cannot remain your wife and you know why.'

He begged I give him a second chance. I shook my head. My mind raked over the debris of my marriage, trying to find one happy moment.

'Louis, I have endured long enough the misery inflicted on me by the malicious clerics within your court. But you

Chapter 12. Determining the Future

know what has been worse than that humiliation? Your gutless inaction: topped by the wicked, cruel, spineless way you allowed our daughters to be taken from me!'

I took a deep breath to control my emotions, my tears, my loathing.

'I was not even allowed to hold them. You have broken my heart.'

I struggled to keep my voice level.

'I can never, never forgive you! Do you think I could ever let you in my bed again to have yet another child removed from my care?'

Silence!

'Get out!'

He crept through the door.

***

For our meeting with the old Abbé, I dressed demurely. It was well known Bernard despised ladies of rank who dressed like *"painted ponies"*.

The meeting went well for me; Louis was shaking, pale faced. Bernard emphasised in plain terms we lacked an heir because Louis and I are cousins in the fourth degree. Louis' great-great uncle, Robert Duke of Burgundy was my great-great grandfather. I am glad Bernard worked it out. I knew, of course, because I had looked up our relationship before the crusade. Our lack of an heir however, I thought was more likely due to Louis' inability to please his wife in bed. I kept that to myself.

To my amazement, the Abbé already had scribed a letter petitioning the Pope on Louis' behalf. All Louis had to do was sign it. I had brought my signed application which Bernard read. He asked who wrote it. When I replied I had, I received a penetrating stare. He grunted it was well penned for one of my sex.

***

Couriers astride swift horses were on their way to Rome carrying our petitions. Within minutes of them galloping over Pont Neuf, I resembled a caged bear. I prayed for forbearance to endure the long wait.

Some weeks after the couriers left, Geoffrey came to attend Louis regarding their continuing disputes over the Vexin, a thin strip of land between Normandy and France. The Dukes of Normandy and the French kings have been bickering over it for as long as I can remember. It swaps backwards and forwards. I knew not who was claiming it as their territory for now, nor do I care, except it allowed Geoffrey and me to find a few precious moments together. As I lay draped over his muscular chest, I told him my exciting news. But he shattered my world by urging me to remarry as soon as I was free of Louis, and to my horror, suggested as a suitable husband his son, Henry! I pounded him with my fists. He pinned my arms to my sides. I bit into his shoulder with all my might, like a rabid dog. He yelled in pain. I am glad I hurt him. Does he think so little of me he can pass me on like some whore or milkmaid – and to his son, for God's sakes, a boy? Damnation on his soul!

I have tried to distract myself by reading. But the book I chose was Greek. Greek reminded me of Geoffrey. I started some embroidery. It was so ill I had to undo it again and again. Amaris said she would fix my mistakes just to get me out of her sight. My ill temper was affecting her too. I stomped back to the library. I saw Brother Joachim had cleaned up the splintered quills and left others. Maybe writing will clear my smouldering thoughts. Jesus, Mary and Joseph – do I have to carve it on my forehead or write in letters higher than a halberd? I do not want another husband! That pup, Henry Plantagenet, will have his eye on my dowry to prop up his struggling and impoverished inheritance. I want to weep but I am too enraged to shed a tear. I will tear the books off the shelves if I stay here. I will adjourn to the archery range. One word of disapproval from Angelique and I will put an arrow through her.

Chapter 12. Determining the Future

***

Another night of tossing and turning had me bleary eyed. Self-pity washed over me. I prayed with all my heart for the Pope's decree as I brooded in the library, the one place I shall leave with regret if I am freed from this wretched existence.

The books are dear friends, more comforting than any damn lover. I blessed dear old King Louis for his inheritance. Reading to him when he was ill all those years ago filled me with pleasure. I felt honoured because I was little more than a child. I wondered what he would think now. I do not believe he would be surprised Louis' and my marriage is a disaster.

I stared at the shelves, their serried rows cleft by narrow aisles. My private writings are stowed away in locked chests for safe keeping. There is only this journal left, some ink, some quills prepared by gentle Brother Joachim. I will miss his kindness, how he has so often calmed my brittle nerves with few words. He knows my moods by the shards of quills on and around my desk which he gathers up and spirits away in the pockets of his robe. New ones appear like gifts from the Magi. The old ink-ingrained desk bears epics of my humour.

***

It is September – I am still awaiting my fate. During this time, I had to go on progress with Louis throughout the Aquitaine to visit vassals; how I wished he had not been there! However, I was reacquainted with Geoffrey de Rançon whom I had not seen since we had left the Holy Land over two years ago. He has regained weight and has lost his haunted look of despair. I told him about my petition to be free of Louis. He wished me luck; expressed kindly I deserved better. Next, he surprised me by saying he was sorry to hear about my bereavement. I looked at him, puzzled. I said I did not understand his sympathetic words. He turned pale. Something was amiss, my heart pounded.

'Milady, have you not heard?'

'Heard what?'

'The attack on Aleppo. Your Uncle, Prince Raymond, was captured and killed.'

My darling Raymond, Papa's little brother, my old playmate, the boy who did not allow me to get above myself, who kept my feet on the ground – no longer! My knees crumpled beneath me. I was helped to a chair, a goblet of brandy wine pressed to my lips. Poor Constance! I will have to write to Nilla, Clotilde, and Jerome. Renée was mother to us all. She will be heartbroken.

When Louis appeared, I screamed at him for his cowardice in Antioch, by reneging on his original promise to help Raymond, leaving him unaided and galloping off to Jerusalem. I yelled how I hated him. How I wished it were he who was dead.

I stayed in Poitiers. Louis, after my tirade, returned to Île de France. I should be enjoying my home, but I swing from melancholy one minute to optimism the next. Since the courier left for Rome, weeks have stretched into months. My rift with Geoffrey of Normandy caused grief and a heavy heart. I still have his chain around my neck, the cleft heart snuggling between my breasts. But like Abraham, Geoffrey is another love unable to be fulfilled by marriage. I tried to dispel the niggling worry I will not be safe alone, yet alone is what I desire. Why must I remarry? It could be another disaster.

***

Eastertide was approaching at the pace of a tortoise when I was summoned back to Paris. The envoy from the Pope has at long last arrived. I left Poitiers at all speed.

Where, as Queen of France, I presided with Louis over banquets glittering with dignitaries, bishops and vassals from our estates across France and elsewhere, I was asked to stand like a common criminal in front of Archbishop Hugh de Sens, the Archbishops of Bordeaux, Paris and Rouen,

Chapter 12. Determining the Future

many lords and the Archbishop of Rheims. Abbé Bernard led the proceedings.

I wore a sombre gown, not wishing to draw attention to my features. A company of knights escorted me into the great hall. My stomach churned. Amaris was my only sympathetic attendant amongst a cohort of black beetles and smug-faced Angelique. At least her sneering brother, may he suffer hell's wrath, could no longer intimidate me. With every inch of pride and dignity beholden to my status as Duchess of Aquitaine, I stood with my head high, presenting an icy, armour-clad demeanour despite the inner turmoil.

Abbé Bernard droned on and on – stiff-necked ass – reading with great deliberation the Pope's screed. He was determined to draw proceedings out to make me suffer. Finally, he pronounced the verdict: I was free. I froze for a minute as the thrill of the end of a life sentence coursed through my being. My daughters were taken as legitimate and would remain in their father's domain or where they have lived since birth, a blessed relief!

In front of Louis was a scroll of vellum containing the Pope's decree with his signature attached as well as the Papal seal. Bernard beckoned me forward, indicating after Louis where I should put my mark. I leant forward over the long table, my breasts almost under Bernard de Clairvaux's nose, I smiled as beguilingly as I could.

'And what mark would that be – a cross, perhaps? It may come as a surprise to you, Abbé Bernard, but I am as capable of signing my name as are the eminent gentlemen before me, but only after I have read the document for myself to make certain I am not putting my name to something not exactly as you have purported.'

Louis, with trembling hand, turned the scroll around. I read it aloud, agreed it was in order.

'Now, your eminences, where would you like me to place my *signature*?'

I took the quill and scribed my name. The date, March 11th, in the year of our Lord, 1152 will forever be engraved, with relief, on my heart. I removed my wedding ring from my finger and the crown from my head and placed them on the document in front of Louis. I turned on my heel and left the chamber.

Chapter 13. Short-lived Freedom

In anticipation, my life as Queen of France was packed away and I was ready to embrace the freed Duchess of Aquitaine. Chests piled high in my dressing room. Louis allowed me to take my jewellery, most of which came from my inheritances anyway, though I left what he had given me over the years to be divided between Marie and Alix. I kept the chest containing the trinkets I have gathered for my daughters, hoping above hope, one day I will be able to give them to my girls.

I told Louis, if he wanted his father's books to remain on Île de France, I would understand. All I wished to take were my father's along with the tomes I have accumulated, my work in Greek, and personal documents and letters. My journals have long been secreted away in custom built chests with intricate locks.

I was about to finish writing, when I was surprised by urgent knocking on the library door. I was confronted by one of my Praetorian Guards. He handed me a missive bearing seals from Poitiers, begging me to read it at all speed. I broke the seals. It was from Guillaume, a senior knight from the Aquitaine. He was only two leagues away from Île de France. He insisted I be ready to leave early on the morrow. It appears word of my annulment has spread even before the ink on my signature was dry. My guard, Antoine, continued they had taken the liberty to load my possessions onto barges on the Seine. As soon as Guillaume arrived, we were to proceed to Orléans by as devious a route that can be found. From now on, my safety was paramount.

I was shocked but thrilled at the same time. To be honest, I had always felt the concern for my safety was exaggerated. Antoine looked so serious however, I did not argue with his directive.

I looked around this haven as Antoine hopped from one foot to the other, frowning I not tarry. Brother Joachim, who was crating my and Papa's books, stopped with a look so harrowing, I could not contain my tears. Protocol or no, I wrapped my arms around this good, kind, saint of a man. Words could not express how much I will miss him. I had begged him to come with me, but his order is in Paris. I have thanked him from the bottom of my heart, in fact I could not find words fine enough to describe my appreciation for all he has done to make my life bearable. I have initiated alms to be distributed to his monastery. I have left him Titan and Mars.

***

My departure was swift. Before cockcrow next morning, without a backward glance, I was escorted to Guillaume, by Antoine and my Praetorian Guards as well as another company of knights from the Aquitaine. Like them, I was disguised as a pilgrim *en route* to a shrine near Orléans. To my surprise and some consternation, I found Geoffrey among the escort. I discovered it was not only Guillaume who had organised my departure. I feared a trap, with me being spirited to Rouen and forced to marry his son. I hissed at Guillaume as to why he was there. He informed me Lord Geoffrey was so concerned for my safety he had offered his personal services for the passage to Orléans, where he would leave us. From there we would continue to Poitiers. What could I say? I had no time for discussion, and they knew not of our affair. Deep in my gut, my last encounter with Geoffrey churned. I could never contemplate renewing the affair – it was over. At the first opportunity, I made it clear he was no longer welcome in my bed. Mounted we set off, his horse's head just behind mine as the sun peeped over Notre Dame.

In Orléans, Geoffrey requested to speak to me in private to explain his reasons for suggesting I marry his son. I glared at him with the eyes of a basilisk. With a raised hand, he

Chapter 13. Short-lived Freedom

ignored my fiery stare, declaring instead his love for me. He stressed my safety and wellbeing were all he wished that they were of the uttermost importance.

'Eleanor, you are no fool. You must know you will be pursued by every mad dog in Christendom for your wealth and beauty. They will snap and snarl outside your walls, waiting for a chink in your defences to break in to carry you off to God knows what fate. Bavaria, Castile, Morocco, Sicily, barbarians – if you thought Île de France was bad, those sons of Satan will be worse, not to mention the self-interested mongrels within your own duchy. Your only other option is to take the veil and somehow, Eleanor, I cannot see you as a nun.'

He began to praise his son Henry's virtues.

I was silent. Around my neck, I was still wearing the cleft heart bearing the bejewelled letter, Gamma. I removed it and held it out to him. The air between us was a wall of ice as the trinket swung back and forth on its gold chain.

'Keep it.'

I flung it to the floor.

***

My heart skipped with joy as the walls of Poitiers loomed as we crossed the river Clain. I was stiff and a little chaffed from the ride as I do not often ride astride. I slid from my horse. Renée clasped me to her bosom as we cried and laughed. Petronilla, Raoul and little Ralph had come from their estates to greet me. The whole palace was out in force, cheering and clapping my return. What a welcome!

I was bathed, pampered, cossetted and fed all my favourite food. The greater part of my belongings had arrived safely at Bordeaux. After their trip down the Seine to the sea, they were transferred to ships to finish the journey. Some gowns and personal belongings had been sent overland to Poitiers, comfort after the rough monk's habit. I could also unplait my hair.

I am back at my old desk in Papa's library, inhaling the familiar aromas of leather, ink and parchment, a breath of sunny air. I feel carefree as I record my recent thoughts and actions. A knock on the door interrupted, followed by a familiar though deeper, voice from my childhood.

'Blessed to see you, Elly!'

I almost toppled off the chair. Standing in the doorway was a powerful, rather austere but elegant figure of a man dressed in a dark Benedictine robe. I have not seen Jerome since he went to the Benedictines after Papa's death fifteen years ago. He always called me 'Elly,' his pet name for me.

We laughed and hugged one another. We did not stop talking and reminiscing till the shadows through the windows had lengthened and the bells were ringing for services in the chapel. I had yet to give thanks for my freedom. I was told Louis was prostrate with grief.

***

There was so much for me to do. I met with my justiciars, my seneschal, constable, stewards and others of my Aquitaine court to begin the process of governance. The last time I had any influence in the duchy was prior to the crusade, which hangs over my head, haunting my dreams. So many men followed my call to arms with ardent fervour, so many are no more. The clergy say these men are martyrs in the arms of God and the heavenly host; but I cannot drag from my heart and mind they are the result of misguided passion on my part. I know I was ignorant about what we were to face, and I know nothing could have prepared me for the horror. But once confronted with reality, the likes of Louis and Conrad still blundered ahead regardless. They took no heed of the tactical advice given by those like my poor darling uncle who had lived in the Holy Land long enough to pass on local knowledge, who tried in vain to warn there needed to be well-planned strategies if their armies were to have a chance against our wily foe.

It was my duty to make reparation to their families. It came to my attention some of their wives, who took over the reins

Chapter 13. Short-lived Freedom

of their estates during their men's absences, have prospered, running them with careful husbandry and prudence. Others have struggled with warring relatives, grown sons with all manner of disputes. Some of the successful women have had male relatives with no previous claim now contending the estates were their rightful inheritances and were feuding with their mothers, sisters-in-law, sisters or female cousins, demanding to reclaim what they considered were their rights. Worse, some of these women have been carried off to wed against their will – my heart sinks.

Petitions were piling up on my desk. I spent hours burning candles to their waxy stubs, reading and rereading these plaintive pleas. The poorer folk, the peasantry, were in dire need. They turned to convents and monasteries, many of which were stretched for alms to feed these poor souls. I found Louis had neglected his responsibilities in many areas of the Aquitaine. He was not popular within the duchy: he has squandered its wealth. Crops, orchards and vineyards have been allowed to wither through mismanagement.

It was going to be a valiant effort on my part to rectify the damage, to regain trust. Some placed the blame at my feet by association with my wretched ex-husband. The Aquitaine treasury had been squandered over and above its support for the crusade.

***

For the next few months, I travelled up and down the duchy, dispensing alms where necessary to monasteries and abbeys. At least, I have my own personal wealth which I was able to separate from Louis and his so-called mentors. Over the years it had accumulated because, except for some personal needs and making the Palace on Île de France habitable, it had remained dormant. Some went on my personal needs for the crusade, but there were funds available. Grandmother Dangerosa, for all her infamy, was an astute woman and I have benefited from the inheritance bequeathed to me.

I had a wonderful reunion with Faydide on her estate. She is running her lands successfully, so far without a male heir. I was a little disconcerted with her warning, not unlike Geoffrey's, I was a prize plum ready to be plucked. I tried to laugh it off, but I realised she was in earnest. She gave me a strange prediction, which was a little too Judith-like for comfort, that I had a greater destiny to follow. Our conversation was hard to comprehend, considering she was doing what I wanted to do without a man dominating her life.

***

I was mulling over this on my return to Poitiers when a great pounding on the library door had me jumping out of my skin. Guillaume burst in. The Duke of Bavaria had crossed our borders with an army of about five hundred men. How did he get across France? Was Louis in cahoots? Guillaume knew not.

'Milady, knights have been sent out to counter this invasion. But you must leave immediately for L'Ombriere. We have horses at your disposal.'

There was no time to change. He threw a cape at me. I ran behind him as he continued,

'Renée and your other maids will follow. Check your stiletto. A bow with arrows is with the horse. Antoine and your elite guards are already mounted. God speed. Go!'

For the first time, I was frightened.

The horse was one of the fastest I have ever ridden. We galloped through Poitiers scattering people in our path. My hair was loose – no time to plait it – and streamed behind me like my personal Oriflamme. By the time we had cleared the city my valiant animal was frothing and covered in sweat. At an inn, we changed horses in haste, speed a necessity. My gown was bunched under me in an uncomfortable swathe of material; my cape was twisted, the bow slung across my body was almost strangling me, arrows bounced in the quiver. We slowed when we came to a copse of trees.

Chapter 13. Short-lived Freedom

Halfway to L'Ombriere there is a swift stream, a tributary of the Dordogne, with a knoll beyond that gave a good view of the surrounding countryside. A guard was set as water was fetched for us and the horses, which after they cooled, could drink. Antoine told me to rest because, as soon as possible, we would continue. I managed to plait my knotted, wind-blown hair. I tried not to panic.

The forested area we had been riding through was light, which enabled us to move at a steady pace. Before long though, the terrain becomes wooded, heavy with spreading oaks and chestnuts, the home of wild boar and other game where the House of Aquitaine has hunted for many years. The terrain is rugged. A wrong step could break a horse's leg.

We dismounted into the dim green depths to attend to the calls of nature. As I adjusted my chemise, gown, and cape, I detected movement, a shadow. I picked up the bow I had laid on the ground and loaded an arrow. It may, I thought, have been an animal sniffling around, but I was taking no chances.

Next, I was grabbed from behind. I screamed before whoever he was could cover my mouth, but I dropped the bow because he was pinning my arms. I managed to elbow my assailant somewhere in his midriff. He cursed in Langue d'Oc, which betrayed his origins. My yells brought help, but he had a knife and an accomplice; the outline I detected.

My guards were cursing like demons. They formed a half-circle, swords drawn, but the undergrowth hampered them. I caught the name, Thierry de Gervaux, one of Geoffrey's self-interested mongrels. I knew if he desired me for a wife or ransom, he would not want to damage the prize. I stopped struggling. His grip relaxed. With a sudden movement, I was able to twist sideways enough to slip from his grasp. There was a twang. Hot blood spurted over the side of my face and gown. He fell to the ground.

The other man bolted. Some of my guards pursued him. Antoine rushed to my side. I thought I too had been hit, though I felt no pain. The blood was Thierry's. He was face down: an arrow through his neck. Simeon was standing over him, bow still in his hand. Two of my guards helped me back to the clearing and my horse. I was hysterical, shrieking at them to wipe the blood off. With water from their sacks, they cleaned my face, doing their best to comfort me at the same time.

My lucky escape brought home the reality of Geoffrey's words. I realised, how Simeon's accuracy and skill in archery had saved me from whatever fate Thierry de Gervaux had in mind. His accomplice was soon caught. It was his brother, Alain. A sword swiftly ended his life. I vomited my guts up.

The L'Ombriere palace staff were horrified by my appearance. Clotilde, like her mother Renée, took me under her wing. I ordered everything I was wearing to be burned, including my chamois boots. Although the tub of soothing hot water by a cosy fire in my quarters eased some of my stiffness, I felt as if I had been flogged. It took forever to get the knots out of my hair. Bed was all I desired.

***

I am recovering from the shock, but it was several more days before I received the news the Duke of Bavaria had been sent back from whence he came after a thorough rout. We could not discover how he got so far through France, but Odo de Deuil was mentioned. I am not surprised. What he thought he would achieve, apart from vindictiveness, I know not. Two other contenders were also brought to my notice: Geoffrey, Henry Plantagenet's younger brother, the other from the House of Champagne. What in God's name did they think they would achieve by abducting me? There would have been an all-out war between our people because I would never surrender the Aquitaine to them. I would die first.

Within my old schoolroom, I have had plenty of time to think. As much as I hate admitting it, Geoffrey was right: the dogs are snapping at my borders, marking their territory.

Chapter 13. Short-lived Freedom

Thierry's spattered blood and Alain's last breath still disturb me. I must consider my options. At present all I am doing is cursing my fate for being born female. I am going to have to remarry. This time, however, I will make certain it is on my terms. Which brings me to young Henry Plantagenet. Somewhere in my memory I think he may have attended Louis' court with his father many years ago, aged about nine or ten, but I cannot be sure. I would have shown little interest in a child.

Apart from his father's undoubtably prejudiced and glorified description of his virtues, I know only gossip about him with few facts. His mother, Empress Matilda, has groomed him to become King of England which has been embroiled in civil war for years. Stephen de Blois, who usurped the throne from Matilda, with his son Eustace, have brought the country to its knees. I suspect Henry Plantagenet is after my dowry. He is supposed to be mature beyond his years, according to his father, but I am nine years older! Not to mention I have been his father's mistress and deep down still love Geoffrey.

Although I have pushed Judith's prophesy to the back of my mind, it niggles. I have tried telling myself it is fantasy. I am never going to marry the love of my life; impossible because the only love I have found is with men I cannot wed. Furthermore, I do not want another debacle in bed. I want some pleasure and to be loved. Nor do I want my education and intelligence unexcepted because I am a woman. Jesus, Mary and Joseph, what a mess!

***

On a pleasant note, Clotilde had recruited more maids to join my court: they are Lucille, Marion and Celeste. I interviewed them and I approve. They all have even temperaments, great senses of humour and make me laugh. Above all they are intelligent as well as capable. Clotilde has grown so like Renée. When we were young children there was rivalry between us for Renée's attention. Clotilde is older than me by about nine months. I remember her telling her mother, when we were eleven or twelve, I was nothing but a precocious, spoilt brat, far too privileged for my own good. Lord be praised she got over that. She is married to one of my stewards and has a delightful baby girl of her own, Emilie. Clotilde has also become a clever apothecary, like her mother. How different these maids are from Angelique and the black beetles. My temperament has improved – Amaris is overjoyed.

I must not procrastinate here any longer. I had received a request from the harbour master from one of the small fishing communities on the mouth of the Garonne. They had a problem where the seawall had partially collapsed in wild weather, so the mouth of the channel the fishermen used to go to sea was silting up. This was making entry and exit to the harbour difficult. They have a young man who believes he has a solution, an ancient Roman method which will re-direct the current when the tides change, preventing future silting. I admit I know nothing of engineering, but I have faith in the inventiveness of the Romans evident here at L'Ombriere and in Constantinople. I told them I would provide funds from the treasury and encouraged the harbour master and the villagers to set to work immediately.

***

God's teeth! I managed to hurt my left knee. I dismounted from my horse as I have done a thousand times, on my return from the harbour, only to put my foot on a wobbly cobblestone and come crashing down on my knee. Grooms ran from everywhere. I knew when I stood something was amiss. I managed to hobble back to my quarters. On examination my knee looked like one of those leather balls boys and young men liked to kick around. Renée was summoned along with Clotilde and, seemingly, all the herbalists in Christendom. I am now wrapped in tight bandages with some foul-smelling unguent about my knee. I have been given a stick to help me walk if needs be but, on pain of death, I have been ordered

Chapter 13. Short-lived Freedom

to keep my leg upright on a cushioned stool.

At least I was permitted to hobble as far as the library. Awaiting were a few letters, mostly of little import. There was one from Guile; I intend to bring him back into my service now he has recovered from the crusade. He was alarmed by my hasty departure from Poitiers and my near abduction. Another from Tarquiri said the same thing. There was a thank you from one of the abbeys with added prayers and, horror, a bulky one bearing Geoffrey's seal.

I sat staring at it, trying to find courage to open it. Well, I cannot read it without doing so. I broke the seal. I was about to smooth out the parchment, when two gold chains fell out on my desk – Gamma and Epsilon. Why? I do not want them. That part of my life is over. I have been struggling, mostly in my bed at night, not to think of Geoffrey; his strong arms, the jousting scars on his body, our passionate love making. Now he reminds me of what I can never have. On my desk was a little wooden box. Papa used to keep little surprises in it for Nilla and me, a pretty pebble he had picked up, a shell from the beach, a little carved horse of bone or some such thing. I dropped the chains in and shut the lid.

I had no desire to read his letter, so I ignored it. When Renée knocked, I shoved it out of sight. She was checking on me to make sure I was not dancing a jig. I had to return to my chamber so she could plaster my knee in more goose fat and the ghastly smelling herb. My protests got me nowhere.

***

Today I hobbled to the garden to embroider with Amaris and the others. Lovely girl, she now has genuine companions. We are all about the same age. Lucille, Celeste and Marion are of noble birth. All have escaped violent marriages. Each had fled to the local abbey near Bordeaux, the same nuns who embroidered my trousseau. I hoped that was not an omen. One of my many cousins, Nanette, is the abbess. But they felt they were not suited for convent life. None of them wanted to return to wedlock. I know how they feel.

The last few days have been mightily vexing. My swollen knee was keeping me cooped up like a Christmas goose. I was able to hobble into the audience chamber to deal with writs and petitions, but I cannot get out and about. My patience is a little thin.

A parcel arrived. What a joyous surprise. Papa's copy of *The Aeneid* has caught up with me. In my haste to leave Paris it was left behind. Dear Brother Joachim has repaired it. It looks almost new except for the tell-tale ink-stained pages. I have had a wonderful nostalgic read. I love the new squeaky bindings as I turn the pages. To breath in the new cover's leather bouquet is heaven sent. What joy!

I was feeling quite relaxed, despite my damn knee. Although the swelling has almost disappeared, Renée will not release me from the goose fat. I would not be surprised if ganders started following me in anticipation.

Of course, all dreamy things usually come crashing to earth. Still unread at the back of my desk was Geoffrey's letter. I decided I had better get it over and done with. He mentioned the trinkets. He says he does not want to be reminded of me because it hurts too much. God's teeth, does he think I want to be reminded of him? He heard of my narrow escape on my way to L'Ombriere; he must have spies everywhere. He also knows how the Duke of Bavaria managed to get through France: he and his men came on barges down the Rhone. Informants had given Bavaria news of my annulment before I received it, so he had a plan in place. Another with spies; in this case, in Rome or Tusculum. Geoffrey warns me the Bavarian Duke will not give up unless I wed another. He mentions not the other two.

I continued to read. Having procrastinated for days, I realised to my horror, young Henry was on his way, less than a day away, by the date on the letter. Dear God, he is almost crossing my moat!

***

Lord Henry arrived with a small entourage, his squire,

Chapter 13. Short-lived Freedom

Sir Robert de Lucy, and a contingent of close knights. I sent messages of welcome but said I could not present myself because I had to attend to urgent affairs of state. Vanity was my major impediment. I did not wish to show myself until my knee was unbound, and I no longer limped. The difference in our ages plagues me. I confided this to Amaris. I have stared at the glass till my eyes watered, looking for lines or wrinkles. Much to my disgust, Amaris found this amusing. She informed me, that as I am one of the most beautiful women in Christendom, I have nothing to worry about. Huh! Besides, she said men are often weather-beaten; Henry may look older than me. I do not know why I am so concerned. I do not want to marry him or anyone for that matter.

I gave him a free run of the gardens and the nearby Roman ruins, and furnished him with books, chess and backgammon for entertainment till I am ready to meet him. I am harassing Renée to remove the stricture round my knee.

***

This morning was bursting with sunshine. Spring is here. My ladies and I were sunning ourselves near the remains of the old amphitheatre. Climbing roses, a multitude of blossoms and, much to my joy, jasmine spilled over arbours, trellises and the ancient stonework. I could not be more delighted with how the jasmine has taken to its new home. The seeds I sent here and to Poitiers from Constantinople and the Holy Land have grown well. The plants were now well established. Their tiny star-shaped flowers filled the air with their perfume. With the roses the combined scent was breath-taking.

The gardens continue down a winding path to the old Roman baths fed by a spa. Grandfather William had them renovated when he rebuilt the exotic Roman folly for Grandmother Dangerosa. I opened it up a week ago. I had not been inside for many years. Nilla and I used to play in there till Papa decided the frescos on the walls were too explicit for our delicate sensibilities. I now agree, though they are beautifully drawn and painted, down to the last erotic detail.

My maids and I were all simply gowned. I was wearing a favourite blue robe. We were chatting and laughing and winding jasmine flowers in each other's hair when we heard a light cough. Lord Henry and Sir Robert had wandered into our circle. At once I knew who was who. Lord Henry is a younger version of his father. I turned my head away and whispered to Renée not to name any of us. The two men introduced themselves and apologised for disturbing our frivolity. Renée made a great play because of modesty, and because none of us were veiled, that she could not formally introduce her charges, but would be delighted to do so when Lady Eleanor agreed. The two men accepted her explanation. Lord Henry expressed his desire to meet the Duchess of Aquitaine as soon as was possible and would Renée pass on his compliments. We all stood to leave. As I limped off with my stick, I glanced back catching Lord Henry's eye. My face reddened because he gave me quite a lascivious grin. Like father like son.

***

Lord be praised, no more bandages or stinky unguent. I sent an invitation to Lord Henry inviting him, Sir Robert and their entourage to a banquet in Lord Henry's honour. The sooner I get it over and done with the better. I have asked Amaris to do a little snooping to find out what Lord Henry's father has said about me.

My next dilemma was to decide what to wear and how I should present myself. I have consulted with Renée who believes I must look my best because I am, after all, Duchess of Aquitaine, though she was muttering about modesty. I accused her of turning into Angelique. She snorted and gave me one of her disapproving looks!

Lucille asked if I would like to wear a purple silk robe. It arrived with my gowns from Paris. She thought it was the most beautiful thing she had ever seen. I had to be reminded because I could not recall it. My other maids were eager to dress the 'doll.' I had a sickening feeling of *déjà vu*, dressed like an ornament for my betrothal to Louis. I left all of them twittering away and fled.

My spirits are low. Why cannot I be left alone? My burdensome existence is at times overwhelming. I took myself for a walk to the remains of Aphrodite's temple, the goddess of love, which overlooks the estuary of the Garonne, where I ran lamenting my betrothal to Louis. I hoped it was not to be *déjà vu*!'

If I must marry, Lord Henry is probably the best of a bad lot. In Poitiers, I questioned Guillaume if he had ever met him. He said he had made his acquaintance at a few jousting tournaments. He observed Lord Henry was smart, a bit over-competitive, could not sit still for a mere second but overall was likeable. Guillaume remarked also, he had a fiery temper when roused. That could be interesting, I thought, knowing my propensity to fly into a rage. Guillaume chuckled. He had witnessed a spectacular brawl in a tavern after a joust in Rouen. Lord Henry took exception to some knights who insulted somebody he knew. Guillaume laughed, 'He is a scrapper when in his cups'.

As I mulled over this. I knew not what to think. Tonight, I will meet him. I will try to be a gracious, charming hostess – not difficult as I have had plenty of practice. Will I be able to come to some conclusion about his suitability as a husband? Who knows? But now I must choose the gown and suffer the hours of being 'adorned.'

***

My chamber was a rainbow of colour and gilt. My maids were looking so eager I could not remain peevish for long. Lucille trumpeted the beauty of the purple silk with such enthusiasm that I selected it. It must be new. I cannot recall having worn it. Marion, pink with excitement, said I would look magnificent. I stopped myself from rolling my eyes.

I spent the rest of the day being bathed, scented and preened. The gown, I must admit, is glorious. The purple silk gleamed, glimmered and rustled. When I think of the labour to extract the excretions from all those little sea snails to make the purple dye, I am agog. Such a time-consuming process to create this most regal of colours. Hours must have been spent stitching the pearls, amethysts and gold thread into the cornucopia-shaped sleeves and down the train like a peacock's tail. As much as I hate to admit it, the work must have been done by the beetles. I have chamois slippers to match.

My breasts were pushed high in the bodice, laced so tightly I hoped I could breath. My shoulders were bare. I decided to wear my Briolette diamond and pearl pendant, one piece I did not sell during the crusade mostly because it is priceless and a family heirloom. I have not worn it often. Louis hated it, considering it ostentatious. My maids were agog at its size. Diamond and pearl drops fell from my ears. My hair was coiled into a golden filigree nest. With the crown of Aquitaine about my temples – I was ready. The pages arrived, beautiful in their golden livery. Like a barque in full sail, we made measured progress towards the great hall.

***

In Papa's library haven, I have had time to ruminate over last night's banquet. The fanfare of my entrance, the long slow parade past the homage of my people and my arrival in front of young Lord Henry were designed to be splendid, to impress. But all I could think was here I am, the walking dowry. But I dare you to compare the outside with the inner Eleanor.

Lord Henry showed polite deference, paying homage to my status. I told him to rise, that we were equals. His eyes are a piercing blue with a wicked twinkle like his father, damn him! His hair, an auburn tangle of curls. The colour must come from his mother. He is taller than Geoffrey but just as powerfully built. As the evening progressed, I noted the

Chapter 13. Short-lived Freedom

familiar naughty sense of humour and mimicry underlying a quick intelligence. He agreed his Greek was ill because, as his father once related, he spent a goodly time avoiding his tutor, to hunt or joust. His voice is deep, as is his rumbling laugh. Henry Plantagenet is ruggedly handsome. I detect a certain irreverence for church and authority. At least we have that in common. He did make a wry comment with a certain wicked glint in his eye, that I no longer seemed to limp. I blushed under the rouge.

I introduced him to the '*satanic*' fork, which he handled with delicacy for someone with large hands. He had a hearty appetite whereas, as Renée would note, I was my usual picky self, this night because of nerves. Our conversation ranged over many subjects. I had an inkling he had been schooled on what not to mention. Music was a safe topic. We both played the lute and liked to dance, though I did little on Île de France where it was considered a lewd activity. He enjoys reading, with his favourites being from Roman history which impressed me. I mentioned Saint Augustine to which he gave a snorting guffaw. Peter Abelard was an interesting topic, with Lord Henry saying he thought him sorely judged. I told him of Nilla's and my escapade into Notre Dame. He was mightily impressed by our initiative.

He brought up the subject of the crusade. Without mincing words, I said it was a debacle. The loss of life saddened me. I surprised him, I think, by declaring we were beaten by a superior foe. The Saracens knew the territory as well as a dog its kennel, and we were disadvantaged from the beginning. He was interested in Constantinople, Antioch and Jerusalem. I said I saw little of the latter, but how impressed I was with Constantinople. I steered clear of Antioch; too many heart-felt memories.

I offered horses and falcons should he and his men wish to hunt. I think he has felt caged over the last few days waiting for me to meet with him. Tomorrow I will join him for a day of hunting, followed by an evening of music and games in his quarters, with my maids and I as his guests.

***

The hunting went well with plenty of game brought home for the table. God be praised, Lord Henry did not think it unwomanly for me to ride at more than a trot. Jerome challenged me to race him back to the palace. He exploited the situation by galloping off before I was ready, so I took the short cut, jumping Diablo over a tricky log we called Loopy Luna as children, because of its crescent shape. I won. Jerome accused me of cheating. He ought to talk! Lord Henry seemed perplexed at our mad banter and comfortable familiarity. I may be wrong, but I think I discerned a look of disapproval.

My maids and I enjoyed our night of entertainment with Lord Henry and his men. When we entered, I noticed a chess game in progress. While Lord Henry was organising pages to pour wine, Sir Robert said he was being thrashed as usual. I told him how I thought he could win, but he would have to sacrifice his queen.

'Go on, I am all ears.'

I gave him a quick demonstration.

'There. Checkmate in four moves.'

I replaced the pieces to exactly where they had been. He looked at me in amazement as Lord Henry approached with wine.

'Lady Eleanor, why do you not play a game of chess with his Lordship?'

Lord Henry, I discovered, does not like to lose. Neither do I. He bit his tongue. His eyes went cold. I will, in future – if there is a future – avoid chess for a while. I suppose I did not help myself by returning the pieces onto the board to where he had made his error. He was grinding his teeth. I suggested we played our lutes, asking him which tunes he liked. Somewhat tight-lipped, he suggested I choose. I played the Moresque. He thawed and picked up the tune with ease. Amaris surprised everyone by performing the dance. The evening, overall, went well.

Chapter 13. Short-lived Freedom

***

Amaris knocked on the library door and entered. She asked what I thought of Lord Henry. I shrugged, saying he was more pleasant than I expected, but I still had reservations. She chided me about the chess and rubbing his nose in his loss. If I become his wife, he will have to put up with more than losing a game of chess. I asked what she and my other pretty spies had gleaned. Marion heard his father had told him not to be taken in by my looks, that I had a mind like an iron trap. How flattering! I was pleased to find he does not disapprove of women with an education, a blessed relief. Sir Robert she said, thinks Lord Henry is smitten. He has not stopped raving.

***

I have turned my attention back to my guest. Lord Henry did not, after the chess game, take leave of me. I escorted him and Sir Robert on a tour of our vast gardens, the herbarium and perfumery. He paid more attention than I thought, showing interest in the plants I had brought back from the Holy Land and Byzantium: the mulberry trees for instance, still small but growing well.

We wandered away from the others to the grove of ancient olive trees. I told him they were planted by the Romans and how we still get a goodly amount of fruit from them, despite their antiquity. I jested I hoped I did not look as old as the trees when, in the next instance, Lord Henry was kissing me passionately, his manhood most obvious as our bodies pressed together. Voices and laughter coming down the path broke his grip. I was not disappointed by his display. I wanted more.

My voice husky, I whispered, 'There is much to show you. Over yonder is the Aphrodite temple, which is aglow at sunset, as is Grandmother Dangerosa's Roman folly. It contains some most interesting frescos. Maybe this evening?'

His blazing eyes and flared nostrils answered my suggestion.

Sir Robert and my maids arrived laughing. I hope I did not look too flushed.

Chapter 14. Tigress Marries Lion

I told my maids I had some deep thinking to do. They were having such a good time with Henry's men I think they were happy to have a night without having to do my bidding.

After my repast, I slipped away to the library. I hid my gown under the desk. My hair was already loose. I wrapped my red, miniver cape about me, and slipped from the palace carrying my lute. I often played on the steps of the temple in melancholy moments, so it would not look out of place should someone see me. Henry was going to be surrounded by an entertaining group of revellers, so I was a little unsure he would take my hint.

I unlocked the door of the folly, trying not to remind myself how I used my infamous grandparent's chamber in Poitiers for my first encounter with Henry's father. While I waited, I reflected. Quite deliberately I was testing this young man. I am almost convinced I could marry him, but I am not going to marry another monk – I would prefer to take the veil. I lit candles, illuminating the frescos in all their exotic glory and hoped the large Roman-styled couch was as sturdy as it looked. I went outside to watch the full moon glow like a giant peach as it rose over the estuary.

Footsteps crunched on the path. Henry crushed me to him in a fiery embrace, our lips full of anticipation. Desire coursed through me. I led Henry to the folly, removed his robe. He had naught on underneath. His erect manhood was impressive!

I had already removed my chemise. I dropped my cape. If he had never seen a naked woman before, he had now. During tactile minutes of bliss, he took my breasts in his powerful hands as gently as one would hold tiny birds. My hair covered us like a cape as I took control, straddling his powerful body. If he wondered how a woman married to wishy-washy Louis Capet knew so much about sensual pleasure, he gave no indication. Like the erotic nymphs in the frescos, I slid my body to consume his engorged member as we became one.

We spent most of the night experimenting, enchanting each other. He was young and vigorous, I sensually experienced. There was something joyous about me being older; we truly were equals. I laughed when he told me I had legs like a boy.

'Really?'

'You have muscles.'

I examined my legs. For fun, we compared the two pairs. Henry's were like tree trunks of power, mine lithe with shapely calves, slim ankles and long feet. Henry's feet looked like they could hold up a vaulted arch. Next, he was tickling my feet ruthlessly. I thought I would have convulsions begging for mercy, arching my back as I kicked, trying to escape. We both fell on the floor where our lips locked together, until Henry's eager probing fingers had us back on the bed.

Towards dawn, I slipped away. Henry was sound asleep, sated. I covered him in my fur-lined cape. I bathed in the warm spa before returning to my bed chamber. I dropped my damp chemise on the floor. Love bites were appearing, purple on my neck and breasts, my pubic bone tender. I nestled my body into my bed, exhausted. Oh yes, Henry, you have passed!

***

I was awakened by Amaris shaking me. Guillaume was marching up and down, wondering where I was. I had a long line of petitioners doing the same. I had overslept. No wonder! I had partaken in some quite vigorous exercise. Amaris, who tried not to look at the tell-tale evidence of my recent activity, dressed me in haste. My hair was matted. It would take ages to brush it out and I had no time. She

Chapter 14. Tigress Marries Lion

bundled it up with pins as best she could and draped a silken veil around my shoulders to hide the love bites, clamping it to my head with a coronet. As I was about to dash out the door, Amaris called for me to wait. I paused. She rushed to me with a damp cloth to wipe the kohl smeared around my eyes and on my cheeks.

'Go!'

I arrived in the audience chamber feeling like I had been dragged from a tavern. With as much dignity as I could muster, I took my place in the centre of the long table surrounded by my justiciars. I received some odd glances; I am usually immaculate. The proceedings of the morning began – the usual neighbourly disputes about estate borders, a ramming of a fishing boat by a disgruntled fellow fisherman about fishing rights, sheep steeling, poaching, and lastly, my cousin Nanette, abbess of the Convent of Mary Magdalen, who was requesting alms for yet another relic.

By the time Nanette put her case to me, my humour had deserted me. I needed fresh air. I questioned her about the validity of the relic. She did not appreciate my query and asked in a petulant tone, if I thought she had conjured it out of her imagination.

'Not at all.'

Nanette intoned it had been brought back from the Holy Land, the toe, ear or some other body part of an obscure saint guaranteed to heal every ague from warts to ingrown toenails. Louis had sworn an oath on another piece of saint ending in the incineration of Vitry-sur-Marne and all its inhabitants. I shook my head.

As she was waxing lyrical in some sort of spiritual trance, I stopped her. I told her in Antioch bits of dead crusaders, even Saracens, were sold in the Suq to returning crusaders as cure-alls for God knows what ailments. Some made quite a profit selling them on to gullible souls who thought their lives would be saved from whatever pestilence was fashionable. I said I needed more proof about the authenticity of her relic and from whence it came before I was going to waste alms that could be used for worthier causes.

Nanette, my holier than thou cousin, and I have never seen eye to eye, so I should not have been surprised at the backlash.

'What would you know, you wanton slut? It is no wonder King Louis annulled your marriage. Incest was it not? "Harlot of Paris" must be high on your list of titles.'

My justiciars froze in their chairs. With a low growl, I rose to my imperious height. I told her to get out. She would not get a sou. Nanette stormed towards the exit almost knocking down Henry as he galloped in exuding youth and vitality, full of confidence.

Without drawing breath, he besought my panel of stunned justiciars and Guillaume if he could have the hand of Lady Eleanor, Duchess of Aquitaine, in marriage.

Vesuvius erupted.

'What! Do you think I am incapable of answering for myself? If you want to marry *them*, so be it!'

My arm swept in a furious arc. I pushed back my chair with such violence it crashed to the floor. I shoved Henry out of the way. The door of the chamber slammed. I ran. My veil and coronet bounced together on the floor as my hastily pinned hair tumbled about my shoulders. I heard Guillaume's voice.

'Lord Henry, stop! Let Her Ladyship go. It will be for the best to wait till tempers are calmed.'

***

What came over me after I had been so abandoned with Henry last night, I cannot explain. Nanette caused part of my outburst, but as I sit trying to understand myself, I realise I am in the middle of a personal crisis. I have come plummeting to earth after the euphoria of escaping the misery of Île de France. The terror of my near-abduction, and the sickening smell of Thierry de Gervais' blood, have catapulted me into reality. I must remarry. I have no choice.

Chapter 14. Tigress Marries Lion

My freedom is slipping from my grasp.

After I ran from the audience chamber, I ended up at the archery range. In fury, I attacked the targets, hitting bull after bull. Henry arrived behind me. He said something I comprehended not. I turned, the last arrow whizzed past him and thudded into a tree behind his head. He roared I could have taken his ear off. I snarled back if I had wanted to do that, I would not have missed. I flung the bow and quiver to the ground, and I pushed past him.

'Milady.'

His voice bellowed, harsh with anger.

'I wish to speak with you.'

I hoisted my gown and ran away from the range, away from the palace, down a forested track to the remnants of an old Roman embankment. I collapsed onto a log, a favourite seat since childhood polished grey from climbing shoes and weather. My breath came in gulps as suppressed tears were released. I was angry with everyone – Henry, Louis, Geoffrey, even Abraham but, above all, myself. With frustration, I pushed back the tangled hair and tried to pin it.

Henry's deep voice behind me interrupted my self-pity.

'Go away!'

'No.'

He sat beside me. I was too tired to bolt. I poked at my hair, pushing it behind an ear. It fell back. With surprising tenderness, Henry tucked the matted strand away.

'Come here.'

The anger had gone out of his voice. I was sniffing, dishevelled. He put his arms around me, pulling me to his muscular chest. He said nothing, I could not. How long we remained like that, I know not. Eventually, he wanted to know why I had given him a night he could only dream about, full of uninhibited passion, when today I appeared to hate him. I said last night was a test.

He dropped his arms to look me in the eye, puzzled.

'For whom?'

'As it turned out, for both of us.'

'Well! I think I deserve an explanation.'

I stared at my hands; blisters were forming from the bow string because I had not donned gloves. I said I wanted to be compatible with my next husband.

'By your reaction today, do you consider we are not?'

'On the contrary, you passed with flying colours. I hope I did, too.'

'Then why will not you marry me?'

'Because – because you have not asked…me.'

With a frustrated exhalation of air, Henry began to fume again. I told him I had drawn up a nuptial agreement. Unless any future husband consents, and signs it, I will never be his wife.

His penetrating eyes drilled into mine as he demanded, 'Where does love come into this?'

Henry leapt up and began to pace, infuriating me. I erupted again.

'LOVE!'

I thundered I knew his father had sent him to woo me for no other reason than for my dowry; told to make haste in case I was carried off by some other ambitious adventurer.

'I am not for sale, *'enri Plantagenet-a*!'

The angrier I became the thicker was my Langue d'Oeil. Henry was taken aback. I think this was the first time he had met a woman who spoke her mind. I reminded him about his aspirations should he become King of England, how he was going to need a fortune to get the beleaguered country back on its feet as well as considerable diplomacy to get the warring factions to unite behind him. Without drawing breath, I ranted, I knew what it was like not to be consulted, to be treated as an ornament. Moreover, I was not a jousting trophy to be put on a pedestal!

'If you want me to be your queen, I expect to be treated with the respect that status deserves. Nor do I want my intelligence insulted. I am not a brainless milkmaid.'

His face had gone quite a furious red. Henry would not keep still, which was making me giddy. He stamped up and

Chapter 14. Tigress Marries Lion

down, saying maybe it was true, but when he met me, he was captivated. Never had he been so attracted to a woman. He found me enchanting, fascinating, beautiful. He wanted to marry me for those reasons, my dowry was no longer of importance. Last night confirmed his love. He thought I felt the same, but now he concluded this was not so, he was mistaken.

We had reached a stalemate. I begged him to sit down or keep still. I told him I had no idea how I felt about him. I did not dislike him. In the short time I have known him, I have discovered him to be more mature, more erudite than expected and his curiosity about life intriguing; also, he was mightily attractive. I had been afraid the difference in our ages would be a barrier but not any more.

I apologised for my emotional outburst. My oh-so-saintly cousin had called me a harlot, which hurt. I added that the months since I left Île de France had been a joyous relief, but my vulnerability as a single woman I found infuriating and hard to accept. I stated I did not appreciate him asking the men who serve me for my hand in marriage when I can answer for myself. I insisted he read the marriage document I have prepared. Afterwards we can talk again. I emphasised he should ask Sir Robert to read it too for his advice.

I stood to leave. I needed to bathe and have my maids do something with my hair.

***

Brushing my hair out was painful. It was full of knots. Amaris kept apologising, which was equally painful. I had to curb my tongue. Now wearing another gown and clean, the library did not give me its usual solace. What a morning! God's teeth, I felt like I was back in the turmoil of Paris.

I did not see Henry for several hours. It would not surprise me if he took to his horse. The document I have drawn up is, I think, fair but it asks a lot of any man. As my husband, he will have all the usual rights to the Aquitaine, its manpower and its produce, but its treasury only if I agree and which I must countersign. The duchy this time will be ruled jointly until any heir I have reaches a suitable age. Should I die before my husband, he will have regency till the child is of an age of maturity. My Chatellerault uncle, Ralph de Faye my mother's brother, will act as regent during my husband's and my absences from my lands and he and Jerome will act as councils when necessary. I have already spoken to both. My husband will have the usual titles, and vassals will be expected to pay homage. To add to this, my future husband will have to agree any children we have will *not* be removed from my care. I will bring up my children till I deem they are old enough to leave my household.

I did not mention Grandmother Dangerosa's treasury. That is my insurance.

***

Without telling anyone, I took myself for a walk to the folly. The scent of last night's love hung in the air. I lay down and fell asleep, mentally and physically drained.

No one could find me. The palace was searched high and low, the herbarium, perfumery and gardens and anywhere else Renée, Guillaume and guards could think to look. The stable had the correct compliment of horses, so they knew I had not gone riding. Henry and Sir Robert joined the search. At last Henry thought of trying the folly. No one else had given it attention because I had shut the door. Henry found me asleep and sent Sir Robert back to tell the palace it could calm down.

He awoke me by arousing my senses in a most sensual way. He proposed to me, saying he would sign the nuptial agreement with his blood if necessary. Simply, I said yes. We locked the door of the folly.

***

We returned to Poitiers. We did not summon the world to our wedding. Protocol dictates I should have asked permission from the overlord of the Duchy of Aquitaine

Chapter 14. Tigress Marries Lion

for me to remarry, and that being Louis, it would have been refused. We were married by the Bishop in the Cathedral of Saint Pierre.

The gown I wore was a sunset of gold silk, glittering with jewels. My young husband wore a simple white tunic. I did not wear the *Knot of Hercules*. It is among my possessions, but I cannot bear to open the chest, nor did I think it appropriate.

Henry slipped the simple gold ring on my finger. After we were pronounced man and wife, Henry wrapped me in an amorous embrace. We had the shortest wedding banquet in history. We re-consummated our togetherness, no longer committing a sin. This was the first time I had woken in the morning with a man beside me. Louis mostly bolted, and my lovers and I had to part to keep our trysts secret. Being awakened by Henry was both a delight and a curious experience. I thought maybe it was the exuberance of youth my young husband was so physically desirous of me. I have since discovered this happened every morning. Interesting!

This morning, though, before I was primped and preened, I was heaving my breakfast in the privy. Counting back from today to the night in the folly was about six weeks. I have missed my cycle. What is it they say about full moons and fertility? In the meantime, I will keep my suspicions to myself for as long as possible.

***

Our progress around my lands of the Aquitaine, Poitou and Gascony to introduce my new husband as my Duke was interesting. Many of my vassals were suspicious of Henry. They feared he will rob them of income, or tax them unfairly to pay for his incursions into England to regain sovereignty. Others were willing to give Henry a little more respect. After all, he was everything Louis was not – athletic, fun loving, enjoying the company of robust men. Henry is good at hunting, jousting, singing and playing the lute. He can converse with all people from bishops to simple peasants. His only downfall is his fiery and unpredictable temper which make many wary. I heard he has been known to throw himself on the ground and writhe in a tantrum like a child. Well, he will only behave like that once with me. I will treat such episodes the way Papa or Renée did with Nilla and me when small, by walking out. No audience, no point!

Henry is wildly demonstrative, which at times is embarrassing, but I am enjoying his attention. Having a moment to myself, though, is hard to find. If I sit down to write, he seeks me out. Worse, he wants to see what I have penned. He is suspicious because I still write in Greek. What I record is none of his business. I told him as much, which he did not like. At times, he can be quite petulant.

So far, we have both managed to keep our tempers in check. I find I cannot remain cross with him for long. He makes me laugh so much with his jests. Where I could not get Louis into my bed, Henry I cannot keep out. I am enjoying being able to sleep the night with him beside me, snuggled up in his arms, a tangle of legs. Apart from having to sneak out in the morning with this early queasiness, I have few complaints. Renée and Amaris are mightily suspicious. However, neither of them, have said anything – yet.

***

While staying the night at one of my estates, Henry was visited by an old acquaintance. While they were quaffing ale and enjoying themselves, I had some privacy to catch up with my journal without Henry peering over my shoulder. When the candles were getting low, I returned to my bed chamber, where I found Henry pacing. He demanded to know in an abrupt manner where I had been. I presented my inky fingers. Then out of the blue, he asked had I had an affair with his father. Thank God in the candlelight he would not have noticed my face pale. I swallowed; my heart skipped a beat. I kept my voice steady; I asked where he had heard the rumour. He told me it was for him to know. I took a deep breath. There was no way I could use seduction to get out of this sticky situation. I had to use my wits.

Chapter 14. Tigress Marries Lion

'My marriage to Louis, as I have explained, was joyless, a misery. On Île de France, I was considered nothing or a witch, depending on which depraved cleric was prattling. I was lonely and unhappy. On two very separate occasions, I fell in love. Both affairs are over and in the past. On the rack, I will never disclose their names. All the rumours you hear about my supposed debauchery say I went to bed with every man in Christendom, including the Pope. If you want to believe those tales, so be it. I have nothing more to say, except, I will treat your illegitimate son as my own. Geoffrey, I believe you named him. Now I intend to go to my bed, you may join me if you desire, otherwise I wish you goodnight.'

Silence hung in the air.

I called for one of my maids to help me undress. Marion obliged. Henry watched from the shadows. He said nothing in reply to my address. After I climbed into bed, his boots hit the floor followed by the swish of his garments from his cape to his hose. His chilly body snuggled against mine. He growled into my neck he did not care about my past love life so long as it was not his father. I shut his mouth with mine and breathed a guilty sigh of relief. He declared how much he loved me.

And what of me, Eleanor of Aquitaine, what are my feelings towards my young husband? He is likeable, but love? I know not.

***

Our journey allowed us to spend a few days with Raoul and Petronilla. She has had another child, a little girl; maybe we can compare notes. Henry and I were slowly making our way north to Normandy towards Rouen, something which I was not relishing. Geoffrey was still in a corner of my heart. I tucked Epsilon and Gamma amongst my jewellery at the last moment; I could not leave them behind.

It was such a pleasure to be reunited with Nilla and Raoul. My sister and brother-in-law approved of Henry, a relief. I told Nilla my feelings for Henry were uncertain, but

I hoped my marriage of necessity was going to blossom into something. The child to be is a joy. Nilla was pleased for my sake.

***

While Henry was out hawking with Raoul, Sir Robert and others, a knight arrived, his horse practically dropping under him. Nilla came looking for me, concerned. I followed her to Henry's quarters where a young man was pacing, looking most anxious. He wanted to know when Lord Henry would be returning. As I was not sure, I asked if I could be of assistance. He must have decided he could trust Henry's new wife because he thrust into my hands a wrinkled missive. The seal was new to me. The young man, Sir Luke, said it was from Empress Matilda, Henry's mother, therefore I was reluctant to open it. I asked if he knew what news it contained.

'The contents are most urgent. Lord Henry must return to Rouen in all haste. His father, Lord Geoffrey, is gravely ill. It is thought he may not live.'

Thank God I was seated; had I been standing I am sure I would have fainted. Sir Luke did not notice the change in my demeanour but Nilla did. How much she suspected of my affair with Geoffrey I know not, but she would have heard rumours. She called for a page who quickly brought refreshments. My body felt drained of substance. I gulped the beverage, not knowing what it was. I started to tremble, and perspiration broke out on my forehead. Nilla had the presence of mind to ask the page to accompany Sir Luke to the stables where the grooms would have a better idea of when the hunters would return.

She sent for Renée, pushed my head between my knees and rubbed my shoulders. Renée ran to my side. She had suspected my pregnancy for some time. Nilla received a frosty glare.

'You know! Why have you colluded to keep Elea's condition secret?'

I sat up. Nilla was about to answer when I stopped her. I told Renée I wanted nobody to know until I was certain myself, and not Henry. She reminded me I could not keep it from him forever, and what is more, he had a right to know. Both, thank heaven, interpreted my shock was due to the baby.

Renée and Nilla helped me to my quarters, where I demanded to be left alone. In my bed chamber, I sobbed into my pillow with an aching heart. No matter how hard I tried to push Geoffrey into the past, he returned to me too often through Henry – a cheeky smile, a twinkle in his eye, the turn of Henry's head in the half-light of a candle. Dear God in heaven, do not let him die, do not take him till I see him at least one more time.

The clattering of hooves dragged me to the window as the hunting party careened into the stable yard. Footsteps thundered upstairs to our wing. Henry ran into my arms, sliding to the floor on his knees, his face buried in my waist. I held him, entwining my fingers in his dishevelled curls. He was no longer the brash young jouster, the tavern brawler, but a vulnerable son. I let him weep, trying not to sob with him. After I helped him to his feet, and sat him down, I asked him when he wanted to leave for Rouen. He wanted to go immediately. Evening was approaching so I asked him to wait till cockcrow the following morn. But he was determined. I said I would follow on the morrow so as not to slow him down. No, he wanted me to accompany him. I warned him I did not know how skilled I would be riding through the night. His answer was I could ride better than most men. He was adamant and in no mood to argue.

Renée threw a fit. She wanted to confront Henry. One of the few times in my life, I over-ruled her. She was not happy. Neither was Nilla. Lucille, who is an excellent horsewoman, was to accompany me.

***

Dressed warmly, with hooded, fur-lined cape and gloves,

thick hose and high chamois boots, I set off with Henry and a large contingent of my guards and Henry's men. The most adept rode in front with flared torches. I was mounted on a sturdy mare whose stamina would carry me through the night to a monastery outside Angers in Anjou. How I did not fall from my horse with exhaustion, I know not.

The good, kind monks took us in, gave us a simple meal of bread and cheese and looked to our horses. There was little heating, so we wore our capes to keep warm. We only had a few hours' sleep before we were on our way again. We travelled two leagues before stopping to stretch our legs. I vomited as discreetly as I could behind a tree, away from the men. As Renée, damn her, had related my condition to Lucille, I was causing her undue worry. Henry, back with the horses, called to hurry while I retched and heaved. All I could do was rinse my mouth and stagger to be hoisted into the saddle. Henry noticed my pallor. I said I was a little tired.

Chapter 15. Burying Gamma and Epsilon

Never have I been so relieved to arrive at a destination. The massive Norman castle at Rouen reared ahead of us. It was a forbidding-looking edifice. Henry is proud of its almost impenetrable fortifications, its sturdy stone walls, moat, portcullis and defensive inner and outer baileys. We clattered over the drawbridge into this protected centre of the castle. Henry leapt from his horse and helped me down. I managed to stay upright. Henry wanted to go straight to his father's bedside. His steward came running, apologising because he was not expecting us so soon. I was surprised there was no welcoming party. Henry gave orders for Lucille and me to be taken to our quarters and asked where his mother was. The steward explained she had been forced to ride to Gisors on the Vexin border with Normandy because of a problem with rebellious vassals and Henry's younger brother, Geoffrey, who had fallen into some sort of trouble on his way back to Rouen. Henry snorted in disgust. I gather there is little love lost between the two brothers. I remembered in horror young Geoffrey had designs to capture me after my divorce. I wondered if Henry was aware of the incident.

As I plodded up the spiral staircase, I was feeling despondent. With all my heart I wanted to visit Geoffrey, but Henry insisted I rest as my weariness was obvious. I would have to wait. I was relieved Matilda was away. I was not looking forward to meeting my formidable mother-in-law. Geoffrey's description of his wife had not been flattering. He called her a harridan.

Lucille and I were led to our quarters. To my dismay, I was confronted with wall to wall rushes. Before we learnt about Geoffrey's illness, Henry and I had sent Byzantium carpets from Poitiers, to be placed in our quarters in Rouen.

All rushes were to be removed and burnt and the floors thoroughly scrubbed ready for the new coverings. The floors were not, we had stressed, to be recovered with new rushes, not even scented.

I wanted to bathe and lie down flat, but I stomped back to the bailey, where I would remain until the rushes were removed, the floors cleaned and my carpets, wherever they were, laid. Lucille offered to supervise. A page was sent to Henry. He went pale one minute and red with rage the next; furious our wishes had been ignored and furious with me for not being more flexible.

I tried to calm the situation by asking after his father. Henry replied he was rambling a bit, and he did not look at all well. He told Henry he was pleased he had arrived home. Henry left me alone, which was what I wanted and needed. Did Geoffrey know I was here?

The steward came with a chair and apologised for the misunderstanding about the rushes. With the Lady Empress being called away, and Lord Henry arriving ahead of when he was expected, the churls had not been supervised, therefore had not done what was ordered. As an expert in detecting the art of prevarication, I suspected Henry's and my wishes had been misconstrued on purpose. I sat and waited. The sun at least was warm in the enclosed confines of the bailey.

Lucille reappeared. All was ready. I inspected the various rooms of my quarters, now to my satisfaction. There was a cheerful brazier burning, Lucille had ordered a tub of steaming water, my bed was readied for me. I let myself be pampered.

***

Someone had thought about my love for writing. I found a table near the window bearing ink, quills and parchment aplenty. It had to be Geoffrey, so he knows I have accompanied Henry, who wants to be with his father as much as possible. I was feeling quite rested now and would have loved to sit with him, but I have not been asked.

Chapter 15. Burying Gamma and Epsilon

As I was about to put away my quill when Henry came in agitated. He had received a letter from his mother, requesting his help. His younger brother is in a lot of trouble or, as Henry says, more likely causing it. His mother wants his aid. Henry must set off on the morrow for Gisors. He is leaving me in charge. Renée and the rest of my maids will be arriving some time before noon today. Meanwhile, Henry's dear old nurse, Maud, has been most kind; another Renée.

We ate together. Henry was pouring his heart out. He was afraid of Geoffrey dying. The responsibilities to fall on his shoulders would be onerous and, although he will have his mother for guidance, the thought of becoming Duke of Normandy was causing him concern. I was silent. His mother for guidance? The words clawed through my gut.

'So, as your wife, and the next Duchess of Normandy, I will be superfluous?'

My hackles were up like a spitting cat. I strode to the door adjoining our chambers, telling him he had better sleep in his own bed as he seemed to have no further use for me.

Henry was now pleading.

'Elea, you know I want you to help, but *Maman* has been running Normandy for years during father's many absences. It would be foolish not to seek her advice.'

'Indeed? Then it is time she retired. What is more, who gave you permission to call me Elea?'

'Jesus, Mary and Joseph!'

He stormed to the door, but he did not pass through. He grabbed me, pulling me to him.

'It has been days,'

He pulled at my gown. It was no use struggling. Henry is no slender Louis who I was equal to in Jerusalem; he is as strong as an ox. His honed dagger sliced through my lacings. I clawed at him with my nails. We fought like two animals. Clothes went everywhere. By the time he had flung me and himself on the bed, we were both so aroused it was inevitable what happened next. My fingers were laced in his hair as I dragged his head to my breasts. How eager, how desirable, under the roof of my dying lover, his son and I moaned our coitus for all to hear.

***

In some respects, farewelling Henry as he set off for Gisors was a relief – I will get some sleep for a start – but I will miss his maddening energy, his quick mind.

It was time for my first visit to Geoffrey. Renée had arrived, so I took her along because I did not trust myself to be alone with him. I was puzzled why he was not being cared for in his quarters, but in a small chamber adjoining the gallery leading from the bailey. Maybe it was too difficult to carry him to the first floor when he became ill.

When Renée and I entered the room, we were overwhelmed by the fetid odour of illness, unclean linens and stale urine. In my present condition, I was forced dry retching from the chamber. I leant my head against the cool stone wall of the gallery, trying not to vomit. It was like old King Louis all over again. How could they do this to him? Why, oh why? Rage overcame my queasy stomach. I returned to the chamber. The family physician, pages, churls and his so-called noble attendants received a tongue lashing. I demanded to be told why the Duke of Normandy was being kept in this parlous state when he was so ill. Mangy curs, I stormed, were housed in better conditions. They reeled at my outburst, grovelling in a babble of voices. Renée, also disgusted by Geoffrey's predicament, wanted to know who was in charge. The ancient family physician shuffled forward. Both of us rounded on him. Behind us a husky, wheezing chortling interrupted Renée's and my tirades.

'Eleanor of Aquitaine, you have not lost the fire in your spleen, one bit. Has not that son of mine tamed you a jot?'

I hoped the pity on my face was masked by my fury. I promised him I would get him out of that hell hole. I left Renée in charge. I grabbed a hapless page by the ear and ordered him to take me to Lord Geoffrey's bed chamber. He scuttled up the stone, circular stairway with me following.

Chapter 15. Burying Gamma and Epsilon

Geoffrey's bed chamber was vast and draughty, but it did possess braziers. Like on Île de France, there were cracked panes in the narrow windows. What is it with these people that they cannot repair broken glass?

The floor was covered in filthy rushes. Without further ado, I ordered a battalion of churls to clean the chamber, to get rid of and burn the rushes and to light fires in the braziers. Next, I had Amaris accompany me with my Praetorian Guard out of the castle to the Jewish quarter of Rouen. Her Hebrew is better than mine. Between the two of us, we would get our needs across.

Our arrival caused quite a stir. We were, I think, the first noblewomen to set foot in this area of the city. I asked a young man if he would take us to the Rabbi. His surprise we spoke Hebrew was written on his face. We were taken to the house of a man with a gentle demeanour. We introduced ourselves and the Rabbi invited us in. Amaris and I explained we needed an excellent physician: someone skilled in apothecary, a man like Isaac was who I had in mind. He said his nephew could be the type of person we were looking for, as he was well qualified in the arts of medicine. I asked to meet him, and he was sent for. While waiting we were served a spiced tisane, so reminiscent of Antioch.

A man of about thirty years appeared. His name is Matthias. He spoke excellent Langue d'Oeil, so interviewing him was easy. Matthias appeared knowledgeable and answered my probing questions in a learned manner. He impressed me. When I told him who his patient would be, he replied it would be an honour to take care of the duke, who was loved and respected in their community. I asked Matthias to present himself at the castle after the noon day bells.

I asked the Rabbi if he could recommend merchants for carpets and tapestries, as well as a glazier. He directed me to the river docks for the merchants and to artisans in the Christian community for the repair work needed for the windows. By the time I returned to the castle, I had been successful, though my personal coffers were a little leaner. I am pleased I had the foresight to bring a reasonable purse with me from Poitiers. At least I cannot be accused of robbing the Norman treasury.

A day that started so full of anger and sorrow, ended well. By mid-afternoon, I had sent the old physician to his home with a pension and installed Matthias. A procession of carts carried carpets and tapestries up the winding road and across the moat. Geoffrey's bed chamber floor was re-covered with splendid rugs from Byzantium, and the draughts blocked by colourful tapestries depicting the tales from the Odyssey. The dreaded rushes were burning in a pyre away from the castle, along with the contents of the filthy chamber Geoffrey had been enduring. Geoffrey's barber had attended to his hair, beard and nails. He had been bathed, dressed in clean linen, his bed sores attended to and reinstated in his bed chamber warmed by glowing braziers The windowpanes remained cracked but would be replaced as soon as the glaziers had suitable glass cut to fit them.

By evening, I was tired but satisfied. I fed Geoffrey the delicious chicken broth Renée had the cooks prepare. As I wiped his mouth, he took my hand. His penetrating eyes might be weary, but the sparkle was still there. I extracted myself from his grip and shooed all who had been helping away. Back beside his bed, I sat out of his reach. Regardless of the temptation, I was not going to be lured into any intimacy with him. He asked how I found Henry, and did I love him.

'I find him…likable. More so than I expected.'

Geoffrey, with a slight catch in his voice, switched to Greek. Henry had brought tears to his eyes by the earnestness of his love for me.

'I am jealous.'

I know Geoffrey was desperate for me to say I returned Henry's affection with the same intensity. Yet I remained silent with my fingers stretched across my tiny bulge, a gesture not missed by his father.

'Do I suspect a child?'

Chapter 15. Burying Gamma and Epsilon

'Maybe.'

'It could be mine.'

His eyes twinkled. I snapped,

'If so, by now I would have given birth, not just a few weeks into my condition.'

'So, you are?'

God's teeth I needed to watch my tongue. I begged Geoffrey to say naught because I had not the chance to inform Henry yet. It was time to get out of there. He gestured round his chamber; before I reached the door, he said,

'Thank you for all this, my darling'.

I closed the door with a gentle click, and beckoned Matthias who was waiting outside.

'Tell me, what ails Lord Geoffrey? Is it possible he will be well again?'

Matthias told me there was a canker deep inside his Lordship only God could cure. He said he can keep Lord Geoffrey comfortable and reduce his pain, which will prolong his life, but we must be prepared that one day God will call him to his side.

The good night's sleep I was hoping for has ended with me burning candles to waxy puddles, as I recorded today's events. I find I am missing Henry.

***

The panes of glass in Geoffrey's bed chamber were now repaired. The chamber was warm and cosy. The tapestries, he said, when I was not at his side, gave him much pleasure. I have been reading to him from the Odyssey. He told me looking at the walls as I read took him inside the epic as if he was part of the saga. I was so pleased, although I feel a little like Odysseus' wife, poor Penelope, left behind to fend off unwanted suitors.

All who were tending Geoffrey were more comfortable, too. The balms, and ointments prescribed by Matthias were improving the sores on his body. Geoffrey had lost much weight, but his appetite had improved with some colour returning to his hollow cheeks. Geoffrey whispered to me it was my presence that had improved his health, but I must remain aloof. It would be folly to allow our love to rekindle. As I expect Henry's child, my loyalty must be to him.

***

About an hour ago, I received news from Henry. He should arrive in Rouen by the morrow with his mother and brother. To be honest, I was not looking forward to meeting either. Overhearing some knights gossiping (how familiar), I heard young Geoffrey is a nasty character. There was intense rivalry between the two older brothers for their mother's and father's attention. Henry is very much the preferred son. There is another brother William, the youngest in the family. He is being brought up by their aunt Sybilla, their father's sister.

Henry said he would like to hasten, but their mother is getting on in years. As Geoffrey is much younger than Matilda, it saddens me he should be the one afflicted. Matilda and Geoffrey have never loved each other and do not get along, their marriage being one of political convenience. What Matilda thinks of me, I have yet to discover. I do not believe she approved of Henry marrying me, except for the dowry of course. When she discovers I have equal control over the treasury, she will not be pleased at all. Geoffrey said once, she is very stingy with her inheritances.

***

Before the noon day bells rang out from the cathedral, a herald galloped into the castle, announcing Lord Henry and his party were but a half hour away. I was veiled and wearing the crown of Aquitaine. It was prudent to be formal for my first encounter with Empress Matilda. As the weather was cooler, I wore a deep indigo velvet gown. My maids had recently stitched golden lions about its hem, my girdle had them rampant along its length. My veil was pinned with a brooch fashioned like Henry's golden broom flower, the

Chapter 15. Burying Gamma and Epsilon

planta genista. Celeste said I looked suitably Norman, except for the crown. I retorted,

'They cannot have all of me.'

I made my way down the stairs into the bailey as Henry leapt from his horse. I was enveloped in his arms; lifted off my feet. So much for careful dressing. By the time he had put me down, crown, and veil were all askew. He was grinning from ear to ear. He crushed me to him kissing me far too passionately, I thought, in front of his mother.

'*Maman*, may I introduce you to the most beautiful woman in all of Christendom, my wife Lady Eleanor, Duchess of Aquitaine.'

I managed to adjust my crown. I bowed my head slightly. She may title herself Empress, but the Aquitaine holds suzerainty over Normandy. However, I needed to be polite. Matilda looked formidable, stern in her heavy veil and wimple. Not a strand of hair was visible, maybe it is grey. I would say she had been handsome in her youth, with strong features. I spoke Latin, she answered me in Langue d'Oeil. I was introduced to young Geoffrey. He looked at me as if I were a piece of sweetmeat, his tongue sliding over his lopsided sneer.

Henry asked after his father. I explained he was a little better since I had taken the liberty to return him to his bed chamber where he was more comfortable. Unless Empress Matilda and the Lords Henry and Geoffrey wished to bathe or change their riding habits, I would be happy to escort them into the Duke of Normandy's presence.

Henry leaned over and whispered softly in my ear he would prefer I went to my chamber. He would visit his father and be with me anon.

'Before you leave, you need to know I have made a few other changes which have improved Lord Duke Geoffrey's health.'

Matilda eyed me with suspicion.

'I have retired the household physician and employed a younger man, more knowledgeable in medicine and apothecary.'

'What!'

Matilda looked as if she had been slapped. She took two strides to face me, difficult because she barely reached my shoulder. I said he had been killing the Duke who was in such a parlous state, in such discomfort, something had to be done, and I was not about to let him die in front of me. Henry was impatient.

'If our father has improved, we cannot complain about something that should have been done years ago.'

He called his brother and they strode off.

Matilda hissed at me like a viper,

'You will pay for this, you whore.'

Sneering down my haughty nose, I hissed back,

'Why? Because I have prolonged his life, when perhaps you want him dead?'

She stormed off. Wait till she sees the tapestries and rugs!

I was pleased to go to my chamber where I removed the veil and crown. I found my hairbrush, undid the decorative plaits and started brushing my long locks. Marion and Lucille popped their heads in, asking if they could help.

'Not unless you want to see me ravished by a rampant lion.'

They turned scarlet and bolted.

A short time later, Henry hurtled into my chamber, greeting me with a querulous,

'You are still dressed!'

I told him he could have the honour of removing my gown but if he cut my lacings, he could weave the next ones. Being undressed, kissed and fondled at the same time was something to experience. He smelt a little of horse combined with a manly odour I found sensual. I was going to have to tell him about my condition, but not yet, in case he had some old-fashioned religious ideas about laying with me.

Henry was on his back with a look of smug satisfaction on his face. I was snuggled into the crook of his arm with one arm across his chest. My hair always gets in the way. As I was attempting to pull strands out from under his shoulder, I told him I had something of import to tell him.

Chapter 15. Burying Gamma and Epsilon

'Ah! You have put tapestries of Roman orgies in *Maman*'s apartments.'

I ignored his ribaldry and told him I was expecting a child. He sat bolt upright, jumped out of bed and started leaping and shouting with joy. The look of him naked with part of his anatomy jiggling and swinging had me crying with laughter. Next, he leapt onto the bed wanting to know what was so funny. I could not stop laughing. I managed to splutter I was happy he was overjoyed. He scooped me into his arms, yelling he had to tell everyone.

'Not disporting yourself like that I hope.'

He became serious. When? I told him six to six and a half months' time. He wanted to know why I had said naught to him. I replied I had been ready to tell him on several occasions, but each time there was a crisis in our lives, and I did not wish to worry him further. He became most serious, gently stroking and kissing my rounding stomach. I am beginning to feel a certain tenderness towards Henry.

***

As I expected, Matilda was furious with what she called my 'interference' in the running of the castle, claiming with disgust I had turned her husband's quarters into a bordello. I retorted I would have to bow to her experience, because I had never been in one. That set her back a peg. She tried another tack. There were more important necessities than tapestries and carpets, along with the cost of the amount of wood being burned in Geoffrey's braziers. I replied, I found it most odd she wanted to deny Henry's sick father comfort.

I am afraid Henry was having to extinguish smouldering coals of hostility between his mother and me. She was most suspicious about my past with Geoffrey. She has not directly accused me of being his mistress, but I feared she was biding her time. I was forced to spend fewer moments at his bedside. Renée kept me abreast of his condition. Between doing his mother's bidding, Henry spent as many hours with his father as possible. Matilda has him on a string.

Young Geoffrey was a fractious nuisance, either upsetting his father and mother or arguing with Henry. Sir Robert said it was forever thus. I did not like the way young Geoffrey looked at me, a sly, lascivious, narrow-eyed stare. He is tall, leaner than Henry, fair-haired, with icy blue eyes. I found his presence disconcerting. He can appear out of nowhere, or one finds him loitering in corners, staring. I am making sure I am never alone with him. I do not trust him.

***

Henry and I had finished dining with Matilda, a somewhat frosty repast with little said between us. Matilda has given no sign of pleasure at the thought of becoming a granddame. I ate little as usual with Henry chivvying me, I was starving our child. In the end the atmosphere ground me down. I begged to take my leave. I was tired. Henry also excused himself to go to his father's bedside. I exited the chamber faster than a greyhound, so as not to be left in Matilda's clutches. I hurried to my quarters. As I approached, young Geoffrey slid in front of my door. He stood there with a slack-lipped leer on his lean, pale face. I stepped back from his reach, demanded he get out of my way. His sibilant snigger made the hairs on my neck stand on end. He whispered, as I liked Plantagenet men, why not try him for a change. My hand closed over my stiletto. Again, I insisted he let me pass or his brother would hear of this intrusion.

'My brother would be far more interested in your affair with our father. It is amazing what you two got up to, very athletic. Those flies on the wall on Île de France were most explicit.'

'And you, you little piece of dog's turd, have a vivid imagination, and can lie in your teeth.'

I knew he was bluffing, he had no proof, but he could cause trouble between Henry and me. He saw the flash of my blade, aware if he tried anything, I could seriously hurt him. As luck would have it, Amaris appeared from the other direction. I yelled at him to move or by Lucifer his pretty face

Chapter 15. Burying Gamma and Epsilon

would not be pretty for much longer. He slunk off. Amaris quickened her pace. I was shaking, my heart pounding as she opened the chamber door for me. I made her lock it before recounting what took place. I was feeling ill. Apart from Henry, the atmosphere within the castle is brittle. I long for my peaceful home.

***

Young Geoffrey took himself into Rouen to carouse in a tavern with some like-minded squires and was now sleeping off his indulgences. Henry and Matilda had duties to perform with their justiciars while trying to keep vigils beside Geoffrey's bedside. I took the opportunity to spend a few hours with his father.

Matthias and Renée are concerned he is finding it more difficult to eat and is in pain. His stomach is mightily distended. I brought a copy of *The Iliad* with me. I asked in Greek how he was. He fumbled for my hand, bringing it to his lips. This time I did not pull away, but gently disengaged his feeble grip, putting my hand on his forehead. It was clammy. He had a fever. I asked Renée for some tepid lavender water to bathe Geoffrey's forehead. As I did so, I whispered what had eventuated between young Geoffrey and me. His father assured me the boy was bluffing. He had never been to Paris and, as far as Geoffrey knew, had no acquaintances there. He said the accusations probably came from Matilda, with his middle son wanting to cause trouble. Satisfied, I told him I thought I was growing closer to Henry. He smiled with delight.

I am trying to put the inevitability of Geoffrey's end to the back of my mind. He is surrounded by clergy and his closest companions. His sister Sybilla and young William have been summoned and will arrive any day soon from Sybilla's estates near Angers. We are all devoting as much time as we can at his bedside.

I was able to spend the morning with Geoffrey. I am weighing up where my emotions lie. I love Geoffrey, except now my love is more for a parent, like Papa. The man lying so ill in his bed has become someone to be tended, not someone I once desired. After he fell into a restless sleep, I left to record events. I have also attempted a few baby garments. Henry is pleased, I think, to find I was beginning to stitch little gowns. What knowledge he has of such things, I know not, but he seemed proud of my humble efforts. As he is worried about his father, I decided not to relate what happened between me and his brother.

***

Henry and I are exhausted. He has hardly left his father's side but needed sleep with instructions to Sir Robert to call him if necessary.

Towards morning, we were awoken by Sir Robert's panic-stricken voice calling Henry. I struggled from Henry's arms while attempting to cover my filmy shift. I shook Henry with dread in my guts. He jerked upright from the twisted bedlinen aware something was amiss. Sir Robert's voice, thick with emotion, urged Henry to hasten to his father's bedside. Henry fell out of bed, grabbed his gown from the floor along with his shoes and flew out the door. By now, Lucille and Amaris were at my side, followed by Celeste and Marion. In the early morning chill, I searched for my chamois slippers. I found them, trying to put them on as I ran. One of my maids threw a cape around my shoulders. I tore down the long gallery towards Geoffrey's bed chamber.

Priests chanted while incense wafted over nuns as they murmured the rosary. I arrived at the end of Geoffrey's bed and clung to its carved wooden foot. In the candlelight, his face was deathly pale. Young Geoffrey wept next to stony-faced Matilda on one side of the bed with Sybilla and William, who had just arrived from Sybilla's estate. Henry stood rigid on the right. Robert looked like he had been turned to stone. I stood frozen, dishevelled, expressionless, which disguised my anguish.

Matilda's icy eyes were fixed on my face, hoping, I am sure,

Chapter 15. Burying Gamma and Epsilon

for a glimmer to betray I had been Geoffrey's lover. Henry started to mumble, 'Papa, Papa!' and began to sob, affecting my composure. My eyes bore down on the almost lifeless figure. Geoffrey seemed to have shrunk. It was as if he was disappearing into the bedlinens, that they were sucking him down like quicksand. Suddenly his sunken eyes flew open. A ripple went around the bed chamber. His chaplain made the sign of the cross. His confessor was muttering the last rites. The priest's chanting seemed to reach a greater fervour. Geoffrey's eyes glided from son to son, to his sister, sliding past Matilda to rest on me. If ever an inner voice could reach the psyche of another person, I willed him not to speak, not to confess. With a capacity of unbelievable inner strength, he spoke clearly in Greek as if we were alone.

'To you, my dearest love, I have given the love of my life. Now, because you carry the love of that love, I can leave this world a joyous man.'

Those were his last words. I gripped the foot of the bed, white-knuckled, every inch of my body wanting to envelope Geoffrey in my arms as he slipped away. Henry was wailing. To stop myself falling to the floor in grief, I threw myself on my husband, I gripped him with all my might, rocking in his arms while he crushed me to him. It allowed me to moan, with heart-wrenching sobs. Henry and I clung to each other, distraught for our own reasons.

***

I felt superfluous as the castle revolved around the sombre preparations for Geoffrey's funeral. I was numb with my own grief. Gamma and Epsilon glinted in the sunshine pouring through the windows, reminding me how Geoffrey challenged my intellect, advised me when it was needed, helped me survive in Paris when I was in despair, gave me joy. Though I fought with all my might against him, he put my safety above his desire for me. He has given me his son, whom I am growing fonder of, day by day. I worried over Geoffrey's last words. Henry's Greek is bad. As no-one else has said anything. I can only presume no-one understood what Geoffrey said in his dying moments. Matilda's grasp of languages was limited to Latin, Langue d'Oeil and a little English.

Matilda I am avoiding. Her eyes, like the arrows of Saint Sebastian pierce my being, too close to destroy my resolve not to break down. So far, she has said naught. I must keep out of her sight.

Poor Henry is bereft; he is organising his father's funeral to take place at the Cathedral of St Julien in Le Mans as Geoffrey wished. Nearby, he lies waiting to leave for his last resting place. I want to return Gamma and Epsilon to him so he can take them to his afterlife in heaven. How I have yet to fathom.

Last night was agony. Henry's brothers Geoffrey and William were greatly distressed. When I was clinging to Henry, I saw the boys, alone, in isolation. Sybilla was weeping in her chair. Matilda just left. Sir Robert, after embracing Henry, went to the priests and Matthias to begin proceedings. I do not like or trust young Geoffrey, but I could not bear to see him standing there like a lost child, William neither. I reached out my hand to them which, after a slight hesitation, they accepted. I whispered to Henry, 'Your brothers'.

We embraced them, letting them cry. Renée came to me, suggesting as there was nothing more for me to do, and considering my condition, I should return to my bed. Henry insisted. I asked if I could say goodbye to a dear friend. Henry, Sybilla and his brothers stood with me as I kissed Geoffrey on his forehead, already cooling. Alone in bed I was grief-stricken.

I prayed to God by recording these events my words will help salve my heart, cleft like Gamma and Epsilon.

***

Geoffrey's funeral procession made its journey to Le Mans, the tolling bells of Rouen receding in our wake. Within the vaulted aisles of the Cathedral of St Julian plainsong

Chapter 15. Burying Gamma and Epsilon

soared as incense hung in the air. We were in the white of mourning. In my hand, I clutched Epsilon and Gamma on their golden chains, hoping above hope, I could drop them in beside Geoffrey.

As I filed past his bier, I made the sign of the cross. As if to steady myself, I leaned over and let the precious tokens of our love slip down beside Geoffrey's shoulder. Nobody seemed to notice the little tinkle, but to me it sounded like a gong. I fought the lump in my throat and the tears. I reached for Henry's hand. He held it in a grip so tight it became numb. It stopped me going to pieces.

We returned to Rouen. The castle inhabitants were slowly returning to their routines. Henry was spending more and more time with his mother. His Aunt Sybilla I found to be a charming woman. I would like to know her better. She left for her estates, taking Henry's younger brothers, Geoffrey and William, with her. William, I found to be more like Henry. There was a mystery woman at the funeral with a small boy. Henry eventually told me she was the small boy's nurse and the boy his bastard son, another Geoffrey. It was a bittersweet meeting. I had to keep my promise to treat the child as my own. I felt pangs of jealousy, emotions I once reserved for Petronilla. I know the child's mother died after he was born but Henry had loved her. He adores the little fellow who was excited to see his Papa. Little Geoffrey looked at me with great suspicion. He looked less like Henry than I expected, except for the colour of his hair and the curls. Matilda was not helping me get to know him. She has a happy rapport with her grandson. Henry says she treats him with far more fondness than ever she did her own sons.

Matilda was making my life difficult. She has not accused, but her sneering lip said it all. Her tentacles have Henry engulfed. To my disgust, he now refers to himself as Henry Fitz Empress in honour of his mother. I was reaching the end of my patience. Henry must take control, but Matilda will cling on till she has sucked him dry.

***

The straw has broken the camel's back. Matilda's snide remarks about guilty consciences sent me to my chamber. Henry entered. With fury I was gathering my belongings.

'What in God's name are you doing?'

'What does it look like?'

'And where do you think you are going?'

'Poitiers.'

'God's Eyes you are. I forbid you to go anywhere.'

'Who and what army are going to stop me?'

Our eyes blazed.

'I have had enough of your mother's insinuations. Furthermore, if you want to believe the rumours about me, go ahead. Your father is dead and buried. Let him rest in peace.'

Henry said he would speak to Matilda.

I stormed off, my gut grinding with the fear Matilda would convince Henry I was an unsuitable mother and have our child removed from my care, something Matilda has insinuated she has no qualms in doing.

Before I could finalise my entourage, I was informed a courier had brought dire news. Louis had invaded Normandy and was determined to take succession of Henry's lands because we did not obtain his permission to marry and ignored his threats to revoke the annulment. He was threatening us with treason. I swallowed my pride to return to Henry's audience chamber.

Henry and Matilda had maps rolled out in front of them. I insisted I speak to Henry about Louis. He said he did not need my interference. I ignored him and his snorting mother. I pointed out I knew a thing or two about Louis' tactics, or lack thereof; after all I had been married to him for fifteen years and had witnessed his actions during the crusade, not forgetting the tragedy of Vitry-sur-Marne and his useless incursion into Toulouse. I emphasised Louis went to war as well as Henry played chess. I cut off his furious expulsion of breath and continued.

'Louis never thinks his actions through to the end. He

leaves himself wide open to surprise attacks.'

I asked to see the maps. Henry said he would listen, but not promise anything. I took a deep breath to control my impatience and indicated where I thought Louis would advance. Henry was grinding his teeth while Matilda could have frozen boiling pitch. I left fuming.

Late evening, I felt the bed sag as Henry crushed in beside me, his freezing feet giving me goose pimples between my legs. My shift was thrown to the floor.

Chapter 16. The Dawning of a Prophesy

Before I left for home, and Henry galloped to war against Louis, he demanded I rein in the writhing snakes and vipers in the Aquitaine or he would hold me accountable. I took that to mean I had regency of my duchy in his absence.

Henry, I was pleased to hear, employed some of my tactics. Using fearless speed, he laid waste to the Vexin and Louis' brother Robert's nearby lands. Louis was in disarray as Henry's men encircled his army like giant crab pincers. To our great sadness, they found Henry's brother Geoffrey had joined forces with Louis because he was angry Henry had not granted lands bequeathed to him by his father. Louis, I heard was unwell with a fever as he limped back to Île de France. What a fool of a man. At least Henry is unhurt and triumphant, though I am not expecting any thanks for my part in his success.

While Henry battled, I left Rouen for Poitiers with my dear loyal Praetorian Guard. What I owed these men for their dedication to duty was priceless. This time however, we were not alone. Henry insisted I also travel with a cavalry chosen by him to make certain his expectant wife came to no harm. Leading his guard was Sir Robert's cousin, Sir Martin du Pres, a man as sound as one could have at one's side. Sir Martin, like his cousin, is kind and level-headed, a jovial man belying a capable swordsman and gallant knight. My men liked and respected him. Both parties had a high regard for each other. I felt safe, in capable hands. Anyone with dubious intent would think twice about plans for an abduction, surrounded as I was by these men.

**

How delightful it was to be in Papa's library, to relax

Chapter 16. The Drowning of a Prophesy

after my long return journey. It was a relief to be away from Matilda's acerbic tongue. But I am missing Henry. For the first few days I felt lost without his mad energy, let alone his beautiful body.

But apart from being away from Henry I was being haunted by a frightening, familiar feeling of despair, akin to emotions I had prior and after Alix's birth. I woke in the night in a cold sweat, shaking. It happened twice. I have told no one. The second time I stoked the fire in the grate, hauled a cape about me, and spent the rest of the night trembling in front of it. Before dawn, I must have fallen asleep. Amaris found me curled up on the floor. I said it must have been a nightmare.

I pushed my worries to one side. This morning I summoned Guillaume and sent a message to Jerome. It was time for me to be brought up to date with affairs in the Aquitaine. Guillaume told me the repairs to the harbour wall and new groyne on the Garonne were moving well. Many of my warring vassals had come to peaceful agreements, for the present. As I know these nobles well, there was no guarantee they will remain so. Two families, the sons of brothers, have been squabbling over who has sovereignty over a bend in the Loire between their estates since my grandfather's rule. Every time the river floods and changes course, there was a dispute. The brothers made Papa tear his hair out. I believe, before he died, he threatened to confiscate their river frontage if they could not agree.

Guile, now back in my service as Seneschal of Poitiers, brought me up to date with his responsibilities. He suggested I let him and the justiciars take care of the administration of the Aquitaine because I should not be taxing myself with governance and its worries at this stage of my (with a little embarrassed cough) condition. Just then, I felt a little fluttering kick as if to say, 'Guile is right, *Maman*; you must consider me.' So instead of arguing, I thanked him. I said I would inform the Duke of Aquitaine what had transpired during our absence if he could give me a written report.

A courier arrived from Henry. The poor man had ridden at breakneck speed as he was ordered to personally deliver the letter into my hands. I told him to take himself off to bathe, eat and rest, allowing my grooms to attend to his tired horse.

Henry's words leapt off the parchment in triumph, screaming with victory over Louis, but he says he must sail for England. Trouble again! As soon as he has settled his mother as regent in Normandy, he will prepare for Barfleur. He knows not when he will return. I will miss him and will pray for him.

The siege of Wallingford Castle, a major stronghold of Henry's loyal followers in England, has reached crisis point with the castle inhabitants in dire need. It has been under siege now for over a year. Those within are desperate. Henry says he has no choice but to go to their aid.

His words of love for me are doing little to quell my growing fear for his safety. He says I will be in his prayers and, with heartfelt joy he wishes the safe delivery of our child.

***

Renée was checking on me; she found me, looking very queer indeed. I started to cry not knowing why except for a feeling of dread. I told her about the two incidents when I woke in the night. The baby was beginning to move – surely not a reason for terror? Renée removed the quill from my grasp. Ink had splattered the page. She took me for a walk in the garden. In its sheltered warmth we sat. The sound of chirping birds, the laughter and chatter of the nearby gardeners wafted around us. She did not speak, nor did I. She waited, holding my hands.

'What is wrong, *Petite Maman*?'

In her gentle, loving manner, she said it was possibly shock from all the events of the last few months – marriage, rushing to Rouen, the baby, Lord Geoffrey's death and Empress Matilda's unkindness. I blurted I was afraid I was

Chapter 16. The Drowning of a Prophesy

losing my wits like I did after Alix was born. I begged her not to let Henry take the baby from me. She calmed me with tender words and sensible advice. No-one, she said, was going to take this baby away: I am protected within the walls of Poitiers and I have my maids and herself to tend me and love me. What would I do without her wisdom? She has calmed my anxious thoughts. What is more, I know I cannot follow my ordained duty if I allow confusion in my mind to take over.

So, I took myself back to the archery range, determined to keep active. A letter arrived while I was firing arrows over my belly. It bore Henry's seal, sent from Barfleur. Now back at my desk, I sliced it open. He writes like he moves, with pugnacious energy, his hand rushes and scrawls across the parchment. He tells me the weather has been appalling, their sailing delayed. He was becoming more impatient as the days stretched into weeks. If the sea does not calm soon, he will take the chance and leave regardless. He misses me with all his being and loves me with all his heart. He hopes I am well, and our baby is growing. He wants me to reply as soon as possible.

I find myself lonely without him. Could I be falling in love with this crazy, energetic husband of mine? I am worrying about him. I pray he will take care. He is a clever, cunning soldier, a natural leader of men – Matilda has trained him well – but even so, I feared he could be too impetuous, too eager, where diplomacy would be more valuable to win over the English barons. I hope Sir Robert can curb his wild enthusiasm. I found a clean sheet of parchment.

My dearest Henry,

Please be careful. Remember the White Ship, plunging your Mother's brother to a watery grave. Do not leave if the weather forbids. I know too well how vicious a storm at sea can be. I do not want our child to be without a father, nor do I want to be without you.

Now, more pleasant news. Our little incumbent is growing fast and is quite active. It must have my 'boys' legs with your vigorous way of moving. At night, it keeps me awake. Like me, it misses your warm embrace. Renée is annoyingly attentive, keeping me corralled like a newly broken filly. I have, however, managed to attend to various charitable deeds. I have by the grace of God distributed alms to the good sisters of the Abbey of Montierneuf on our behalf as Duke and Duchess of Aquitaine and Normandy and Count and Countess of Anjou. I have confirmed and continued all privileges granted by my family since they were granted by my great-grandfather.

I have restored a small area of forested land to the Abbey of Saint-Maixent. Louis, or probably Suger, meddled in the distribution of this woodland early in my previous marriage without consulting me, revoking the abbey's entitlement. Abbot Peter has sent a plea begging to have the valuable asset returned to the abbey. On reviewing their entitlement, I could not see any limitation, on our behalf as Duke and Duchess of Aquitaine and Normandy, as to why the Abbot's request cannot be fulfilled.

Finally, I visited Fontevrault to meet with the charming, virtuous abbess, your Aunt Isabella. It was a quick detour on my way home to Poitiers. Of course, it has great significance for my family too. Now that we are husband and wife, and in my present condition, I wanted to gain inspiration from the prayers of the good sisters for what may unfold in our lives together.

I have conferred on them five hundred sous from our treasury, affirming the continuous support from my father and my forebears. In a separate report from Guillaume, I am including all that has taken place in the duchy during our absence.

I beg with all my heart for you to take care on your travels and travails in England. May God shine his light down on you. You are daily in my prayers.

Your beloved wife,
Eleanor, Duchess of Aquitaine and Normandy
PS The snakes and vipers are behaving themselves.

My missive is on its way.

***

Today I inspected Nilla's and my old nursery. It has been refurbished; a crib lies in wait. I peered into it. A soft lamb's wool shawl was folded within. I lifted it to my nostrils and felt its softness against my face, before replacing it. It had belonged to Nilla and me and had been kept by Renée for a new Duke or Duchess of Aquitaine. My eyes blurred as I wondered about Marie and Alix. I sighed and neatened the pile of swaddling clothes nearby with the little gowns I have stitched, a lump the size of a turnip lodging in my throat.

Chapter 16. The Drowning of a Prophesy

I suspect, from my previous experiences, I will give birth soon. Renée is hovering. Although I miss him, it is for the best Henry is not here for I fear he too would be another falcon over its prey. To be honest, all I want to do is get this baby out into the world. My patience is on a knife-edge.

***

Our son was born in the early hours before dawn on the 17th day of August in the year of Our Lord 1153, two weeks ago. As I write this, he is beside me in his crib. We have named him William after my father and Henry's grandfather. Like his sisters before him the birth was excruciating. Renée told me the process was supposed to improve with each child. I beg with all vehemence to differ. I hear my howls and curses reached new dimensions.

But when William was placed in my arms, never have I experienced such overwhelming rapture. If maternal love can be delirious, it is how I felt. I put my baby boy to my breast in wonderment. His instinct said suck, and he did. Renée said he had to be bathed, after which she would bring him back, warm and swaddled. But panic overtook me, so she was forced to bring his bath to him, while I, an eagle ready to swoop, watched them wash and dress him in front of me. Renée handed back my little bundle. His eyes were shut tight, his little rosebud mouth pursed, satiated from his mother's breast. All that was missing from this perfect moment was his Papa.

Propped up on pillows while cradling this tiny, joyous miracle in my arms; out of nowhere echoed a voice from the past, Judith's prophesy:

'You will marry the love of your life. You will bear him many sons.'

My heart was swelling, full of love for my energetic, adorable, maddening man. I have lived with an ache since Papa's death, a yearning to love and be loved other than fleetingly, often with despair. Whether it was for self-preservation, I know not, but I had built a wall and moat and persuaded myself my status and dowry would always be barriers to love within marriage. My mind has jousted with Judith's prediction. I tried to convince myself it was superstition. But, like a blinding flash, dawned the revelation; Henry is the one, the love of my life.

***

To my darling Henry, love of my life,

We have a son. As agreed, he is William.

He is well and bonny. He has hair the colour of your curly mane. Renée says there is something of my family around his eyes, though he has your mouth and determined chin. God be praised, he has missed my nose. His lungs are lusty. I cannot take my eyes off him. Thank you, my dearest, for making him with all the pleasure his conception gave us. I too am well. I long for your next letter.

Your beloved wife,

Eleanor

***

Several missives arrived in a batch from Henry. I smiled as I tried to comprehend his scrawl, his words running across the pages like a spider; its eight legs dipped in ink. He ran out of patience waiting for the overcast skies to clear and winds to abate. His voyage across the Channel was rough and hazardous. God be praised he, his men, horses and provisions all arrived safely, albeit scattered up and down the British coast. Once assembled, he and his men charged off to relieve the siege at Wallingford. His supporters' predicament was grim, worse than expected, but his speed of attack caught Stephen's army by surprise, and they capitulated after a brief skirmish. Thank God for Henry's military skill.

After his success at Wallingford, he followed with victories over Malmsbury and Warwick Castles and surrounding towns. The inhabitants have been struggling with the deprivations of basic needs: starvation is rife because they have been unable to tend their gardens, crops and animals, as they fended off Stephen's or Eustace's constant raids.

Chapter 16. The Drowning of a Prophesy

The rate at which Henry was travelling and his assaults put Stephen and his followers to flight, most of them Henry says, opportunistic riff raff. Archbishop Theobald of Canterbury has begged Henry and Stephen to come to a reconciliation before the whole country is ablaze. Henry is in my heart and prayers. I hope he is being prudent and patient, somehow, I think it unlikely.

I broke the seal of the next letter. Lord have mercy! Stephen's son Eustace is dead after laying waste to East Anglia. Henry says he choked on something he was eating when he had repaired to Bury St Edmunds. I must say I am not saddened. Eustace was an evil, sadistic animal from all reports. Stephen has made Henry his heir. This is Henry's due. Although I do not see eye to eye with Matilda, she was wronged by Stephen who usurped the English crown, her rightful inheritance, because she was a woman. It must stick in her craw though, that I will become Queen of England, even if it is by dint of my marriage to her son.

I had to pause to comprehend our future. Pride fills my heart. One day I will be Queen of England! My destiny, my ordained role will be fulfilled. I know I can be more than an appendage to Henry, more than an ornament. I pray with all my heart, because of the obligations we face, Henry will allow me to be his queen in more than name only, so I can fulfil my purpose.

Henry says Stephen has adopted him. (I am not sure how Geoffrey would feel about that, or Matilda, though she is more pragmatic). It has been documented, witnessed and a treaty drawn up and signed by the Archbishop of Canterbury, many bishops and earls. Stephen took Henry to London where he has been accepted with cheering and displays of relief by the people, who after so many years of war and destruction can at last see a glimmer of peace.

I opened his third and bulkiest epistle. Out fell a gold bracelet shaped like a lion and curved as if it is chasing its tail. Its eye sockets house fiery rubies, its mouth clasps a perfect pearl. On a piece of vellum, Henry has written, this time with care:

For my Lioness, the love of my life, for the birth of our Lion Cub. I weep with pride and thanks. May God bless you both, my loves.
Henry

I slipped the bangle around my wrist. It fits perfectly. My heart is bursting. When will Henry return? I want his arms around me. I want him to hold his son.

***

Writs for my signature piled up on my desk. In a fit of exuberance, I sent Guile off for a well-deserved rest. I must resume my duties, but I cannot drag myself away from being *Maman*. Little William fills my days with wonder. I do have a wet nurse, Millicent, but I have elected to suckle him myself, though she takes him at night. Renée, not very subtly, said William was not a doll.

When two of my more irritating vassals turned up in my audience chamber, ready to commit bloodshed over a land dispute, I realised I was tardy in my duties. I needed to balance my new role better. I had to find the noble's petitions amongst the pile on my desk. At least, I read quickly. As so often happens with family arguments, a will was involved and a very convoluted inheritance through marriage dowries, death of a first wife, remarriage and stepchildren. My two petitioners were arguing each was wronged and deprived of what was his right. I requested they provide me with copies of all documents for my perusal. I thought I had a copy of Cicero on my desk.

That was just one of the headaches, growing cobwebs around me. William was crying and demanding my attention. Renée was nagging Guile should be here, my maids have pursed lips: even sweet Amaris was telling me there is no such thing as a perfect mother. God's teeth, I needed that copy of Cicero. Jerome appeared, hearing my cursing from a back corner of the library. I yelled at him. William's cries reached a higher pitch. I thumped my desk, hurt my fist and upturned the ink.

Chapter 16. The Drowning of a Prophesy

Jerome thundered,
'Elly! Calm down!'

I grabbed my screaming infant and stormed off to my quarters, breast milk seeping through my gown.

Who am I, Duchess of Aquitaine or mother of William? Can I be both? Renée was shaking her head with disapproval. William was distraught and not suckling as normal. He is three months old and has yet to know his father. After much frustration, my son was satisfied, but I was not. My pride was keeping me from consulting the mothers around me. I was overwhelmed suddenly by feelings of resentment against my beautiful baby.

Back in the library with a pile of petitions and writs in front of me, I felt alone. I have left William, asleep at last, with his nurse. Except at night, this is the first time I have done this. I feel guilty. I see Jerome has cleaned up the ink and a copy of Cicero is smirking in front of me. A deep voice behind asked if I had finished throwing my tantrum. I reminded him I am sure his abbot would be only too delighted to have him back.

'Whatever pleases you, Milady.'

The library door shut with a determined click. I burst into tears. I needed Henry.

Renée, knocked. As she has done forever, she came to my side and as usual waited for me to calm down. I blurted out, Angelique, Matilda, everyone, knew I would be an unsuitable mother. What is more, I am proving I am also unsuitable for my ordained destiny. I am not doing my duty. Papa must be rolling in his grave.

My darling sweet Renée chuckled. I was shocked. I snapped,
'This is not funny!'

She gave me one of her sensible talks: said I was trying to accomplish too much. She suggested I should wean William. I was aghast. I feared he would love his nurse more than me. Renée answered nothing would break the bond between William and me. I would not be leaving him in another household, I would be here for him, and I could perform my duties. She suggested I work to a schedule to accommodate my role as mother with the diligence needed for my regency. She ignored my pouting, kissed the top of my head and left. Right as usual!

Calmed by Renée's advice, I set to the pile of scrolls of vellum and parchment on my desk. Later, with the sun throwing long shadows over the shelves of the library, I had sorted the documents into two piles. Those needing only a signature were complete; the more complicated petitions were ready for deliberation, their complainants listed to be summoned to appear before me and my justiciars. My breasts were now ready to explode. How was I going to wean William? Little by little.

Time to write these days is limited. This is one activity I must ration. At long last I have weaned William. It has not had a detrimental effect on the little fellow. He squeals with delight when he sees me; gives me gummy, dribbly smiles and gurgles with joy. My temper is better.

Henry continues to thunder around England making gains among the barons and settling the population. The clergy approve his actions. He writes often about his activities, his letters full of affection. He misses me as I miss him. Four or five letters will arrive at a time followed by interminable gaps as I wait for the next courier.

***

I am now on progress. There are estates I must visit. My retinue, though, can no longer take to the road with ease: babies have so much paraphernalia. William's entourage seemed greater than mine. To begin with, he was a little anxious, but he soon settled into my nomadic journey. I have managed to visit members of my crusader army, from the simple foot soldiers to my nobles. Of course, Faydide, Tarquiri and the other women were on my list. They fussed over William, praised his looks and placid demeanour and congratulated me for finding a husband who is compatible with my needs and temperament.

Chapter 16. The Drowning of a Prophesy

I visited the families of men who did not return, to make sure they were not destitute. It gave me joy to be able to distribute alms, to make certain no one was without. I know this will be ongoing. It was humbling to see how many of these women and their children can prosper on so little. Many of the smaller convents and monasteries served their villagers with little more than God's devotion.

Lands neglected by Louis are prospering again. Grain, wine and olives and other fruits have been harvested, sheep are woolly and being fattened on salt marshes, such a relief. After my return to the Aquitaine I feared it would take many seasons for the duchy to recover from the fifteen years of Louis' misrule.

As I wound my way towards the north of the duchy, a missive from Henry caught up with me. It had been following like a tail wind. It was disturbing because he reports my movements have been receiving unsavoury attention from France. Henry fears William and I could be in danger. He demands I make my way to Angers, well protected within his domains. Why Louis is behaving belligerently, I know not. Our marriage has been annulled. He needs to accept I have remarried. More infuriating, he is still clinging to the title, Duke of Aquitaine, to which he has no right!

***

We rode into Angers surrounded by curious inhabitants all interested in Count Henry's wife and son. It is fascinating to see where Henry was schooled and lived as a little boy. Poetry, music and philosophy thrive here as they do in the Aquitaine.

After we had settled in our quarters in Angers, we were indulged with a banquet as sumptuous as any in Poitiers where I was introduced to their famous white wine which I did enjoy. Entertainment was similar, to ours in Poitiers. The troubadours were excelling themselves, especially Bernard de Ventadour, a surprising visitor. It had been many years since I was amused by his talent. In the past, he has penned many flattering poems and songs in my honour; tonight, he transcended his usual standard. I blushed at the adoring attention poured upon me. Whether it was the wine, or I was lonely for a handsome man's attention, but I found myself behaving more like my flirtatious younger sister than the sensible wife of the next King of England and mother of his son. I pulled myself together. I did not want to be lured into a tryst I could lose control over, so I took my leave of the festivities and headed to my bed chamber. Bernard had, however, taken my flirtatious frivolity too seriously. He pursued me. Before I could stop him, his arms were around me, his mouth on mine, his hands travelling to where they should not. I shoved him away with all my might, sending him crashing to the gallery floor. My face blazed with embarrassment and fear. I hissed at him that by Satan should Henry discover his unwarranted advances, not only would his life be forfeited, but so would mine. I kicked at his prone body and tore to my chamber where I slammed and locked the door.

I sat on my bed head in my hands. Were there any pages, churls or guards in or near the gallery? Plenty of people would have seen me leave but how many noted Bernard following? There was a tap on the door – I jumped out of my skin. It was Amaris. In a panic, I told her what had transpired. She said Bernard returned to the hall soon after he left, red-faced and limping. Good, the kick I aimed at his groin must have connected. But I am agitated. I have fallen in love Henry, the last thing I want is for some stupidity on my behalf to sully our marriage. I know Henry does not comprehend the 'rules' of Courtly Love and the troubadour tradition. He does not understand these poems and songs of love are innuendo and nothing serious.

You are a fool, Eleanor!

The next day while I was mulling over my silliness from the night before, a courier arrived with an epistle bearing Henry's welcome seal. I read by now he will have arrived at Portsmouth ready to set sail for Barfleur. Thank God! I could

Chapter 16. The Drowning of a Prophesy

leave for Rouen.

***

William was grizzling. Today, he wanted to cling to *Maman*. I tried an experiment by perching him in front of me on my horse. I used a few yards of cloth and tied him to me the way peasant women working in the fields have their babies slung about them. He enjoyed the distraction, soon laughing and gurgling with gleeful pleasure. Renée threw a fit, chiding I was endangering the life of mine and Henry's heir. Our progress was mightily slow, but the men were delighted to see him with me. Soon I was surrounded by knights wanting to peep at the little fellow. William's little head was nodding after a league, so to placate Renée and Millicent I sent him back to the carriage. Its rocking kept him asleep. Millicent thinks his first tooth may be emerging, which is why he is crotchety.

I am scribbling this at the same monastery where Henry and I stayed during our breakneck dash to Rouen when poor Geoffrey was taken ill. The monks love William. He is being spoiled. Our more measured passage allowed us to enjoy their simple monastic life and join in their prayers. I gave thanks for my blessings in giving birth to my beautiful son. He is almost seven months old now; such a bonny baby, so handsome. His hair is growing, except for a little bald patch on the back of his head like a monk's tonsure. It is the colour of autumn leaves, his eyes have darkened, more like mine. Lord be praised he has a retroussé nose, but a very set Plantagenet jaw – oh, and my pouty lips. Let us hope the jaw does not indicate the stubbornness of both parents!

On the morrow, we will leave for the last leagues to Rouen. I had requested, before I left for Poitiers, Henry's and my chambers have fireplaces installed. Braziers are all very well, but unless one sits on top of them, they are not very warming.

***

Matilda was waiting in the bailey when we clattered over the drawbridge; most unexpected. Her greeting was cool but polite. She asked where her grandson was: a surprise because she had shown little prior interest. I said he was a league or two behind. I had hastened to have everything ready for his arrival and comfort. She snorted that his needs had been considered and there were fires in the new fireplaces. I thanked her and asked if she had heard from Henry. As it happened, she knew less than I did, having received naught from him since he left London. I did not enlighten her about what I knew. At the speed Henry travels he could be right behind me.

Henry's and my quarters were warm and welcoming. I wanted to bathe, I smelt of horse. By the time, a tub and hot water were prepared William, my maids and the rest of the escort had arrived, followed by a courier from Henry. His mother was thin-lipped when there was no missive for her. Henry was lazy, writing in mine he had no time to pen lines to his mother when he knew I would pass on his information. Mid-morn on the morrow should see my dear Henry arrive. I am excited but nervous. The behaviour of Bernard de Ventadour is still at the back of my mind.

My hair was washed on my arrival; today it was brushed and gleaming. I desired to look as beautiful as I could be. Gown after gown I rejected, unable to make up my mind. My maids' suggestions caused more confusion. Bells were ringing out the hours and I was still in my chemise. I gave up and let them choose. They unanimously decided on a shimmering golden silk gown embroidered with silver flowers resembling jasmine and broom. Pearls edged the sleeves, with golden topaz gems spilling from the long trumpet-shaped sleeves. The front of the bodice was laced with gold and silver woven cords. I have taken to wearing my veil long and flowing instead of pinned around my face. Celeste said it made me look serene. That will be the day! Before Amaris added rouge and kohl, I examined my face for lines. I was becoming obsessive, but I have been out in

Chapter 16. The Drowning of a Prophesy

the elements for days. My women stood around smirking. Renée had been massaging a sweet-smelling lanolin into my skin, but it can be greasy; I do not want to look like a basted duck. In amongst my jewellery we found a coronet I inherited from my Grandmother Dangerosa. The golden circlet is rimmed with pearls and studded with topaz. It matched my gown perfectly. I wore my pearl cross and Henry's lion bracelet was on my wrist. Little William was dressed up too, wrapped in the soft lamb's wool shawl used by Nilla and me.

I was ready. I fidgeted from one foot to the other waiting for Henry, thinking he would never arrive when a herald galloped across the drawbridge. He announced Lord Henry was on his heels. I was manoeuvred down the circular staircase. Millicent carried William till we stepped onto the cobbles of the bailey, where she handed him to me. Matilda too was waiting. I had been telling William for days he was going to meet his Papa. He put his head on my shoulder; his thumb was getting a good suck. I prayed he would not scream at the sight of the 'strange man'.

We could hear the drumming of hooves moving at speed. Henry's destrier thundered into the bailey, frothing and foaming, the poor animal almost rolling its eyes. With his attire all awry, Henry catapulted in front of me. His eyes were blazing with love, passion, lust – God knows what roared through his brain. The world existed with only him, me and William in it. The breeze ruffled my veil, the half-asleep babe opened his eyes, father and son gazed at each other. William stretched and yawned. I held out the now wriggling bundle with the rust-coloured hair. I whispered, 'Hold him'.

Large, powerful hands, as tender as he caresses my body, clasped his son to him in wonderment. Lord be praised, William did not yell but stared at his father with his big eyes.

'This is your Papa, William.'

To my relief, William uttered a happy gurgle, reaching out to Henry's face with a dimpled hand. Henry's eyes streamed with tears.

My eyes raked over Henry. His hair had darkened to a deep chestnut, a rugged beard covered his once smooth chin, his face was weather-beaten and tanned. He looked up from his baby boy, his eyes glistening in wonderment. Dear God, Geoffrey had come back in the guise of his son. Is this why he has become the love of my life? A thrilling shiver ran down my spine. A ghost of a voice echoed.

To you, my dearest love, I have given the love of my life. Because you carry the love of that love, I can leave this world a joyous man.

Who was Geoffrey speaking to, me or his son, the man now carrying the baby? Was this the unravelling of the mystery of Judith's prophesy, the truth of my destiny? I felt for a moment as if I were on the outside looking in.

The magic of the moment was interrupted by jingling harness, snorting horses and grunting men as they dismounted. William sneezed, making us all laugh. Matilda made her presence felt with a heavy sigh of annoyance because Henry had said naught to her. He gave her a peck on both cheeks and announced he needed to bathe. I whispered, 'No! Come now'.

William was handed back to Millicent.

***

Henry told me later I looked ethereal, silhouetted against the sun, dressed in gold. Like me, he had felt enveloped in the moment as if we belonged outside this world with our son, one of the cherubim. He told me I had given him the greatest treasure of his life.

In the privacy of my bed chamber, we undressed each other. My golden gown tinkled to the floor, an embroidered jewel box. Henry smelt of horse and sweat, his hair woolly, his beard rough, but pleasant. Our love making was slow and sensual, a pleasure to all our senses from taste to touch.

We were given a day of freedom to be together. I piled my hair in a knot on top of my head and bathed with Henry which turned into an orgy of a water fight. We dried naked

Chapter 16. The Drowning of a Prophesy

in front of the fire. Time meant nothing to us as we climbed back into bed. The bells from the distant cathedral chimed the hours; we fell asleep in each other's arms.

Henry woke as the sun was setting and announced he was starving. He flung a clean tunic over his nakedness and strode to the door to send for food and wine. He threw off his gown and bounced back into bed. The bed creaked and groaned.

We fed each other cheese, oysters, bread and other morsels. The wine was rich and red. Speech between us was unnecessary when touch was all we needed. Henry announced when I was Queen of England, he intended to ravish me while I was wearing only my crown. Only if you wear yours, was my retort.

Now Henry was sublimely sated, I had to tell him what occurred between Bernard de Ventadour and me in case someone caused trouble between us. I did not hide the truth I may have given Bernard the wrong idea by being a little skittish, but I impressed on Henry it was Bernard who broke the troubadour's code of honour by pursuing me. He said nothing, but his brain was grinding and growling. After what seemed like an eternity, he propped himself up on his elbow. His eyes bore into mine.

'I believe you, but if you ever, ever, betray me, you will not see the light of day.' I reached between his legs and squeezed gently.

'And if you ever, ever, betray me, you will be singing higher than a choir boy.'

***

The next day was a celebration of Henry's triumphant and safe return to Normandy. Matilda was more than proud of her son's achievements. Henry's brother William had ridden to Rouen to celebrate Henry's return. Both William and Geoffrey were overjoyed Henry's exploits in England were successful. Geoffrey, who had been welcomed back into the fold, showed genuine pleasure, but I still do not trust him. He makes my skin crawl.

Henry was welcomed by the people of Normandy, Maine, Poitiers and Anjou. Many had travelled to Rouen to pay homage to Henry and thronged the streets where we rode with pride to their cheers and ovations. This was also their first introduction to William, Henry's heir, who I carried with all the love and pride of a lioness for her cub. William rode with me, perched on my saddle, laughing and squealing with joy. The elegant hispano placed his feet with care on every cobblestone as if instinct told him he was carrying the most precious of chevaliers as he moved with the grace of his breed. Henry does not like me riding my stallion, Diablo. But I trust him with my life. I have known him since he was a foal. We have a bond.

Henry looked magnificent, robed in his regalia. His barber had trimmed his shaggy locks and beard. Sir Robert complimented us. He said we were the most handsome couple in Christendom – Henry on his shining black steed and I on my white.

It was a day of celebration for all, a day to give thanks. We attended a special service in Notre-Dame-des-Pres. This was a bitter-sweet ceremony because the last large Plantagenet occasion in the cathedral had been a memorial service for their late Duke, Geoffrey.

***

Matilda has set up house in the palace near the cathedral outside the castle walls to give Henry and me and our increasing entourages more space. Matilda is happy with the arrangement, and so am I. At last I do not have to spend my days trying to avoid her. Henry, on the other hand, was grumbling because he now must mount a horse, take guards and travel half a league to consult his mother. Walking, he says, would be demeaning to his status. I was hoping the new housing arrangements would have Henry consult me more, but unless there is a necessity to discuss the Aquitaine, Matilda has priority no matter how much I fume.

And fuming I am, after such a glorious renewal of our

Chapter 16. The Drowning of a Prophesy

love. Henry was snooping around wanting to know what I had written in my journal because I am still writing in Greek. I told him again what I put in my journal was none of his business. He thinks it is. He does not understand why I do it, though I have explained it so often, I feel as though I may turn purple. Papa started it with Nilla and me when we were about nine or ten as an exercise to practise our writing. I enjoyed jotting down my thoughts and observations, so I continued. To placate Henry, I read what I wrote about our triumphant parade amongst our people and said it was about as exciting as my writing gets – except when I wrote about husbands being pests. When I asked him if he had something better to do with his time, his lips and tongue fluttered over my neck and he nibbled my ears.

That was the end of a few quiet moments in front of my desk.

***

We have had two peaceful months. Henry has been able to rest a little, to hunt and enjoy some jousting, which I hate. To my dismay, he was dislodged from his horse. Although not seriously hurt, he jarred his hip. I recommended Renée's smelly goose fat and herb remedy. One sniff and he refused. He said he would rather limp. It has slowed down our exercise, though. Not that he sleeps in his own bed, regardless of his sore hip, preferring as he does to warm his freezing cold feet on me. I do love him.

We have been able to relax to music and other entertainment as well. Henry's hip has stopped his dancing, but we enjoyed singing together and playing our lutes. Chess is a sore subject – his impulsiveness undoes him – so we play backgammon where we are more evenly matched. Sir Robert whispered to me one evening: Bernard de Ventadour has been banished on Henry's orders. I felt my face flame with embarrassment.

William has another tooth. He had bright pink cheeks and was not his usual cheerful little self. Now the little white protuberance has broken through his gum, he is happier. Millicent gives him hard crusts and the rind of cheese to gnaw, which makes me laugh. He swaps what he is chewing from hand to hand, examines it like a precious jewel before popping it in his mouth again. He looks so funny. Hands and face are something to behold. I find this messy occupation challenges my fastidious nature. Millicent has learned to wipe hands and face before William reaches for *Maman*.

Our peaceful sojourn was interrupted. A courier arrived early this morn with several missives for Henry and me from Guile and Jerome. Some of my unruly vassals are causing trouble by threatening to besiege castles of their neighbours. Henry accused me of being too soft on them and has decided to gallop off with an army of Normans to bring them to heel, once and for all. To be honest, they are a nuisance. After they have experienced Henry's wrath, they may think twice about causing trouble in the future. I have my doubts, however. But I am happy for him to take the responsibility, electing to stay in Rouen. The tell-tale stomach-churning mornings have started, and I have again missed my cycle. I will wait till Henry returns before I burden him with worries about me, nor do I want him fussing, Renée is bad enough. He can learn about our next bundle of joy on his return. Lord be praised, his hip is better.

In his letter to me, Jerome confirmed information from Paris; Louis has remarried. His new wife is a Spanish princess, Constance of Castile. She is young; I pity her having to endure what I have escaped. Dear Lord, I hope she will be happier than I was. Jerome says she is only educated in womanly pursuits and the French consider her a far more suitable wife for Louis. Jerome gloats they are mightily vexed Henry's and my first child is a son. I pray our second child will be too, to rub salt into the wounds. I hope their spies have also told them I nursed William for twelve weeks, he is happy and loves his mother and father, and they adore him. Moreover, he lives within my court.

At last, Louis has given up the title of Duke of Aquitaine.

Chapter 16. The Drowning of a Prophesy

It galled me he thought he could continue to claim it. After all, Henry is Duke of Aquitaine now.

***

In the past, I have tried to keep my discomfort to myself, but today I consulted Renée. In her vast knowledge of herbal remedies, surely there is one to help my grinding stomach. She recommended we try a tisane of ginger steeped in boiling water with some honey. I am willing to try anything! For once, I am going to obey and have more rest. What is more, I am happy, and I am trying not to be impatient when all my maids and Renée are fussing.

My routine now revolves around William who is such a delight. He is a striking child. His favourite toy is a little felt horse, which he must have about him at all times. He will not sleep without it. Many a panic has taken place if *Maman* cannot find it. Yester morn, the whole household was in a fit looking for Horsey, found in the end, in my bed chamber behind a chest where it had fallen. He can crawl like a demon and pull himself up on chairs and stools. Millicent thinks by the time Henry returns William will be walking. He will be one year old. I am amazed how quickly a baby can progress.

***

Henry hurtled back to Rouen, sliding from his horse, exhausted. Much to my consternation, he looked haggard. William was so excited to see him, walking a few steps before plopping onto his little derriere. Henry picked him up, but something was amiss. Was it his hip? Maud, Millicent and Renée noticed too that Henry was not his usual exuberant self. I let him carry his excited gibbering little boy to our chamber and sent pages for food and drink, and warm water so I could bath him. William played about his feet. He wanted to climb on to Papa. Before he left, Henry was throwing William into the air and tickling him till he cried with laughter, but Henry had no energy. Although the little boy screamed, I had to insist Millicent take him away.

Renée approached Henry, begging his pardon while she placed a cool hand on his forehead. When he did not complain, we knew he was unwell. She sent a page to fetch Matthias. When the tub was filled, I helped him undress. He looked drained. When he stepped into the water, his body shivered. A few weeks ago, he would have wanted me naked beside him. This was a frightening experience. He said little as I washed his back.

'What ails you, Henry?'

He replied he knew not what was amiss, but for the last two days, he felt hot one minute, cold and shivering the next. They had stayed on the banks of the Eure on the Norman border where they were plagued by mosquitoes; I could see many red, itchy bites on his arms. My heart sank. Diseases spread by mosquitoes can be serious, often fatal.

Matthias arrived and, with Renée, combined herbs into an unguent to attend to the bites, binding them to prevent Henry scratching the persistent itchiness. We helped him into his bed. He had a fever, so they gave him a mixture to try to break it. I sat beside him, praying with all my heart, begging God, the Virgin, saints and angels to watch over my love. Do not take him from me!

Matilda was summoned. She was distraught should Henry die. I sponged his burning head with tepid lavender water. Throughout the night, Henry raved and ranted with delirium. If only my tears could cool him, for I wept enough to fill a lake. Sometime during the night, I fell into a deep sleep, fatigued at his side.

***

Each day ran into night. For four days, Henry tossed and turned. Prayers were chanted in the cathedral and at his bedside. Rouen had fallen into silence. My head ached, I felt limp, I did not want to think of the future. All those around Henry's bedside were weary. I, a picky eater at the best of times, could not swallow a morsel. The thought of life without Henry hung over me like an evil spectre. William wanted his Papa, a new word I had proudly taught him, which he was chanting like a little monk.

I wanted to shake Henry, to scream, 'Don't you dare die on me!' Instead, I collapsed over his prone body, wetting his chemise with tears I thought I had drained. A deep voice vibrated through me, 'Eleanor, you are soaking me. Do you want me to drown?'

I sat up. Henry's eyes were open, tired and haggard, but open. His arms wrapped around me. I kissed him all over his face till my lips felt chafed. Everyone was cheering, weeping, praying, uttering, 'The Lord be praised.'

It was several more days before he was strong enough to exit his bed, but his appetite had returned. We fed him delicious broths, chicken, beef or vegetable. Soon he was demanding more substantial food. William could visit, saying Papa, which had Henry grinning from ear to ear with pride. Now I could inform him of my good news. He looked at me with his face bathed in joy like spring sunshine. He enveloped me in an embrace of sweet tenderness. He whispered, 'When?'

Chapter 17. A Destiny Fulfilled

Trouble has reared again on the Norman, French border. The Vexin, the Vexin, the Vexin –that disputed tract of land between Louis' Franks and Henry's Normans. Papa used to say there would always be conflict between Normandy and France over the Vexin, the moat, portcullis and wall between the two. Kings and Dukes from both sides have been trying to besiege it over eons. They have taken it in turns to batter it into submission to keep the other at bay.

No matter how hard I begged Henry to let his army and the Franks battle it out between themselves, he was determined to bring them to heel though he was just out of his bed. We had one of our screaming arguments, but I might as well have saved my breath as the rear of his horse disappeared across the moat. A silver goblet bounced off stone, leaving a nasty red stain on the Byzantium carpet.

While he was reducing the Vexin to rubble, a most official looking cylinder of gold arrived for Henry. I slid the missive from its gleaming office. It bore an ornate seal I did not recognise. My palms felt sweaty. This was no ordinary missive. I looked at the heavy vellum scroll and asked the courier if it was urgent. The courier said it was the most important epistle he had ever the duty to deliver. Henry's return was still unknown. I was now more than curious but reluctant to break the seal of such an official looking document. As much as it irritated me, I sent for Matilda, saving some dignity by requesting she come to the castle. She arrived in more haste than I expected. Her intake of breath when she saw the seal alerted me, she knew the author.

'Should I open it, do you think, Milady?'

'Give it here.'

I was too quick, however. I slid my stiletto under the hardened wax, unrolling the velum.

Chapter 17. A Destined Fulfilled

'Well, what does he say? It is from Archbishop Theobald of Canterbury, is it not?'

My eyes scanned the page. I gasped! I leant against the table for support.

'Stephen is dead! Henry is king. His Grace demands his presence as soon as possible in England.'

A strangled expulsion of air escaped from Matilda's lips. She sat heavily into a chair as I handed the missive to her to read while I tried with whirling emotions and pounding heart to come to terms with my new status as Queen of England.

***

Henry arrived back from the Vexin, triumphant. I met him in the bailey as he leapt from his horse. He looked dashing, invigorated. One would never have thought he had been so ill. He strode towards me.

'My Queen' – something Louis had never said.

He drew me to him. I could hear his heart beating under his dusty tunic. Amid horses, knights and indeed the whole world, Henry can create an atmosphere like he and I are alone within the welkin and its stars. My rounding stomach pressed close which he noticed through layers of material. His arm around me, we walked quickly to our quarters, leaving Matilda snorting her disapproval in the background. We have much to discuss, a multitude of plans must be made. But no, Henry's priority, sweaty or no, was my arousal, my body. We can talk later, he said.

***

Henry was like a whirlwind consulting his mother (which annoyed me), sending couriers hither and yon, particularly to England and making plans for all our domains from Normandy to the Pyrenees. It took days for him to find time to discuss the Aquitaine. I had to ask for an audience with him. He harrumphed but agreed to spend time with me to discuss my affairs. I wanted to return to the Aquitaine to put my house in order. I needed to talk to Uncle Ralph de Faye, Jerome, my seneschal and other justiciars. They have already been notified of Henry's and my ascension, but I have much to organise before I can leave for England. Henry thinks, in my condition I should not be doing anything, let alone mounting a horse. I pointed out, William had many a ride before he was born, including one hectic gallop through the night to be at Geoffrey's bedside.

Well, we had another argument. In the end, I got my way, but I had to leave William with Millicent and Maud as I galloped off. My maids, less accomplished horse women and poor Renée, were forced to ride with me.

The future governance of the Aquitaine is of major importance. Over and above is the treasury which must be handled with diligence and care. Guillaume will remain Sergeant at Arms. I have brought in Saldebreuil de Sanzay, an old and close associate of Papa's, and a Chatellerault relative. He was Papa's constable. I gave them the responsibility as overlords in Henry's and my absence. Uncle Ralph, as planned, will be Regent. I feel these men have the right balance of expertise and honour for one another. They are also respected by the clergy throughout the Aquitaine. The last thing I wanted was to have the Pope, any Pope, throw an interdict over my lands as I stepped into my role as Queen of England.

**

Henry tells me many palaces and castles in England are in neglect or damaged due to the civil war. When we arrive in England, he wants me to supervise the rebuilding and refurbishment of the palaces of Winchester and Westminster to make them comfortable and fit for a king and queen. After they are habitable, we can turn our attention to others like Windsor and Woodstock. I have raided the Poitiers palace storerooms for carpets, tapestries, and furs, wool and feathers for mattresses. There are chests that belonged to Papa, now empty. They are beautifully crafted, many with inlays of

Chapter 17. A Destined Fulfilled

different woods, some with gold. I have never thought of touching them for purely sentimental reasons, but now, they can be put to good use. Other furniture can be sourced after I arrive in our kingdom.

Papa's library will continue to house my private journals and papers within their protective chests. Jerome has been instructed how to open them if necessary. I have abandoned taking books, hoping my new dwellings will contain libraries, but I do have *The Aeneid*. I have been learning English, knowing it would be sensible to have a rudimentary grasp of the language. It is improving, though I have not been practising as diligently as I should. My pronunciation is rather heavily accented, worse than my Langue d'Oeil which still has hints of Langue d'Oc, and I get the order of words muddled. 'Practise, Eleanor.' I can hear a ghostly voice from childhood hammering about Latin verbs. Darling Papa!

A courier arrived from Nilla. I did not visit her on my mad ride to Poitiers because Raoul was unwell. In eagerness, I broke her seal. I read with disbelief; Raoul has died. My poor, poor baby sister! I ran to Renée. She, too, was devastated. I have told Renée to pack her goods and to travel immediately to Raoul's estate to be with Nilla, to give her and her little children succour. As soon as I am finished here, I will join them. With a heavy heart, I have sent a sad letter to Henry, begging him to allow me to bring Nilla and her three little children with us to England.

It was with great sadness I said farewell to my beloved Aquitaine. I will return, but who knows when?

***

A forlorn party trudged into the bailey at Rouen. Henry was waiting for us. He hugged Nilla to him, his commiserations full of tenderness. I was touched. Poor Renée was so exhausted and heartbroken for her other 'little girl' she looked dragged down. Maud, bless her, came to the rescue, taking Renée under her wing. Millicent brought a rather sleepy William to me. We had arrived late in the afternoon and he had not had his usual nap. He squealed with delight, 'Maman, Maman.' He has grown! I kissed his happy little face, crushing him to me. He was intrigued by his older cousins and they with him. At least that meeting was joyous.

As soon as we had everyone settled, I concentrated on Henry who wanted to be alone with me. Together, we had much to discuss. Henry was happy with the judiciary I have put in place in Poitiers, approving my appointments. He knew some but not all. I was pleased he trusted my judgement – and so he should!

'We will make a queen of you yet.'

I reminded him not to take me lightly. After all, I have had more practice at being a queen than he had at being a king.

'Touché.'

I thought, 'Checkmate', but said naught.

Henry approved of the items I had gathered for our residences in Winchester and Westminster. Henry repeated how both had suffered during the civil war and how beautiful they were in their early days. He wants them not only to be our primary residences, but establishments where we can carry out governance as well as entertainment.

Henry is almost ready to leave. Matilda will manage the affairs of Normandy and act as Henry's Regent (as usual). I have given him a list of all I will need to take from here as well as the baggage of my entourage.

'Forty-two gowns, fourteen pairs of shoes...how many feet do you have, Eleanor?'

I had no idea I had so many gowns or shoes, but his querulous tone annoyed me. Before I could utter a word, he went on listing items of my wardrobe, from fur-lined capes and mantles to woollen undergarments. I scolded him. Surely, he did not want me to be cold or look like a peasant. He muttered how he would never be able to understand women and their attraction to gowns and baubles.

Chapter 17. A Destined Fulfilled

***

At last we stood on the dock at Barfleur. All our possessions were loaded onto the barques and galleys to take us to England. I knew Henry and I would embark on different ships in case of accident, but Henry, without consulting me, announced he wanted William and me to travel apart. My maternal instincts flared. To separate me from my baby boy in unfamiliar surroundings was, I raged, detrimental for William. Henry insisted and tried to remove him from my arms in full view of our entourage. William screamed; plump little fists clinging to my gown. I gripped William and told '*enri Plantagenet-a* if he dared tear William from my arms, he would travel to England alone. I would in all haste return to Poitiers. Furthermore, not a sou would I sign for his beleaguered kingdom now or in the future.

I think for the first time Henry realised how binding was our marriage contract. He could have all the funds he needed, but I had to countersign the document to release them from the Aquitaine treasury. He stormed off. I had won that round, but I was so angry. I was distressed Henry could deign to think William could travel on perhaps storm-tossed seas without the comfort of his mother's arms. I wanted to return to Poitiers.

As it happened, we had to wait days to depart. The weather was most inclement, with high seas, driving rain and unhelpful winds. Henry became more irritable by the minute, pacing, cursing and no doubt driving the harbour master to despair. When we could leave, we were not speaking to each other.

With Henry's ship already out of the harbour, I boarded with my little boy. Now suspicious of sailing and not understanding his parent's fury with each other, he could not be calmed, as sobbing and hiccupping we settled ourselves in our cabin. I handed him to Millicent. She gave him her breast while I, my gut wrenching with maternal jealousy, watched on thinking, 'That should be me.' After the comfort of the breast, she handed him back to me. I caressed him, stroking his tawny head. Poor little darling was exhausted. With 'Horsey' for comfort, he stuck his thumb in his mouth and fell asleep in my arms.

The trip was not smooth. We were tossed like a cork. My maids suffered. William, praise God, slept through it beside me in my bunk bed. I wondered how Nilla and her children were faring.

After an unsettled trip, the seas calmed as the English coast emerged through the gloom. Towering white cliffs loomed ahead. I spoke to the captain who said with the wind in our favour, we should reach Portsmouth after the eight bells of noon, late afternoon at the very least. The coastline seemed vividly green, deeply wooded with many tiny inlets, Henry's and my kingdom.

As I jotted down what I was seeing and what I was feeling, I could only hope our ill-tempered departure from Normandy was not auspicious, that our arrival in England will lead Henry and me to find an even path. I want to do my duty by him and our country. We have much to learn.

***

Mid-afternoon, the barque gently bumped against the dock, not in Portsmouth but in Osterham near Southampton. Sailors secured ropes fore and aft before the gangplank was lowered and we disembarked. Henry was already ashore. I could see his fidgety pacing as I stepped onto England's shore wearing the crown of Normandy with William on my hip. Before I could put our son and heir on his two feet, Henry was in front of me. After the animosity between us at Barfleur, I stiffened, not sure how he was going to react.

'How was your crossing?'

'A little rough. William slept next to me, a little apprehensive at the beginning, but Horsey and I were able to reassure him and give him comfort.'

I knew I was laying it on, but Henry must understand there are times when a child needs its mother.

'You are spoiling that boy.'

Chapter 17. A Destined Fulfilled

'Good.'

Henry tried to take him from my arms. William tightened his grip; Papa was not his favourite person at present. It was 'Greek' day. I have been following my father's method of teaching foreign tongues by speaking to William in a different language each day. I said in Greek, Papa loved him. Henry's frustration was bubbling to the surface. William, thank God, let go and went to Henry, one little fist firmly gripping Horsey's leg. Henry blew on William's neck, which always sends him into tickly giggles. My baby boy relaxed, so did his Papa.

I observed the surroundings of the dock. It was busy with activity as our chattels were being unloaded. However, there was an air of neglect. The busy men looked as if they needed a good meal. Their clothes were patched and worn. Some of the buildings along the dock had suffered fire or had been ransacked, many were derelict. My heart sank as I realised the accounts of how England's civil war had torn its once mighty prosperity apart, were stark in front of me.

Horses and carriages were waiting for us. My maids were relieved they were on dry land. All had suffered mal-de-mere. As Henry and I walked towards our horses, my eye caught what I thought were two piles of rags – until they moved. There, crouched in a huddle, was a woman with a child: bowed down, filthy with matted hair, almost unrecognisable as human. I froze. Henry turned to see why I had stopped. At my waist I carry a small purse. I could not pass these poor souls and not leave alms.

'Eleanor, you will be penniless before you reach Winchester if you stop for all the poverty you will encounter.'

'So be it. But God help me if I cannot, as Queen of England, help these two sad relics of humanity.'

The haunted eyes stared at me, taking in the riches of my gown, cloak and crown. I pressed a gold coin into her grimy hand.

I asked, in my newly acquired, but most ill English,
'What name do they call thee?'

She frowned before she registered what I had said.

'I am Flora, this is Meggin. Who are you?'

'I am Eleanor. I am King Henry's wife.'

I gestured to Henry.

'God bless thee both. Thou hast come to save us from evil.'

I smiled.

'And may God bless thee also.'

Henry came and took my arm, smiling too.

'We will do our best, with God's help, to make thine lives better. It will take time, but we will not give up till we do.'

Henry's English was much easier to understand. I looked at him with pride – my king, bad temper and all.

Our horses were waiting. The animals had arrived from Normandy a few weeks ago. I was not allowed, by Henry's furious decree, to send Diablo. So, I sent Diablo's sister, just as beautiful, but at times far more cantankerous. I call her Rebel; Henry says we are well suited. Both our horses are as magnificent as their breeds can be.

It was quite a procession our entourage made on its way to Winchester where I had my first glimpse of one of our future homes. In the distance, the palace looked magnificent in its Norman splendour, but as we rode closer, a mighty, jagged, fire-ravaged wing was revealed. I tried to be positive and remarked to Henry most of the structure seemed to be intact. He raised his eyebrows; the only habitable section was the great hall and the east wing. The kitchens, however, were in the west wing which was consumed by fire after being struck with balls flamed in pitch and fired from catapults by Stephen's forces.

The surrounding town had withstood most of Stephen's fury. We were housed comfortably with the Archbishop of Winchester and other loyal nobles, a little scattered, but for a few days it would not be inconvenient. We were something of a novelty. I was proud of how honoured Henry was received. He was treated as greater than human, a Greek god, who had tamed the seas, produced a son (not solely by

Chapter 17. A Destined Fulfilled

himself), stolen the beautiful French queen to make her his wife and would restore England to prosperity by clicking his fingers. I am apprehensive about the population's confidence we can create miracles: the expectations we can drag this beleaguered country back to prosperity in the blink of an eye. The degradation I have seen so far was worse than expected. If England were not going to be hard work for years to come, the tales, songs and hearsay praising Henry would be the stuff of sagas. I will have to keep a tight rein on the Aquitaine treasury, or I can see rebellion breaking out amongst my vassals. They and Uncle Ralph will be at my throat should Henry suggest raising their taxes to pay for England's repair.

***

I heard some barons were quaking in their boots, but we were royally welcomed by a great number who paid us homage. They had been rallied by Archbishop Theobald, who I found was a kindly man of deep intellect. I also met another, somewhat flamboyant, character, Thomas Becket. He is Henry's chancellor, a tall aesthetic man of about my age with dark hair, balding a little, wearing clothes fit for a king. Henry's gown looked quite plain by comparison. I do not know what to make of Master Becket.

After securing the English treasury at Winchester, we progressed to London. The palace of Westminster is a sad relic of its former glory. I have visions of introducing the new Gothic style of architecture for its rebuilding, which has become popular in France and the Aquitaine. The building was in a worse state than Winchester, uninhabitable, having been looted and vandalised by Stephen's rebels. We are residing at the Palace at Bermondsey on the opposite side of the River Thames from the Tower of London.

Our journey through the London streets was mightily received. Vast crowds cheered joyously, calling Henry the 'Peacemaker.' My heart swelled. Beside me on his prancing steed, he looked so handsome, so regal. He looked at me with love written over his face. Who would have thought we left Normandy screaming at each other? Praise be to God Henry does not seem to sulk; he is quick to anger but quick to forget. I need to be more humble; to rein in my pride.

***

Preparations are being made for our coronation in Westminster Abbey. Henry is to continue the tradition begun by his grandfather – he will be crowned with his great-grandfather William's crown. Mine is not unlike the French one I wore for years and is almost as heavy. Our gowns have been especially made for the occasion. Mine is samite, heavily embossed in purple and scarlet, embroidered in gold and encrusted in gems and pearls. The train seems to go on forever. Many pages will be helping me move. The under gown is lined with fur.

Henry has been groomed for this day. He has vowed to avenge his mother, to reclaim the kingdom stolen from her by the betrayal of men she trusted. Regardless of Matilda's and my differences, she has my admiration for what she tried to achieve. I pray to God we can fulfil the destiny wrenched from her by Stephen and his collaborators.

The night before the coronation, the banquet went on forever. My appetite was worse than usual as platter after platter arrived in front of Henry and me. Even Henry's hearty appetite was diminished. We both drank too much wine. I was nervous, not because of the onus to come but about stupid things like tripping on my gown as I walked down the aisle of the abbey or falling on my face while dismounting from Rebel. When we had performed our duties, we took our leave. After all, it was going to be an eventful day on the morrow.

Henry waited for my maids to disrobe me. He snuggled against me. I heaved myself over to face him. In the dimness of my curtain-draped bed I gave him my blessing for what is ordained for him and promised I will support him with my life. His reply was a gentle kiss. He placed his hand on my

Chapter 17. A Destined Fulfilled

expanding belly as our baby danced a Moresque within. I hoped we could sleep.

***

On the nineteenth day of December in the year of Our Lord 1154, I was awakened by Amaris before dawn. Henry had already left my bed and gone to the chapel to prepare his soul for today. Should I have joined him? Probably, if I had risen in time, but I have prayed and now I need to be readied for the day ahead. It was going to take hours to be dressed. In the still dark of the English winter, shivering with cold, I went to my dressing room. My maids, who had been up long before me, had ready a steaming tub of water surrounded by braziers to take the chill off the air. The torches flared, casting shadows.

Normally being bathed, perfumed and preened was relaxing, but my stomach was full of fluttering birds, and it was not my unborn child. My copious mane had been washed the day before, so I did not have to go through the nightmare of drying my tresses in the cold of the morn. Regardless of the braziers, my teeth chattered as I was dried and wrapped in heated towels. Marion had warmed my under-shirt, so it was a comfort to don. Thank God we brought these garments from Normandy. They are woven of the finest lamb's wool, seductively caressing one's body. My chemise was of finely woven silk edged in lace with rampant lions and broom flowers embroidered around the hem, bodice and sleeves.

At last, the weak sun started to filter through the small windows of this quaint Saxon palace. My hair, piled on my head till I was out of my bath, was brushed till it gleamed. To keep warm, I was wrapped in one of my fur-lined capes.

Henry wanted my hair to be left flowing. My maids decided it would be sensible to plait from either side of my temples and pin it below the line of the crown; otherwise, I would have hair blowing over my face on the way to the Abbey. The remainder of my long tresses fell in their usual wavy curls to below my waist. I did not wear a veil because of the crown to come. I wore a simple cross of amethysts and pearls with similar earrings, my mother's. I had to remove Henry's lion bracelet. It had not been off my arm since he sent it to me. My assortment of rings except for my wedding ring were placed in a chest. They would get in the way of the one placed on my finger as Queen of England – married to Henry and his realm, it seemed.

The time came to be dressed in the gown. All the lacings had been adjusted to accommodate my belly. It took forever to be tied. The cornucopia sleeves reached the hem, with gems and pearls cascading and spilling down their length and folded back to show off the under garment. Amaris tied the last lacings of gold cord down the back of my bodice. I had been standing for what seemed like hours. With relief, I lowered my aching arms.

The only thing left was the girdle. How it would sit around my waist was going to be interesting. Several were spread out for me to choose, all woven in gold thread, each one suitable, but I needed something special. I asked Celeste to bring the chest containing the *Knot of Hercules*. I opened the lid. It had been shut for years, last opened all those years ago on Rusuca. I was afraid its contents could be tarnished or would bring back memories I had put behind me. In the brightening light, it still gleamed as if new. My curious maids gasped. Only Amaris knew from whence it came. Judith's voice echoed as clear as the day she intoned her prophesy. The first part had come true, the second part, '*You will become a great queen,*' was still unanswered.

I decided to wear it. Getting into it without undoing the knot was challenging. I could not step into it because of my train. Amaris stood on a stool, loosened the girdle a little and manoeuvred it over my head and past the flowing sleeves. With a few wiggles, it reached my middle but slid below my bulge. My maids hitched it to the centre of my back where it sat neatly above my train before tightening it, so its length rested partially above my belly. The Knot was manoeuvred below my abdomen where it sat comfortably. It enhanced my pregnant stomach a little but there was no disguising my condition, nor did I want to disguise it. I was a little concerned the girdle might slip down and hobble me when I walked. Marion found some pearl tipped pins and along with an anchoring stitch here and there, it was secured so it would not move. By now, I had been standing in the one spot for so long, I had pins and needles in my legs.

Henry arrived. He, too, was beautifully dressed in his regalia. For once, he did not look as if he had thrown on his clothes while he was dashing to mount a horse. His barber had trimmed his hair and beard. He looked like he had been scrubbed, and so handsome, my heart lurched. He came forward, eyeing the girdle with its eastern design of rubies and pearl fringing. With his head on one side, he remarked he had never seen anything like it and where did it come from. I told him it was gifted to me in the Holy Land. I had never worn it because there had never been an occasion worthy enough until now. Satisfied, Henry took my arm, the pages took the weight of my train, Amaris carried my fur-lined velvet cloak.

In the courtyard of Bermondsey Palace, our horses stood gleaming, caparisoned in scarlet and gold to carry us across the Thames to the Abbey. It took time to arrange me on Rebel: for once, she did not toss her head or jiggle her reins. Maybe she was aware of my destiny. My fur cape was draped around my shoulders, covering my gown till my walk to the altar. Gloves warmed my cold hands, the sun shone in the winter sky.

The crowds who had gathered were shouting and cheering their approval as we paraded to our coronation. My nerves returned; my baby joined in with my churning stomach. Was it aware of what was to befall its parents? The heavy responsibility descending on Henry and me was a monumental weight of proportions unfathomable.

At Westminster Abbey, Henry leapt from his horse with easy athleticism. I had to be hoisted down via the mounting box like a knight in full armour. Maids and pages, like an armada, flustered around. Amaris removed my cape revealing my gleaming gown and took my gloves. The liveried pages swooped on my train. Henry took my arm, steering me through the portal of the Abbey. We paused. Henry's eyes pierced mine. My hand tightened over his. Down the central aisle to fanfares and ethereal descant voices, past my darling sister Nilla and her children, Henry's brothers, Sir Robert and Henry's knights, high-ranking clergy, lords and nobles of all ranks; past my wide-eyed little William and Millicent, Amaris, Lucille, Marion, Celeste and my beloved Renée, we paraded. Across the transept we moved with stately step, to stand in front of the altar. I was so nervous I thought I would faint.

We knelt. The ceremony began, the thurible swung, incense swirled. The Archbishop of Canterbury intoned his liturgy. Amen!

Theobald raised the crown of William the Conqueror, placed it on Henry's head, and another he placed on mine, a ritual as old as the Abbey itself. A fanfare from a legion of trumpeters heralded our crowning as the roar from a multitude of throats, *Vivat Rex, Vivat Regina*, soared through the arches to the heavens. The Abbey bells rang out with joy.

Retracing our footsteps to the entrance, we stopped next to William. I was too burdened by my gown to pick him up, but Henry did, bless him. Poor child was overwhelmed. I was terrified he was going to scream in fear at these beings who resembled his parents but were dressed in mighty regal garb. Henry put William down. So, with dear Horsey clutched in his fist and thumb, much to Henry's chagrin getting a good suck, our little heir toddled down the aisle, holding his father's hand to greet the waiting crowds. We paused as the populous roared their approval, *'Waes Hael'*!

Millicent took William. In my ear, Henry had to shout we would walk. We set off among the excited, cheering, tumultuous multitude. We tossed gold coins into the throng. Hands, large, small, often grimy, were thrust out. My stomach was stroked and admired; I was considered good

Chapter 17. A Destined Fulfilled

luck. Before the bridge to take us across to Bermondsey, we remounted our horses to cross the Thames for the banquet to celebrate our crowning, euphoric at our reception from the good people of London.

When I was crowned Queen of France, I was fourteen years old, a frightened girl. I am now thirty-two. I thought it might be *déjà vu*, but no. With the chanting, the plainsong, the choir, the incense and the Archbishop of Canterbury intoning prayers, I was transported into another realm. As I write, I find it hard to put words to the experience.

I felt Papa was holding me aloft in his arms, saying this is what you were born for. This is your ordained destiny, to be crowned – Queen of England!

www.ingramcontent.com/pod-product-compliance
Lightning Source LLC
Chambersburg PA
CBHW031137160426
43193CB00008B/174